BX
9715
.M87
1994

Murdoch, Norman H.

Origins of the
  Salvation Army.

$32.00

DATE			

BAKER & TAYLOR

Origins of the Salvation Army

Origins of the
Salvation Army

Norman H. Murdoch

The University of Tennessee Press • Knoxville

Library of Congress Cataloging-in-Publication Data
Murdoch, Norman H.
    Origins of the Salvation Army / Norman H. Murdoch. — 1st ed.
    p.   cm.
    Includes bibliographical references and index.
    ISBN 0–87049–858–4 (cloth: alk. paper)
    1. Salvation Army—History.   I. Title
BX9715.M87   1994
287.9'6'09—dc20   94–9334
                                                          CIP

To
Henry D. Shapiro and H. F. McMains
Walter and Irene Murdoch
Grace M. A. Murdoch

Contents

Preface ix
Acknowledgments xiii

Part I.
American Revivalism and William and Catherine Booth, 1829–65 1
    1. The Salvation Army's Roots in American Revivalism 5
    2. The Booths as Wesleyan Revivalists 21

Part II.
Founding an Urban Home Mission, 1865–79 41
    3. An East London Home Mission, 1865–70 43
    4. Failure in East London, 1870–77 71
    5. Forming a "Salvation Army," 1877–79 88

Part III.
Christian Imperium to Social Reform: The 1880s 113
    6. A Christian Imperium's Growth and Stagnation 115
    7. Wholesale Salvation: Darkest England's Social Reform 146

Epilogue 169
Appendices 173
Notes 181
Bibliographical Essay 215
Index 221

Illustrations

1. James Caughey, American Methodist Evangelist 7
2. Charles Grandison Finney, Author of *Lectures On Revivals* 13
3. Phoebe Palmer, American Methodist Lay Revivalist 17
4. Catherine Mumford, Just before Her Marriage to William Booth 23
5. William Booth Preaching in East London 44
6. Christian Mission Headquarters on Whitechapel Road, East London 54
7. Christian Mission Membership in London Districts, 1871–77 82
8. Christian Mission Membership in the Provinces, 1871–77 83
9. Entire Christian Mission Membership: Decline in London and Growth in the Provinces, 1871–77 83
10. Elijah Cadman, a Converted Chimney Sweep 92
11. Poster of "Two Halleluja Females" 107
12. "The Salvation Army," New York, 1880s 116
13. Six "Hallelujah Lasses" Who Helped "Commissioner" George Scott Railton 119
14. The "Booth Dynasty"—A Christian Imperium—Dissensions in New York in the 1890s 124
15. Thomas E. Moore, the Army's Schismatic American Commander, 1884 128
16. Salvation Army Charioteers Taking the Gospel to English Villages 131
17. English Lady-Preacher of the Salvation Army in Swiss Tavern 135
18. Robert Harris's Salvation Army Parade, Toronto 137
19. Catherine Mumford Booth 148
20. William Booth 149
21. Frank Smith, the First "Social Wing Commissioner" 153
22. Suzie Forest Swift 156
23. Prayer Meeting at a London Salvation Army Factory 158
24. Making Up Bundles of Firewood at Salvation Army Factory, East London 160
25. William Booth 170

Preface

In this book I aim at something new in the treatment of Salvation Army history. Heretofore the army, like many religious organizations, has chosen historians who saw it as God's special creation and chose not to view the army in relation to events of a specific era. Such a stance is often taken by apologists for an aging movement, to legitimize its continued existence. It does not help us understand how the army's founders, William and Catherine Booth, spoke to their time. Whether or not a person speaks for God to an age is a theologian's problem. But, as Cushing Strout put it, "To be a historian is to seek to explain in human terms. If God speaks, it is not through him."[1] I cannot divine, then, whether or not God spoke to the Booths. I can only document how they spoke to their age through the army they created. The Booths' gift was their grasp of Victorian language, both religious and social. They were not mystics or recluses, but a man and a woman alive to the flow of events. Ideas they absorbed from American evangelists in the 1840s and 1850s they made congenial to their time and place.

To avoid the pitfalls of hagiography, I shall present these actors in the human theater of Victorian society. Howard R. Murphy chastened one contributor to the Salvation Army's official history for being more inclined to "vindicate the Army's leaders rather than explain them; . . . more interested in being inspirational than in being penetrating; [with] no evidence of either historical perspective or historical curiosity."[2] Not all army history has been done badly, but much has been commissioned by the army to justify its leaders' actions. A new history is justified because of the army's international importance. Murphy argued that "the scholarly community has a legitimate interest in the Salvation Army, which has a significance in modern history that its members may or may not appreciate."[3] Since Murphy wrote in 1965, there has been no attempt to provide a critical history of the army's origins, which point to tension between its revivalist and its social missions.

Five issues suggest the need for a new Salvation Army history. First, more must be said about the transatlantic genesis of the Booths' religious experiences. American revivalists' visits to England in the 1840s led to the founding of a revival mission in East London by the Booths in 1865. To grasp these American revival ideas is crucial to understanding the army's origins. Indeed, the Booths' affinity for American revivalism in 1853 led them to consider moving to the United States, as William's revival preaching would be more accepted there. They felt that the English resisted aggressive Christianity.

Second, few realize that the Booths' mission did not succeed in London's slums.[4] Booth founded his mission as an evangelistic outreach to what he termed London's "heathen masses," but within a decade his mission stagnated. It grew only when it moved beyond East London to provincial English towns and villages in the 1870s, areas already evangelized by other nonconformists. In the 1880s, growth came with expansion to America, Australasia (Australia and New Zealand), Europe, India, and Africa. Growth, mostly in Anglo-American towns, obscured the fact that the army had failed to gain a foothold in urban slums. How did Booth respond when critics exposed his failure to bring the gospel to the "lowest of the low?" He quickly adopted a social program in the late 1880s.

Third, the Booths reveled in revivalism's freedom-loving, antisectarian nature but imposed a rigid sectarian discipline within the Salvation Army. As revivalists, the Booths relied on spontaneous lay and female ministry. After 1865, however, as leaders of a sect, they institutionalized revivalism. In so doing, they introduced tensions between revivalist freedom and denominational discipline. The army gradually buried revivalism's creativity and its lay initiative under regulations more odious than those Booth had escaped when he resigned from the Methodist New Connexion ministry in 1861.

Authorized histories emphasize approved expansion, but the Salvation Army's growth came largely through the unsanctioned efforts of lay persons who pushed the mission beyond its home base and financial resources. In 1872, for example, a lay missioner took Booth's ideas to

Cleveland, Ohio, without Booth's blessing. In 1879, a family migrated from Coventry to Philadelphia, to establish the first permanent branch outside Britain. Yet the army in America prefers to celebrate the 1880 "official" opening of its work there by Booth's "commissioner."[5] In the 1840s, Booth had rejoiced that "separation between layman and cleric [had] become more and more obscured."[6] But forty years later, in his own sect, he instituted rigid separation of "officers" and "soldiers," with a system of military ranks. W. T. Stead saw in 1891 that "succession from Caiphas" (the high priest at the trial of Jesus) was just as much alive as "apostolic succession." The Salvation Army had not avoided the separation between clergy and laity any more than other denominations had.[7]

Fourth, the army developed from simple, almost democratic beginnings in 1865, to an imperial structure in the 1880s. Some argue that military government sparked growth after 1878, but research denies a link between autocracy and success. In fact, the army's failure to grow to a size Booth predicted was the result of his autocratic polity. By the mid-1880s, this failure to gain a lay membership in the slums led Booth to divide the army's energies between social services and evangelism. The working class was becoming less subservient; it wanted a voice. While Victorian love of the military bolstered Booth's autocracy, his military mentality kept his army from adapting to more democratic times. Like Victoria's British imperium, Booth's Christian imperium faded with the onrush of democracy. The reluctance of imperial systems to die created major difficulties for the Salvation Army as for the British raj.

Fifth, the army took on the character of its Anglo-American cultural environment; it was not unique. More synthesizers than originators, the Booths owed a debt to every person they met. For all their Christian militancy, they did not cut themselves off from secular ideas, money, or honors. They lived by the Apostle Paul's adage, becoming "debtor[s] both to the Greeks and to the Barbarians; both to the wise and to the unwise."[8] Flexibility led the Booths to achieve a catholicity that narrow sectarianism would have denied them. They overcame Methodist sectarianism to found a worldwide movement that reflected nineteenth-century Christian ecumenism. They built an international empire, tightly controlled at the center yet made up of discrete parts. Booth's imperium was a single state, but great tension existed between London's headquarters and colonial commissioners. Tension also existed within the imperial family, between paternalistic William and his lively progeny, who took command positions around the globe. Attempts to create a separate American Salvation Army in 1884 and 1896 found William unalterably opposed to nationalist fragmentation. His desire to form a worldwide Christian imperium brought General Booth great success and significant frustration.

Acknowledgments

My debts fall in two bundles. First, I owe an intellectual debt to Henry D. Shapiro, H. F. McMains, and Mark A. Lause, masters of direct yet gracious criticism. Between 1981 and 1992, the University of Cincinnati provided several research grants that permitted me to go to London. Sally Moffitt and Daniel Gottlieb, librarians at Langsam Library, University of Cincinnati, offered gracious help. Salvation Army archivists in London and New York generously assisted me, as did British Library curators. John and Frederick Coutts, Edward Carey, Walter Squibb, and Glen Horridge represent salvationists who shared ideas even when, on occasion, they did not agree with my interpretations. Patrick Kumpf provided essential technical assistance. Editors at the University of Tennessee Press were meticulous in their care of the manuscript and directions to the author.

Second, my greatest debt by far is to my wife Grace and to our children, Randall, Amy, and Ryan, who demonstrated great patience in not taking offense at my diversions. My parents, Walter and Irene Murdoch, initiated my interest in Salvation Army history and acknowledged with forbearance the critical stance I took with regard to it.

The work itself, despite the visible evidence of many invisible hands, is my own. Its conclusions are not those of a deity; I claim no special revelation. They are human assessments of an intricate and absorbing human institution.

PART I.

American Revivalism and

William and Catherine Booth, 1829–65

Posters announced: "War! War! In Whitby! 2,000 Men and Women Wanted to Join the HALLELUJAH ARMY!" Formerly a nearly illiterate, hard-drinking boxer and chimney sweep, Elijah Cadman came to Whitby, Yorkshire, in late 1877. A town crier announced Sunday services at Saint Hilda's Hall, at which twenty-five individuals professed conversion. Cadman then trained converts as preachers, singers, and soul-fishers. His methods, like those of others in William Booth's Christian Mission, included visiting door-to-door in slums by day and preaching at night. When slum denizens threatened to cut his throat for denouncing their hellish lives, he retreated through the streets, singing and waving a huge umbrella. Publicans organized gangs to break up processions of missioners who wore a strange array of military caps. Police, worried about disrupters' power to upset an uneasy neighborhood peace, ordered Cadman to move on. At Cadman's chapel, many wept as a sister preached; others led sinners to salvation: backsliders, a rank infidel, a poor street girl. Soon Cadman rented a hall for congregations of three thousand on Sundays and fifteen hundred on weeknights. Typical of Booth's missioners, Cadman had been converted through Wesleyan influences in 1864, at age twenty-one; he had joined a Hallelujah Band wearing Garibaldi red shirts at Rugby the next year. He rejected "ordinary ministry" because he did not believe in a paid clergy. In 1876, he met Booth at his Whitechapel headquarters and in 1877 became the first captain of the "salvation army."[1]

Unless one fathoms early influences on William and Catherine Booth, the Salvation Army's founders, one cannot appreciate the methods they used. The principal influence on the Booths and on early mission evangelists like Cadman was that of American revivalists James Caughey, Charles G. Finney, and Phoebe Palmer, who preached in England in the

1840s. Their "American methods" converted sinners by "scientific" means, through advertising meetings in rented halls, preaching and praying for specific results, bringing sinners to open confession of sin at a penitent form (communion rail), and training converts to win others. Understanding this legacy and that of British Methodism is critical for comprehending the history of the Salvation Army. The Booths' views on theology, organization, nonsectarian, aggressive revivalism, lay participation, and Wesleyan disciplines of behavior, adopted between 1844 and 1865, well before they founded the army, changed little up to the time of Catherine's death in 1890.

William's limited theological training, just six months in 1852, led Catherine to compensate for his deficiencies. Prior to their marriage, she spent her leisure in exhaustive study, the fruits of which she passed on to him. Their dogma was John Wesley's Arminian theology of "free salvation for all men and full salvation from all sin." Ideas of exclusive election (predestination) were abhorrent to them, as were theories that permitted a believer to engage in antinomian (sinful) behavior. The Booths' Wesleyanism stood midway between extreme Calvinism and such mid-nineteenth-century heterodox expressions as transcendentalism and free thought. Faith, repentance, and restitution for past wrongs brought conversion, and conversion led to holy living. Salvation included both new birth (conversion) and an experience of holiness (entire sanctification) that endowed a believer with purity and power. The Booths adopted these doctrines, along with biblical trustworthiness and trinitarianism, as the creed of the East London mission they founded in 1865.

The Booths also acquired from Palmer and Caughey, and from Finney's fear of ministerial education, a belief in a lay ministry for men and women alike. When attempting to discern why the clergy lacked fire, revivalists identified the problem as formal training. Seminaries were the bane of inspired preaching. Yet, while Booth shared this notion, like many itinerants he himself accepted ordination, even though it meant submitting to the inconvenience of six months of seminary education. He lived with a tension between a desire for knowledge and credentials, and a fear of education's corrupting influence. Although he opened training institutes for Salvation Army officer candidates in 1880, proposed a university of humanity, and accepted an honorary degree from Oxford, he never abandoned his revivalist's distrust of education.

The Booths equivocated on other issues, too. They loved Wesleyan discipline but despised its lack of focus and authority. They loved autocracy's efficiency but denounced its inflexibility and its tendency to allow men of limited vision to gain power. Imagined offenses caused the 1851 Wesleyan Conference to take away William's and Catherine's memberships. In 1861, William resigned from the Methodist New Connexion, when its conference refused his request to follow what he saw as God's call to evangelism. On the other hand, he had resigned Reform Methodist pastorates in Walworth and Lincolnshire because reformers would not give him ample authority. Conflicts between love of freedom and love of discipline pursued him as he founded an East London mission with a democratic Wesleyan Conference system in 1870. Later he altered the mission's polity to an autocratic (many said despotic) military system in 1877. Booth sought a plan that would reproduce aggressive first-century Christianity. Could a movement be at the same time liberating *and* authoritarian? Despite intimations that, as early as 1849, Booth had conceived of a model utilizing military command structures,[2] it was not until 1878 that he put it to use, when he renamed his urban home mission a "salvation army."

The preeminent influence on the Booths throughout their lives was American revivalism, brought to Britain by Methodist evangelists Caughey and Palmer and the Presbyterian Finney. As early as 1846, as a teenage lay preacher in Nottingham's Meadow Platts, William was employing revival techniques before anyone had informed him that he was not even a certified "lay preacher." By 1865, he had had nearly two decades of experience testing these principles of evangelism in streets, in secular buildings, and in homes. He prayed with sinners at church benches and preached for sinners to turn from unrighteousness to God. He took converts' names and added thousands to church rolls.

Caughey, Finney, and Palmer had no truer disciples than the Booths. To them, next to the Bible, no book was so precious as Finney's *Revival Lectures*; no friend so dear as Caughey; and no example of female ministry so impressive as Palmer. Methods learned in the 1840s later became Salvation Army rules. Probably the most important feature of revivalism was public speaking by laymen and laywomen. Caughey, Finney, and Booth had become revivalists before being ordained, and they suspected that clericalism was the nemesis of true religion. From 1859 on, Catherine took a public stand in favor of female ministry, taking her husband with her, in spite of his earlier reluctance to extend this privilege to women. After defending Phoebe Palmer's ministry in Sunderland, Catherine decided to accept a public role as a preacher. Thus the Salvation Army developed out of the Booths' early development in British Wesleyan and particularly out of American revivalism. Aided by thousands of Wesleyan recruits like Elijah Cadman, who also embraced these methods, the army spread through the Anglo-American world and to "missionary lands" as well.

1.

The Salvation Army's Roots

in American Revivalism

When eight religious emigrants clad in military garb arrived at Battery Park, New York, in March 1880, they were returning to a scene from which their general, William Booth, had derived his revival methodology. Soon after arrival from London, George Scott Railton, Booth's commissioner to America, conducted an afternoon meeting at Mrs. Doolittle's Five Points Mission, founded in 1850 by Phoebe Palmer. The *New York Herald* depicted the "motley, vice-smitten, pestilence-breeding congregation" as "negroes, dancing girls, saloon-house tramps, sandwiched between well-dressed visitors." The service began with Methodist hymns, unknown to the slum-dwellers. Railton encouraged sinners to repent and go to heaven. Ladies prayed with outcasts "as tenderly as if they were about to die millionaires and leave the ladies a safe full of government bonds." The *Herald* reported that Railton asked one young black woman, "'Are you a Christian?' 'No Sir.' 'Why not?' 'Kase de Lord ain't in me no more.'" Railton assured her that "'the Lord wants you to come back.'" She ended the chat with, "'I guess Ize too bad today.'" Salvationist services included singing, short prayers, exhortations to be saved, personal interviews to get sinners from the pew to a penitent's bench at the front, and a personal testimony to confirm new-found faith.

The reporter properly identified the "English Salvation Army," but familiarity with earlier American revivals would have shown the army's methods to be those that Caughey, Palmer, and Finney had impressed on the Booths in the 1840s. By the time British salvationists came to New York, not even they were aware of their methods' origins, although Railton noticed that nearly every American, including the young black woman, "knows what being saved means," and that thousands of American evangelicals, mostly Methodists, aided his enterprise.[1]

American revivalists had gone to England soon after the 1783 Peace of Paris ended the American Revolution. First to arrive was Lorenzo Dow, in 1799. An eccentric asthmatic and epileptic, Dow helped to found the first English camp meeting at Mow Cop in 1807 and helped to merge revivalist sects into the Primitive Methodist denomination in 1811. Like later revivalists, Dow focused on England's Wesleyan heartland—Derbyshire, Nottinghamshire, and Leicestershire—an area similar to upstate New York's "Burned-Over District," in that many revivals were held there.[2] The area, in 1829, was the birthplace of William and Catherine Booth.

Caughey, Finney, and Palmer arrived in England between 1846 and 1866 to introduce "scientific" methods of winning souls to Christ—methods that, if effectively employed, would assure conversions. This methodology captured the attention of the Booths in their youth, became their obsession as adults, and gave their Salvation Army its aggressive character. Revivalist independence contrasted with Methodist discipline, to which discipline both Booths became converted. Their dynamic autocracy evolved from these contrasting systems: aggressive, individualistic revivalism and rigid, bureaucratic church polity. Of the three revivalists, Caughey, whom the Booths knew personally, provided the best model of how the new methods worked. Finney, whom historians generally have viewed as father of the new methods, was best at describing the techniques in book form. Palmer, a lay evangelist, offered the Booths an example of a female preacher, and her books on holiness doctrine provided them with a terminology for their preaching. Both female ministry and holiness doctrine became key ingredients of the Booths' mission after 1865. When the Salvation Army added a social service program in the 1880s, it mixed revivalism with late-nineteenth-century social Christianity in a manner characteristic of evangelical societies founded in the 1850s, including the YMCA, the YWCA, and the WCTU. The army still claims allegiance to its revivalist heritage.

While English Methodism long had influenced Americans with books and tracts, confident American Methodist revivalists now convinced British evangelicals that they could be a social force. By 1829, Methodism had become America's largest sect. It had grown from less than ten thousand members in 1780 to about five hundred thousand, penetrating the growing northwestern cities. American methodism's strengths were: (1) an optimistic Arminian theology that held that people were prime actors in their own salvation; (2) a flexible structure that permitted individual initiative while imposing control over untrained, free-wheeling clergy-

James Caughey (c. 1810–91), the American Methodist evangelist who, in Catherine Booth's words, "prayed for us most fervently . . . expressing the deepest interest in our future. . . . [I was] almost adoring his very name." Courtesy of the Salvation Army National Archives and Research Center.

men; (3) diminished distance from pulpit to pew; (4) a millennialist dream of an improved Christian state with a thrifty working class, which gave Methodism a reputation for social reform;[3] (5) an appeal in both urban and frontier areas. Methodism opposed infidelity and popery and appealed to the poor and the rich through itinerant preaching, protracted meetings, and active lay and female involvement.

James Caughey was the American who most influenced the Booths. His sway began in 1846, when William first heard his electrifying preaching in Nottingham. Thereafter, Booth bore Caughey's stamp. Caughey had been born in southern Ireland on April 9, 1810, of Scottish ancestry. In 1827, he took a position at the Methodist Sunday School Association in Newburgh, New York. As a flour-mill worker in 1830, he was caught up in a revival at Troy, in New York's "Burned-Over District." As a probationary preacher in the Troy Conference in 1832, a deacon in 1834, and an ordained elder in 1836, he learned Hebrew and Greek adequately to study the Bible. English Methodists labeled him "well read, a philosopher and a clever man." He believed in the potential conversion of mankind and in providential intervention by God and Satan in daily activities. His claim to having had supernatural visions disquieted Methodists, who feared the impact of Millerite millennialism (an American sect that emphasized the imminent return of Christ, to the neglect of common Christian doctrines).[4]

In July 1839, as Caughey was considering a marriage he apparently wanted to avoid, after three days of prayer a voice informed him, "the will of God is that thou shouldst visit Europe." By now he was an experienced revivalist. He had been a circuit rider in upstate New York and had held a successful revival in Montreal. At Pittsfield, Massachusetts, he converted over three hundred in six weeks. But, as he prepared to go to Britain in September 1840, with enough money for a two-year stay, he did not have an extensive reputation. After brief missions in Quebec, Caughey arrived at Liverpool in July 1841 and attended the Wesleyan Methodist Conference at Manchester. He had a letter of introduction from New York's Bishop Robert R. Roberts. Thomas Waugh, a respected Irish Methodist, invited Caughey to Dublin, where, contemporaries claimed, his conversion of seven hundred people in five months was "unequaled" in Methodist history. He moved on to Limerick and Cork, hostile Roman Catholic towns where he found that his methods were better suited to stimulate Protestant churches than to expand Methodism in unfriendly climes—a discovery that Booth later made in city slums. Expecting to return to America, Caughey asked the Troy Conference to grant him a settled pastorate, but in the interim he received an "impression" that placed Liverpool "constantly before me, although I have no official invitation."

Hearing from the Holy Spirit was excuse enough to skirt a bishop's authority in New York, where revivalists had such freedom. He divided his six weeks in Liverpool between successful work in the North Circuit and unsuccessful work in the South.[5] His major revivals after Liverpool were in Birmingham and in the Yorkshire cities of Leeds, Hull, Sheffield, Huddersfield, Boston, and York, where churches experienced impressive membership gains after a period of stagnation and decline. He went to Nottingham, Chesterfield, Dorchester, Macclesfield, Wakefield, Gateshead, Scarborough, Lincoln, and Sunderland—all cities where Booth would preach in the 1850s. In six years of campaigning, with brief periods for recuperation and two trips to Europe, he counted twenty thousand conversions and nine thousand persons sanctified.[6]

Sheffield was an ideal social environment for revival success. A predominantly working-class city with iron and steel industries, it had a population of one hundred thousand. The religious climate included an evangelical Church of England and a revival tradition which dated to 1794–96, when William Bramwell, an exceptional English evangelist, preached there. Methodism was the strongest sect, although from 1834 to 1844, it had declined from 4,950 to 4,307 members. Caughey disliked what he termed the city's "Chartist conspiracy"; he opposed "secret combinations of workmen" and the collapse of social order. But his visit fell between peaks of Chartist activity in 1842 and 1848. Historian E. P. Thompson argues that working-class allegiance shifted between religious fervor and political activism. Methodists infiltrated the Chartist movement, in terms of both men and ideas. Chartists sought a working-class parliamentary vote and representation, ideas which reflected the sentiments of upwardly-mobile Methodist workers. Due to Methodist influence, Chartists used models of camp meetings and love feasts in their endeavors. After achieving a decade of growth in Sheffield in 1834–44, now respectable Wesleyan Methodists wanted a role in the social and political system.[7]

Sheffield fell prey to Caughey's reasoned emotional appeal. Before his arrival in May 1844, Methodists saturated the city with handbills and showbills heralding his meetings. When he arrived, he preached as many as ten sermons a week. His pulpit presence was commanding; height, keen eyes, and attractive dark features attracted attention. His "bell-like" voice was unforgettable, and his tongue was packed with attention-arresting Irish-American idioms. But his forte was the use of anecdotes and a frank denunciation of sin. He avoided speculative theology. He incited fear with vivid pictures of hell's fury and God's looming judgment, then abruptly shifted to evocations of Christ's mercy and love. He addressed individuals in the congregation without mentioning names: "There are several characters here before me tonight, my discourse will particularly concern." He then gave them a special message and even prophesied their imminent death, hoping for an immediate conversion. His theatrical manner deeply impressed young Booth and taught him methods that he later used in his own preaching. Caughey's social message encouraged converts to make restitution of property and to embrace teetotalism, though the British Wesleyan Conference had ordered chapels closed to teetotaler meetings in 1841. It associated such issues with excessive lay influence. But in Sheffield, Caughey found Methodists who had accepted abstinence since the mid-1830s.[8]

Caughey's emphasis after preaching was on "knee work," his term for prayer. This included the "American device" of calling penitents to the communion rail (also called a *mourner's bench* or *penitent form*) to pray following a sermon. He told penitents how to get free from sin while the congregation shouted, prayed, or sang. He went from pew to pew inviting "anxious enquirers" to go forward. Caughey, like Wesley before him, deplored fits of wild frenzy. After conversion, Caughey pleaded for an instantaneous "entire sanctification" experience which gave believers purity and power. He recorded each conversion and sanctification, noting that converts included both the "educated" and "those of the baser sort." But an English historian of revivalism argues that "Shopkeeper Wesleyanism had arrived." While a few of the 80 percent non-Methodist converts were wild characters, as Caughey claimed, most were between sixteen and thirty, of evangelical upbringing, who had experienced conversion in earlier revivals of Aitken, Miller, and Bramwell.[9] Since Dow's time, Methodism had become respectable, and open-air preaching had declined. Church members' children were easier revival targets than "papists", infidels (non-believers), or socialists. Converts were primarily Methodists; 20 percent came straight from the membership rolls. They simply could not recall a time when they had been converted.

In 1846, the year Booth first heard Caughey at Nottingham, "all hell" let loose against Caughey at Hull, as chartism revived in the Midlands. At Huddersfield in 1845, socialists had attacked him in a public debate as a hindrance to the working-class cause. The *Whig Morning Chronicle* viewed his 1846 Birmingham revival as evidence of popular ignorance, demonstrating a need for improved education for the masses. It charged him with fostering family disunion, spiritual pride, and religious excitement, adding, "Nothing that has grown of the transatlantic fusion of Puritanism and democracy ever produced a more appalling frenzy than the ministrations of Mr. Caughey have engendered among the sturdy hammerers of the iron town." Caughey's enemies despised the contrived nature of his revivals: his use of a penitent form, his individualized "death warrants," and his planting of "decoy penitents" at the mourner's bench to entice the shy to come forward.[10]

Caughey's independence from conference discipline owed much to his income from books, portraits, and occasional gifts from the congregation (the Booths later sold the same trinkets to build their income). Wesleyan conferences heatedly discussed his case but took no formal action until 1846. That year Jabez Bunting, a "High Church" party leader, asked the conference "affectionately" to request the New York bishop to recall Caughey, on grounds that he "has now been for several years in this country . . . subject to no ecclesiastical supervision, responsibility or control, such as those to which all other Methodist ministers . . . are required to submit; [and] that such an irregularity is dangerous to the good order, peace and unity of our Body." Threat to authority caused "settled ministers" to point with envy at their itinerant brother's freedom. Caughey had come to England without an invitation and had remained for five years without any official connection to a Methodist conference. His popularity had kept him in demand even when circuit superintendents preferred that he stay away. More ominous, he had encouraged "irregular ministers," uneducated men like Booth, who might overrun the denomination.

August 12, 1846, with his chief defender absent, the conference ruled that Caughey be denied the use of Wesleyan pulpits. Then, after participating in revivals and temperance meetings of other Methodist sects in the Midlands and North, he bowed to his bishop's "earnest request" that he return home. When his partisans, mostly laymen, protested the censure, the conference raised questions about his position on slavery, which in 1844 had split American Methodism into northern and southern churches (he opposed slavery), and about the accuracy of his revival statistics. His return to New York in 1847 left behind in the Wesleyan Conference a storm of controversy over revivalism and lay authority.[11]

When Caughey returned to Britain in July 1857, his fame was considerably augmented, possibly due in part to his unceremonious departure in 1847, but also due to the publication of his *Letters,* which described his English revivals. At Sheffield, where he was popular and where Reform Methodism was strong, the Booths went to hear him preach. Catherine wrote to her mother that Caughey was "a sweet fellow, one of the most gentle, loving, humble spirits you can conceive of. He treated me with the greatest consideration and kindness; conversed with William on his present and future position like a brother, and prayed for us most fervently." Next day Caughey baptized the Booths' second son, Ballington.[12] Caughey preached at Hanley, Manchester, Hull, and Louth in 1858–59, and claimed over eight thousand conversions and three thousand entirely sanctified, by count of church secretaries. His third visit, in 1860 to 1862, was again directed at Midlands cities— Lincolnshire and the North, in United Methodist Free Church chapels— with one southern three-month visit to Bristol in 1862. He compiled a

record of seventy-five hundred converts. His last visit came during a period of ill-health and a decline in revivalism. Still, working in the South,
he stirred up revival in London in 1864, and in Exeter in 1865–66.[13] Booth
last met his revival mentor in New Brunswick, New Jersey, in 1886, during Booth's first American tour. A Salvation Army officer reported the
reunion at a crowded theater where Booth was preaching:

> In that period of silence prior to the opening remark, a stooped figure,
> clad in a black cloak hobbled down the aisle leaning heavily on a cane. All
> eyes were fixed on him. His hair was snow white and his face showed the
> effect of the passing of time. . . . An officer bent over the shoulder of the
> General [Booth] and whispered, 'General, that is Dr. James Caughey.' The
> message galvanized the General into action. Leaving his seat on the plat-
> form, he climbed over the orchestra pit and swiftly made his way up the
> aisle to meet the old man.
>
> 'Dr. Caughey,' exclaimed the General. 'William,' said the old man and
> they embraced each other and kissed each other on the cheek and under
> the barrage of the amazement of the crowd, [Booth] led the old man to a
> seat on the platform. In his address that afternoon, . . . Booth paid high
> tribute to the man who placed his feet upon the path which had made him
> successful as a soul winner.[14]

Booth was Caughey's heir. Caughey convinced Booth that converting the masses was possible through scientific, calculated means. Revivals which were planned, advertised, and prayed for would succeed. From
the time they met in 1846 to his death in 1912, Booth was consumed
with the idea of winning souls through mass meetings, house-to-house
visitation, and personal witness. That was the legacy of James Caughey,
who died in 1891 at age eighty-one, largely forgotten, despite his influence, not only on the Booths, but on all British evangelicalism.[15]

Charles G. Finney, credited by many as the main designer of
revivalism's "new methods," at any rate was the major promoter of those
methods. In 1837, his *Lectures on Revivals of Religion,* which became the
Booths' prime text and later was required reading for Salvation Army
cadets, was published in England. *Lectures* put in writing what Booth
had seen at first hand in Caughey's meetings. Booth's first biographer
noted that "among the few modern books which have received the

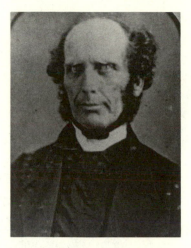

Charles Grandison Finney (1792–1875), wrote *Lectures on Revivals,* which greatly influenced Catherine and William Booth. Their approach to revivalism copied Finney's "American" methods. Courtesy of the Oberlin College Archives.

hearty *imprimatur* of the Salvation Army have been Finney's *Revival Lectures* and *Autobiography*." George Scott Railton, Booth's mission secretary in the 1870s, placed Finney above Wesley and Whitefield as Booth's model for sermon making.[16] Catherine often remarked on the parallels between the careers of Finney and her husband. The clergy rebuffed both for their preaching manner and unconventional educational backgrounds. Both refused to become ministerial trainees when that meant embracing Calvinist dogma. To Catherine, Finney was "an American William Booth." When eldest son Bramwell became ill due to mission work in 1876, she sent him on holiday to Scotland with a copy of Finney's *Theological Lectures*. In 1852, when William's vocational problems depressed her, she wrote, "I often wish I could have an hour's talk with Finney, I think he would be able to advise me. He would understand me."[17]

Finney's *Lectures* advised on "How to Preach the Gospel." The Booths and hundreds of others committed to memory his manual for successful evangelism. Like Caughey, Finney stressed prayer, "an indispensable condition of promoting the revival," and preaching, preferably without notes. Colleges and theological seminaries did not encourage preachers to talk extemporaneously to people. Finney argued that "ignorant Methodist preachers, and the earnest Baptist preachers" were more effective than learned Presbyterian divines. He wrote about how to do house-to-house visitation, how to get anxious enquirers to seek conversion, how to get new converts to testify in public meetings, how to hold meetings in unconsecrated halls (schoolrooms, barns, theaters, music halls), and how to encourage women to pray in public. His books allowed the Booths to recall each new method; the Bible and Finney's *Lectures* were their two primary texts.[18]

Finney's first tour began in November 1849 in Cornwall and the Midlands and lasted until 1851. Some saw him as a replacement for Caughey, who had left in 1847; but Finney, inconsistent in his appreciation of the unlettered, considered Caughey's work to be "unintelligent bluster and excitement." Finney began in Houghton, Birmingham, and Worcester and was in London by 1850, at a time of economic prosperity that had brought young William Booth to the city to find work in a South London pawnshop. Finney's success had come in small towns, but in London he preached at Moorfield Tabernacle, John Campbell's pulpit that challenged German higher criticism in England. The congregation was accustomed to Finney's analytical approach. The lawyer-turned-preacher aimed his two-hour sermons at "laymen and women [who] represented a huge army, underutilized, badly deployed, and lacking in motivation." He asked them to seek "perfection" as a means of achieving personal and social progress.[19]

Laymen posted showbills, handed out leaflets, and carried placards in the streets. The religious census of March 30, 1851, reported that "thousands" were unable to get into the tabernacle's three thousand seats to hear Finney. Although reluctant to use Methodist bookkeeping, Finney recorded converts from various classes. Generally the literate middle class marked the upper limit of his appeal, and tradesfolk and poor working people the lower limit. But he noted with pride that at Houghton he met "Old John Clark the drunkard," "Barnes the Blasphemer—Ellis the pugalist [*sic*]," and "Bass the harlot." Yet, despite his pride in reaching the outcast poor, the submerged masses and the upper class were still beyond revivalism's reach.[20] While Finney was at Worcester in 1850, a group of wealthy men offered to build a "transportable tabernacle" for him to use in revivals among the "masses," but local ministers warned against preaching "in an independent way." Later Finney had second thoughts about his decision to accept the clergy's advice. In the 1870s, evangelist Dwight L. Moody adopted portable tabernacles in England and America, and wealthy admirers offered Catherine Booth a tabernacle of her own.[21]

Finney's second British tour came in 1858–59, when revivals in America, Ulster, Wales, Scotland, and England confirmed the existence of a transatlantic community. English evangelicals copied "correct" American methods to increase church growth. In America, over half the white populace was under twenty in 1850, and many converts were Sunday School children. American and English revivals were mostly urban and northern. American Methodist membership grew by almost 22 percent in 1857–58; by 25 percent in New York State. Historians cite some causes of the revival: guilt over speculative business ventures; anxiety over a changing society, as floods of immigrants, primarily Irish and German Catholics, were arriving; and an urge for a homogeneous society built on Protestant republicanism and free of papists, infidels, and socialists. Abolitionist debates split denominations and created openings for freelance revivalists. In 1846, interdenominational cooperation increased, as the Evangelical Alliance began to gather evangelicals into united prayer meetings, often held under the auspices of the newly founded YMCA in nonsectarian halls or Union Tabernacles.[22] Revivalism played the vital role in nonsectarian transatlantic cooperation.

An 1853 religious census indicated weaknesses in religion's working-class appeal, particularly in English manufacturing districts where Caughey had found success prior to chartism's rise in the late 1840s. In 1855, the Wesleyan Conference started daily services for workers. Congregationalists and Baptists, who generally feared emotionalism, began workers' meetings in halls and theaters with popular preachers. Thousands attended the Baptist C. H. Spurgeon's services in London's Exeter Hall and Surrey Gardens Music Hall.[23] Even Anglicans used revival methods. Robert Aitken held high-church revivals in Cornwall, the "Black Country," and northern England; and low-church folk engaged in outdoor preaching to "the humbler classes of society."

By early 1858, revival news from American newspapers and religious papers saturated Britain and spread American-style revival methods. Union prayer meetings and the 1846 organization of the Evangelical Alliance reduced sectarian rivalry. Lay persons contributed to revivals and to sectarianism's decline, although less than in America where preachers were less dominant. In late 1858, Finney conducted revivals in Cornwall before moving on to South London's Borough Road, where he chided English evangelicals for reluctant attempts "to move large cities." He spent the summer of 1859 preaching at four East End United Methodist Free Chapels but was not nearly as successful as Richard Poole had been in 1857 or Caughey in 1864. His age and a lack of a denominational ties worked against him. But Finney, through his involvement in antislavery, temperance, and Sabbatarian crusades, infected a generation of Anglo-American preachers with his ideas on perfectionism, revival methods, the importance of the laity and women, and the need for an urban ministry concerned about social issues.[24]

Phoebe Palmer, a third major American revivalist in England in the 1850s, was born in New York City in 1807, where she lived most of her life. In her, the Booths found an example of female ministry and an exponent of holiness which fit perfectly with the influence of Caughey and Finney. A lay Methodist evangelist, she came forward in an era of increasing female interest in voluntary agencies to support temperance, abolition, and suffrage. With her husband, Dr. Walter Palmer, she shared the social reform concerns of pre–Civil War evangelicals. Together they founded New York's Five Points Mission in 1850, the first Protestant institution for slum work. The couple did not support abolition. Indeed, Phoebe's friends, Bishops Janes and Hamline, invented the silence policy on the issue. Phoebe hoped that, by cooperating with the Methodist hierarchy, she could protect the holiness movement from schism, but silence did not keep Methodism from splitting into northern and southern branches.[25]

In 1835, she began her Tuesday Meeting for the Promotion of Holiness for women in New York City. Twice she and her physician-husband moved into larger homes to accommodate the meeting. Phoebe was "sanctified" in 1837 and opened her Tuesday Meeting to men in 1839. She swayed numerous Methodist leaders and reached such diverse intellects as Finney, Frederic Dan Huntington, and Professor Thomas C. Upham. From 1850 on, the Palmers spent half of each year at camp meetings and revivals in the eastern states and in Canada. Phoebe stressed that holiness resulted from an act of commitment to God in faith. Holiness was an experience that God gave suddenly in response to that commitment. Her most famous book, *The Way of Holiness* (1850; 1856 in England), had appeared in thirty-six editions by 1861. During 1859–63, their first stay in England, 17,634 were converted and 2,287 sanctified. But Phoebe Palmer's health broke after the 1862 Wesleyan Conference denied her access to its pulpits. After that, her English work was almost totally in United Methodist Free and New Connexion chapels of the Midlands and North,

Phoebe Palmer (1807–74) was an American Methodist lay revivalist. Rev. Arthur A. Rees's attack on her Sunderland, England, revival led to Catherine Booth's written defence of "Female Ministry" and the commencement of her public preaching ministry in 1859. Courtesy of the Billy Graham Center Museum.

with about a hundred saved weekly. The Palmers' four-month Welsh campaign in 1862 produced over 1,000 converts; and early 1863 revivals in Wolverhampton, Birmingham, and Walsall rivaled Caughey's success. After they returned home in October 1863, Dr. Palmer purchased *The Guide* and *The Beauty of Holiness*, and Phoebe became editor of the combined journal with a monthly circulation of thirty thousand. By 1886, there were 238 imitations of her Tuesday Meeting in America and England.[26]

English Methodist acceptance of "female ranting" had rapidly declined after an 1803 Wesleyan Conference restricted women's public role. Nonetheless, women continued as itinerants in Primitive and Free Methodist pulpits. By the 1850s, support for women's public role was increasing. In 1859, Phoebe Palmer emerged as the sort of "decorous, middle class" female preacher whom English Methodists could admire. She would modestly step to the front of a chapel after her husband had opened the service and the host minister had said a few words. She then spoke in the nave, not presuming to occupy the clergy's pulpit preserve, simply giving her personal experience. When a Congregational minister, Arthur Augustus Rees of Sunderland, attacked this ministry, he drew Catherine Booth's wrath. To counter Rees's tract, "Reasons for Not Co-operating in the Alleged Sunderland Revivals," she wrote a pamphlet on "Female Ministry." Catherine's decision to preach and the Salvation Army's female ministry can be traced to Phoebe Palmer.[27]

It is fair to claim that the Booths were products of revival ideas carried to England by Americans and that the Salvation Army is the fruit of that influence. The Booths' theology and revival methods were gifts from three American revivalists. There is no evidence that the Booths' mentors knew each other, although on occasion Finney, Caughey, and the Palmers were in the same area. They avoided proximity. Finney said that "he could do nothing after Mr. Caughey," who evidently had outshone him at a conference in Cincinnati in 1854. Nor is there evidence that the Booths worked with any of these itinerants. The influence came through exposure to their meetings, their books and tracts, and their fame. British itinerants who followed the Americans included a small number of revivalist ministers from Methodist conferences, among them Booth and James Codd Milbourn, another Caughey disciple. A larger group of independent lay preachers, patterned after the Palmers, included Reginald Radcliffe, who helped Booth settle in London in 1865, Harry Grattan Guiness, Brownlow North, Gordon Forlong, and Hay McDowell Grant. A working-class lay group included the ex–chimney sweep William Carter, Richard Weaver, Joshua Poole, converted railroad laborer Mr. Bradford, and William Pennefather and George Pearse, who helped the Booths after 1861.

American revivalists opposed sectarianism and invigorated the religious press; even secular newspapers gave them headlines. They supported Evangelical Alliance union prayer meetings and revivals. The Palmers' Newcastle revival of 1859 was hailed as an "Evangelical Alliance Revival." Along with English imitators, including the Booths, the Americans saw British evangelicalism as hamstrung by sectarian rivalry. Caughey told American backers that sectarianism "runs very high in England." Union meetings, according to Phoebe Palmer, attracted criticism in England. Although the Americans were mostly denominational evangelists, each was forced to find work beyond sectarian boundaries, as was Booth when he resigned from the Methodist New Connexion in 1861. Their need to move beyond denominations grew out of the church bureaucracies' unwillingness to adopt measures which might appeal to the emerging working class. Yet, although revivalists' music-hall preaching showed some effect on the masses, in nearly every case the revivalists soon gave their "spontaneous movements" institutional form, to keep them alive. The Booths in 1865 founded their East London Revival Association, which by 1878 had grown into a bureaucratic Salvation Army.

Revival methods aimed at immediate response. Caughey and the Palmers invited penitents to a mourner's bench or asked them to raise their hands to indicate a desire that prayer be made on their behalf. Finney adopted that Methodist method, but he held special services for enquirers in Presbyterian or Congregational churches. The Booths employed all three methods. Revivalist theology was Arminian, although Finney would not have used that term for fear of alienating Presbyterians. None of the revivalists we are considering here was a mystic with novel theological ideas, although the group's members did not lack personal peculiarities. They were conventional evangelicals who held the Bible to be God's Word and heaven or hell to be the future abode, respectively, of those who accepted or rejected grace. They were millenarians with hope for the age, as voiced in William Arthur's tracts, *The Conversion of All England* and *May We Hope for a Great Revival*. Such grand phrases forecast Booth's "Food for the Millions" shops of the 1870s and his scheme to organize world missions in 1888.

The Americans were largely responsible for membership gains in Welsh and English Methodism, from 444,369 in 1859, a low point since 1849, to 565,272 in 1863. The trend reversed after they left in 1866. The Methodist New Connexion peaked in the mid-1850s, but growth of other Wesleyan groups coincided with the 1858–59 revival. The revivalists exaggerated their influence outside evangelical denominations. They attracted few Catholics, Unitarians, or Quakers; the vast majority of converts were unregenerate evangelicals. About half of Caughey's converts were under twenty. Seldom were social outcasts present; revivalists appealed to the "respectable," or at least to the "working class," and a majority of converts were female. At times the revivalists had a significant, if fleeting, effect on social behavior. They encouraged abstinence and attacked wife-beating, gambling, prostitution, and theater-going. But by 1866, as the number of unconverted adherents diminished, Methodist and Baptist growth declined, and Caughey, Finney, and the Palmers returned to their New York homes.[28]

Many agreed with John Stuart Mill that revivals appealed to "narrow and uncultivated minds," being "at least as much the revival of bigotry." But revivalism fostered interdenominational fraternity; evangelism by the laity, including women; and a doctrine of Christian perfection. Revivalism's most lasting institutional legacy is the Salvation Army. As

American bread cast upon the Atlantic, Booth's Christian Mission arrived in Cleveland in 1872 and in Philadelphia in 1879. The Booths' army institutionalized revivalism's "new measures." Understanding the Booths' enthusiasm in their formative years (1846–65) for the ideas of revivalists James Caughey, Charles G. Finney, and Phoebe Palmer, establishes an essential introduction to Salvation Army history.

2.

The Booths as

Wesleyan Revivalists

Two experiences in the 1840s preordained the vocations of William and Catherine Booth, namely, their conversions to English Wesleyan Christianity and their exposure to American revivalist methods. Their later interest in social reform grew out of this early spiritual formation. To their deaths they continued evangelistic preaching, which they enjoyed more than the social services they devised to keep their Salvation Army alive in the multiethnic Anglo-American cities of the 1880s. Revivalism gave the Booths their methodology and their aggressive spirit.

William was born on April 10, 1829, in a Nottingham suburb. His parents, Samuel and Mary Booth, were of the laboring class. Despite his father's pretense that he had fallen from wealth, the family was desperately poor throughout William's childhood. St. John Ervine, William's most accurate biographer, describes Samuel as "an illiterate speculative builder." Ervine chides Harold Begbie, an earlier biographer, for a "curious attempt to prove that the evangelist of the poor was born of a substantial middle-class family which had fallen upon hard times."[1] Mary Moss, Samuel's second wife and William's mother, was a rural cottager's daughter. Neither parent had much education, although both became expert at veiling their low estate.

William's childhood was unhappy, due to his mother's anxiety over his father's speculations. William described his father as "a Grab, a Get [who] knew no greater gain or end than money," fearing that this materialistic bent had become part of his own nature. A family friend described the elder Booths as "proud and very reserved"; they "felt their position acutely, and wished to keep to themselves." William seldom spoke of his parents, although he visited his mother regularly and, after his father's death, aided her financially to the end of her long life on January 13, 1875.

The family returned to Nottingham in 1835, after four years on a ten-acre farm. Thereafter, William attended Mr. Biddulph's school, an experience of which he kept no cherished memories, although he studied there until he was thirteen. The Booths were not religious, but they expected their children to attend the parish church where William was baptized. When he was six, he signed a pledge never to drink alcohol, but at thirteen his mother convinced him of beer's medicinal usefulness, and he broke his pledge. In later years, his formidable wife caused him to abstain totally. In 1842, with the Booths in financial disgrace, Samuel apprenticed William to a Unitarian pawnbroker in Nottingham's slums. Five months later Samuel died, leaving his family in poverty. Mary moved to a small shop in a poor district, where she sold toys and household wares. At this point of despair, William began attending a Wesleyan chapel, becoming a member of Brother Carey's class.[2]

Catherine was born at Ashbourne, Derbyshire, about thirty-five miles from Nottingham, on January 17, 1829, to Sarah and John Mumford. Sarah was an exceptionally devout woman, and John was a Methodist lay-preacher, a wheelwright, and a carriage builder. Of four children, only Catherine and John survived. John left for America at age sixteen.

Catherine's early education was under the puritanical rule of her mother, who claimed that Catherine had read from the Bible at age three and had read it eight times by the time she was twelve. The family moved to her maternal grandfather's home in Boston, Lincolnshire, in 1833, where Catherine's father John became involved in the rising temperance movement. His social interests liberated Catherine somewhat from her mother's narrow views. She became secretary of the juvenile temperance society and wrote articles for temperance magazines. At twelve, she commenced a two-year stint at a Boston girls' school, where she finally escaped her mother's close supervision to be exposed to girls her own age. Her interests were geography, history, and theology. She read Wesley, Fletcher of Madeley, translations of Neander's *Ecclesiastical History*, Butler's *Analogy of Religion,* Bunyan's *Pilgrim's Progress,* and Sir Isaac Newton on prophecy. But she particularly enjoyed Finney's *Lectures on Revival* and his works on theology.[3]

Although William and Catherine had very different childhoods, Catherine's deeply religious and William's only superficially so, both experienced religious crises in their teens. William's was due to his father's death; Catherine's resulted from her father's turning from a narrow path of Wesleyan temperance to alcoholism. Although neither was able to

Catherine Mumford just before her marriage to William Booth in 1855. Courtesy of the Salvation Army National Archives and Research Center.

identify the time of conversion exactly, both felt a deep sense of sin and a desire for God. Each needed a father-replacement.[4] Most converts of itinerant evangelists were in their teens; perhaps teenage crises led many to similar resolutions.

William's conversion may have happened in a Nottingham street, at Broad Street Wesleyan Chapel, or during a prayer meeting. Although he could not recall the moment, he credited the eccentric lay preacher Isaac Marsden with stirring his heart by warning that souls die every minute. But an act of restitution, after a long siege of conviction, may have been the real turning point. William, in what he described as "a boyish trading affair," had made a profit while leading friends to believe that he had done them a favor. In thanks, they gave him a silver pencil case; he experienced great guilt until he confessed his deception.[5] Catherine re-called that, around age seventeen, after "a great controversy of soul" which went on for six weeks, words of a hymn gave her assurance of salvation on June 15, 1846. No great sinner, she could not "remember the time when I had not intense yearnings after God."[6]

After conversion, William found the exemplar of his life's vocation, a father figure, in American revivalist James Caughey, who arrived in Nottingham in 1846. Three months of prayer and reports of success else-where preceded the revival, which Booth termed a "remarkable religious awakening." Erik H. Erikson wrote that lonely youths seek recruitment "by an ideological movement in need of needy youths." Such a dynamic marked William's commitment to saving souls by methods "dictated by common sense, the Holy Spirit, and the Word of God." He joined friends who set out to apply Caughey's principles in the impoverished Meadow Platts neighborhood and became "a leader in the fight." According to his memory forty years later, the plan involved giving nightly open-air addresses, at which they invited listeners to a cottage meeting. There, lively songs and short exhortations led to on-the-spot conversions to Christ at a table in the middle of the room. They visited the sick and converts, whose names and addresses they recorded. On Sunday they marched to the chapel, where authorities sent them to the free seats at the back door. When converts died, they held their funerals. In short, Booth wrote later, "we had a miniature Salvation Army," based on the principle that "human nature was as religiously impressionable if not more so in its poorest, most ignorant and wretched forms as in any other."[7]

While employing Caughey's methods among Meadow Platts' poor, two new crises fueled William's religious fervor. His friend and fellow slum evangelist Will Sansom died. Then the Unitarian pawnbroker Francis Eames fired Booth for refusing to break the Sabbath by working past Saturday midnight. "Narrow escapes," scattered through evangelical literature, no doubt reinforce a convert's beliefs. To William's surprise, Eames rehired him just seven days later and gave him charge of the business, while he took his young bride to Paris. At the time, William was working from early morning until seven or eight at night and evangelizing in the evenings and on Sunday.[8]

Booth had not considered entering ordained ministry but found himself drawn by its promise of security. Here was a conflict he would feel throughout his life. He loved freedom, Christian primitivism, and revivalism, on one hand, but, on the other, he desired clerical notice. He found a need within himself to become a "regular" preacher. As early as 1846, his minister, Samuel Dunn, urged him to go "on the plan" as a local preacher to villages. Becoming a local preacher was the first step into Wesleyan ministry. Such men preached when a "regular" ordained minister was unavailable. Booth declined, but in 1847 he changed his mind and became an accredited, unpaid local preacher.[9]

In 1848, health problems delayed William's studies for the ordained ministry. He was out of work for a year at the end of his six-year pawnbroking apprenticeship. At this low point, he found that "no one took the slightest interest in me." He spent his time reading Finney's *Lectures,* and sermons and books by Whitefield and Wesley. In fall 1849, he moved to Walworth (London) and worked "practically [as] a white slave" in a pawnshop. Although lonely, this was the year when he began to preach in London chapels on spare evenings and Sundays. If a "call to preach" came to him in this period, William made no reference to it. Here he honed his personal discipline, in six "Resolutions" similar to those Caughey had made in the 1830s. They attest to William's Wesleyan preference for rules of behavior over speculative belief systems. On October 6, 1849, he wrote:

> I do promise—my God Helping—1st That I will rise every morning sufficiently early, say twenty minutes before seven o'clock, to wash, dress, and have a few minutes, not less than five, in private prayer. 2nd That I will as much as possible avoid all the babbling and idle talking in which I have lately so sinfully indulged. 3rd That I will endeavour in my conduct and deportment before the world and my fellow-servants especially to conduct myself as a humble, meek, and zealous follower of the bleeding Lamb, and by serious conversation and warning endeavour to lead them to think of their immortal souls. 4th That I will read no less than four chapters in God's word every day. 5th That I will strive to live closer to God, and to seek after holiness of heart, and leave providential events with God. 6th That I will read this over every day or at least twice a week. God help me, enable me to cultivate a spirit of self-denial and to yield myself a prisoner of love to the Redeemer of the world. Amen and Amen.—William Booth.
>
> I feel my own weakness and without God's help I shall not keep these resolutions a day. The Lord have mercy upon my guilty soul. I claim the Blood. Yes, oh Yes, Jesus died for me.[10]

His family found this faded paper at his death.

Biographer Harold Begbie wanted to prove that William had an official-professional ministerial calling during this period when he was a lay preacher, although William, as Begbie put it, had "only the earnestness

of a good layman," since the Wesleyan Connection had not ordained
him. But William, in an 1849 letter to a Nottingham friend, expressed his
attitude toward unordained lay ministry in positive terms and also indicated an early fascination with the jargon of aggressive, militant Christianity in a letter to a friend:

> Grasp still firmer the standard. Unfold still wider the battle flag! Press
> still closer on the ranks of the enemy, and mark your pathway still more
> distinctly with trophies of Emmanuel's grace, and with enduring monu-
> ments of Jesus' power! The trumpet has given the signal for the conflict!
> Your General assures of success and a glorious reward; your crown is al-
> ready held out. Then why delay? Onward! Onward! Onward! Christ for me!
> Be that your motto . . . your battle-cry . . . your war note . . . your consola-
> tion . . . your plea when asking for mercy of God.[11]

In 1850, a dispute which had begun at the 1846 Wesleyan Conference over Caughey's revivals entrapped William. Jabez Bunting, president of the Theological Institute, opposed reformers' plans for local autonomy. Bunting's conservatives preferred connectional control over
ministers, congregations, and orders of service. Reformers soon formed the
United Methodist Free Churches, a revivalistic branch of Wesleyanism. Although Booth had played no part in the 1849 schism, his Walworth
Chapel pastor suspected him of reformist sympathies and, when Booth
resigned his local preacher's license, denied him his quarterly ticket of
admission to class meeting, effectively excommunicating him. His love
of revivals, his association with Caughey and Dunn, and his unexplained
resignation of his local preaching license led to expulsion. At points
where he himself was disciplined, Booth the disciplinarian does not give
clear reasons for the exclusion.[12] His leaning toward autocratic order sug-
gests that his own organizational bent would have been in the direction
of Bunting's strong hierarchical control.

In the wake of Booth's problems with the Wesleyans, Edward J. Rabbits, a boot manufacturer and Methodist reformer, became interested in
him as a preacher. In April 1851, Rabbits asked Booth to preach for three
months for a stipend of one pound per week. It was common for wealthy
benefactors to support preachers of their own choosing at their own
chapels. Booth worked as Rabbits' hired preacher from April to June

1852. One day Rabbits invited William to his home for a temperance meeting, to recite a lengthy, grotesque American poem, "The Grog Seller's Dream." Catherine Mumford, a deeply religious young woman with social-reform notions, also was there. William's recitation touched off a discussion in which Catherine made her strong abstinence views known. Besides helping Booth financially, Rabbits had introduced him to his future wife.[13]

Beginning with their second meeting on Good Friday, April 9, 1852, William and Catherine, both twenty-three, entered one of the more remarkable male-female relationships in religious history. This period of emerging female equality saw the formation of notable pairs both inside and beyond evangelicalism. The Finneys and Palmers were yoked in ministry. In English politics, Sidney Webb and Beatrice Webb, and the Queen and Prince Consort, provided images of productive companionship. The sphere of endeavor for women of talent was expanding. A key reason why the Booths, both dominant figures, were able to sustain a loving relationship was that they kept their activities separate. Catherine said that she feared preaching in William's presence. When on the same platform, they spoke deferentially of each other. Although Catherine acknowledged William's "headship," his frequent travel allowed her to control their children's lives. Catherine educated them almost solely at home, due to fear of outside contamination. At dinner William and Catherine sat side-by-side; there was no head at their table. A relationship that might have been filled with conflict was a marriage of romantic love until Catherine's death in 1890.[14]

By July 1852, at the end of his three-month commitment to Rabbits, William looked for a solution to his vocational dilemma, now all the more serious since, on May 15, he and Catherine had become engaged. Of Rabbits' reformers, William said, "They did not want a parson. They reckoned they were all parsons." Booth was no democrat, even when he questioned those in authority over him. His passion for control outweighed his theoretical love for the "priesthood of all believers." His July 1852 break with reformers led him to take Catherine's advice that he look into joining the Congregational Union, formed in 1831. There were signs that the Union had diluted its Calvinism and might ordain a Wesleyan. Her pastor, Dr. David Thomas of Stockwell New Chapel Congregational in South London, proposed that Booth talk with Dr. John Campbell, at whose tabernacle Finney was then preaching. Booth's friendly meeting with Campbell was followed by unfriendly ones with other Congregationalists, who argued the reasonableness of Calvin's doctrine of election. Maybe Finney's threat to hyper-Calvinism had caused them to close ranks against what they saw as an antinomian intrusion. Booth declined a Calvinist conversion, but later, in 1864, during another period of vocational uncertainty, he again sought to join the Congregationalists.[15]

In fall 1852, reformers from Spalding, Lincolnshire, invited Booth to take charge of their circuit.[16] For eighteen months he preached there and corresponded with Catherine in London. Their letters reveal their minds, as they tried to agree on many issues that would occupy their lives. These included education, health, clericalism, holiness, and the locale and nature of their work. They pondered Finney's methods for transforming the church into an agency of spiritual reform. On issues of abstinence and the place of women in the church, William would later become Catherine's reluctant convert. In the *Methodist Times,* he proposed an amalgamation of reformers with the Methodist New Connexion or the Methodist Association, but the New Connexion declined because of the "more democratic tastes of the Reformers." The Booths were drawn to the New Connexion, a federation of local churches with more central control than the reformers' independent congregational system. Catherine read that the New Connexion had come out of methodism's first schism in 1797, and had been "founded on a plea for democratic government." She measured a sect's effectiveness by how much it resembled first-century Christianity and wondered if the New Connexion was vigorous enough to "promote the ultimate prosperity of the Church?" In her view, aggressive Christianity could not "triumph till disentangled from the gigantic systems of worldly policy which men have identified it with."[17]

In 1852, frustrated by the reformers' disorganized ways, Booth resigned his Spalding post and applied to the Reverend William Cooke for candidacy in the New Connexion ministry. He rejected the temptation to become a nonsectarian lay revivalist like contemporaries Richard Poole and Richard Weaver and attended Cooke's seminary at Camberwell, South London. Here he found the theoretical less appealing than the practical and sacrificed his study time to evangelistic work. He did sufficiently submit to Cooke's rule to impress this tutor, who indoctrinated students against what Wesleyans termed "worldliness" and drilled them through criticism of weekly sermons; doctrinal essays; and lessons in elocution, grammar, rhetoric, logic, composition, church history, and elementary Latin and Greek. After lessons, students did practical mission work in the neighborhood. Fortunately for Booth, Cooke valued the evangelist over the theologian and asked the 1854 Conference to assign Booth to a London circuit, with opportunities for itinerant evangelism elsewhere. Booth became resident minister for a new Packington Street Chapel in Britannia Fields, Islington, under P. T. Gilton's frigid oversight.[18]

From 1854 to 1857, Booth was a New Connexion evangelist. He spent several weeks at each chapel, using the methods of Finney and Caughey to enliven Methodist congregations. On June 6, 1855, he and Catherine were married at Stockwell New Chapel in the presence of William's sister, Catherine's father, and the caretaker. The following March 8, the first of their eight children was born. They named him for William Bramwell, the English holiness preacher.

William became convinced that he was a born revivalist, and his conviction that Finney's methods were sheer genius deepened. He wrote to Catherine, "Nothing moves the people like the terrific. They must have hell-fire . . . or they will not move." Why was it churches "advertise for money, but are ashamed to advertise for souls?" He was obsessed with making the church as efficient in its mission of salvation as it was in its concern for its own survival. He placed converts' names in an address book to visit them systematically. He employed converts in "salvatory" work "almost on the instant" that they were saved. He saw "respectable seat-holders" as his chief nemesis. Yet he hoped that respectable folk would notice his ministry. When his meetings became emotional, he feared that their support would slip.[19]

Catherine warned William to curb "mere animal excitement" in his services and reminded him of Caughey's "soft, heavenly carriage." The latter did not shout; his dignity was a more potent weapon than noise. If her views on revivals confused him, he could find them "exactly in Finney's *Lectures on Revivals*," which she deemed "the most beautiful and common-sense work on the subject." William was delighted when listeners compared him to Caughey, and he sensed he might someday "do something for this poor perishing world . . . to realize the big desires that have existed in my breast . . . to save thousands and tens of thousands." Catherine deplored his revivalist ego yet admired his aggressiveness. In this period, he expected an average of twenty converts nightly, about six hundred a month. Catherine warned him in 1853 that ambition was his "chief mental debasement." But after their 1855 marriage, she saw that he was a man of many doubts and that his boasts masked deep anxieties. She became his champion, believing, as she told her mother, "if God spares him, and he is faithful to his trust, his usefulness will be untold, and beyond our capacity to estimate." She had just seen a crowd jam a Sheffield chapel to hear him preach "one of the mightiest sermons" she had ever heard.[20]

Temperance was another topic of correspondence between the two. Before their marriage, Catherine wanted William to stop treating his dyspepsia (indigestion) with alcoholic remedies, the common cures of the age. Even as common a remedy as aspirin was not invented till 1899. When he wrote that he "had to have brandy twice," she responded that she had "lost faith in brandy." When he asked her opinion on port wine, commonly used by Wesleyan clergy, she would "hear of [his] taking it with unfeigned grief." "I abominate the hackneyed but monstrously inconsistent tale—a teetotaler in principle, but obliged to take a little wine for my stomach's sake." She invited him to "wage war with the drinking customs." Catherine, an abstinence worker from childhood and the daughter of an alcoholic, was the force behind making the Salvation Army the world's largest abstinence society by the 1880s. By then, she had weaned William from medicinal uses of the beverage. Social historian Brian Harrison credits the Industrial Revolution with inspiring Methodist adoption of abstinence in the 1850s. Abstinence appealed to Methodist frugality, and the need to have a sober, stable workforce on Monday mornings led Methodist factory managers to support it. For these reasons, clergymen joined the war against the traditional "Holy Monday," which farm laborers customarily had used for recovery from weekend binges.[21] But Catherine's moral enthusiasm for abstinence went beyond economics.

The couple's health, especially his dyspepsia and her back ailment, were themes of their letters. Catherine's passion for hydropathy made her the family theorist on both physical and moral redemption. At times of exhaustion, they retreated to Matlock for hydropathic cures at John Smedley's spa. William commenced cold baths at Spalding in 1853. Cold water cures, a favorite of Victorians, became an official Salvation Army treatment in the 1880s, when the Booths opened an army officers' rest center at Matlock. Later, in writing to salvationists, William proposed hydropathy as a remedy for fevers, smallpox, liver inactivity, sore throat, inflamed eyes, bladder or urine distress, abscesses, diarrhea, and cholera. His obsession with dyspepsia bordered on the neurotic. Harriet Beecher Stowe claimed that it was nearly impossible for a confirmed dyspeptic to be a good Christian, "but a good Christian ought not to be a confirmed dyspeptic."[22]

In family discipline, the Booths were puritan-Wesleyans. They denied themselves fancy clothes, jewelry, and millinery adornments such as feathers; were strict Sabbath-keepers; and avoided tobacco. For health reasons, they were avowed vegetarians. As for childrearing: children should be whipped, as Susannah Wesley had taught, but they must not be humiliated. Always interested in rules for practical living, the Booths produced Wesleyan disciplines in the 1880s, which they renamed *Orders and Regulations* to fit the Salvation Army's military metaphor.[23]

The Booths embraced a Wesleyan holiness doctrine of salvation from all sin, a point on which traditional Wesleyanism and mid-nineteenth-century American revivalism agreed. Both systems proposed a two-step process of salvation—first, conversion as a remedy for basic human sinfulness, and, second, a perfecting and empowering experience that brought more godliness to human behavior. The second experience they termed entire sanctification, holiness, Christian perfection, or (in John Wesley's simple phrase) "perfect love." Although the Booths themselves had private, unemotional religious experiences of conversion and sanctification, they insisted on public experiences for their converts.

This emphasis on experimental salvation led them to be disinterested in "speculative" theology, formal education, and intellectualism. Neither had much formal schooling. Catherine's mother's dictum was: "If you want your child well trained, train her yourself." Still, both Booths saw the importance of study, at least in areas calculated to improve one's soul-winning methods. Neither read novels—Methodists, like the puritan fathers, saw them as clouding a Christian's view of the world as it was; novels romanticized the human condition and desensitized the soul to its depraved condition. Theater, of course, had the same effect.[24]

These prohibitions led the Booths to adopt anti-intellectual outlooks. Biblical literalists, they took little notice of higher criticism or theories of evolution, even though they were contemporaries of Joseph Ernest Renan,

Charles Darwin, and Herbert Spencer. They confined their interests to the moral universe, and, even in that sphere, they were concerned only with God's redemption of the world. Begbie labeled William a "Hebraist," Matthew Arnold's word, pointing to Booth's alleged Jewish ancestry and his puritanical habits. Booth, said Begbie, "had something of Carlyle's contempt for Art, Science had no vital attraction for him. The sports and amusements of mankind filled him with contemptuous ignorance." After listing Booth's intellectual deficiencies in fields including psychology, philosophy, physical science, architecture, painting, and classical music, Begbie wrote, "Booth was born a provincial, and he remained a provincial. He was not born a Hebraist, but he made himself the most uncompromising Hebraist of his time." William left Catherine and their son Bramwell to deal with ideological critics, both secular and ecclesiastical, while he kept to his purpose.

But Begbie went too far when he said we must judge Booth "a man who, for the sake of Christ, denied his period and lived without enthusiasm for human inquiry." Booth's sense of his era, at least in the orb of human reform, was the essential quality of his success. It was the age of the common man, and Booth adapted religion and expressions of social concern to fit his time. He did not lack curiosity, he simply lacked time. Philistinism requires leisure. William grew up in poverty and lived most of his life with the threat of financial disaster looming over his family and their organization. Catherine did not preach out of singular religious motives; she preached to support their large family, which could not have survived without her income.[25]

Catherine's ideas on women's rights to preach had both Wesleyan and American revivalist roots. Her views first appeared in 1850, when she wrote to her Congregationalist pastor after he had demeaned woman by terming her man's intellectual inferior. Concerning woman's inferior position, Catherine's assertion was that nurture, not nature, had crippled the female intellect. Seven months after their 1852 engagement, she told William that only when women are "educated as man's equal will unions be perfect." William, a man of his era, held that woman had a fiber more in her heart and a cell less in her head. At this time Catherine did not deny the curse on Eve for her disobedience at the Fall, but she condemned the argument that woman was inferior; a Christian husband's love for his wife nullified all but "the outward semblance of the curse."

In 1855, she faced him with the issue of equality in the pulpit. He responded, "I would not stop a woman preaching," but "I would not encourage one to begin." When she began to teach Sunday School at his Brighouse Chapel in 1857, she wrote to her parents: "If I get on well and find I really possess any ability for public speaking, I don't intend to finish with juveniles." She thought that, if she had been brought up among Primitive Methodists, she "should have been preaching now."

The final stimulus to Catherine's preaching came in 1859, when she read Rees's pamphlet attacking Phoebe Palmer's preaching. She wrote to her mother, "Would you believe that a congregation half composed of ladies could sit and hear such self-deprecatory rubbish?" She then wrote a tract, *Female Ministry: Woman's Right to Preach the Gospel*. She argued that women's "graceful form and attitude, winning manners, persuasive speech, and above all, a finely-toned emotional nature" ideally equip them for public speaking. And, if "the Fall" set occupations, men should "till the ground" as God commanded. But if men escape drudgery to find refined tasks, why should women be confined to "the kitchen and the distaff" on account of Eve's sin? She denied Rees's charge that "female ministry is forbidden in the Word of God."

On Whitsunday in 1860, after she had published *Female Ministry,* Catherine preached her first sermon at Gateshead's New Connexion Chapel. Feeling "the Spirit come upon" her, she strode to where William was concluding his sermon and said, "I want to say a word." He introduced her and sat down. She told of her struggle over a public ministry, which had led up to that moment. Many wept as she concluded, and William announced that she would preach that night. Thus were launched thirty years of preaching in Britain, during which time, many agree, no man exceeded her in popularity or results.[26]

The Booths' Wesleyan, middle-class sense of vocation created tension in the roles of family provider and revivalist. At times William indicated that he could have gone into business and that, if he had, he would have been successful. After all, he had inherited "the grab, the get" from his father. In 1876, while preparing son Bramwell to succeed him as superintendent of his London mission, he considered sending him to college, but ended by preferring "a modified amount of mission work and a simultaneous course of study," particularly in systematic theology. One difficulty was "the effect [on other missioners] of my son being at

College." But later, two younger sons, Ballington and Herbert, attended Dr. J. B. Paton's theological institute at Nottingham.[27]

By 1865, when the Booths threw their energy into making revivalism a practical solution to the spiritual poverty of the Victorian city, they had a firm grasp of Wesleyan and revival ideas. In the 1850s, as Caughey, Finney, and Palmer conducted revivals in the Midland cities where Methodism was particularly strong, William demonstrated that he could convert thousands of working-class Englishmen to the gospel. Revivalism gave the Booths their methodology and spirit, but as Wesleyans they found that it conflicted with orderly discipline. The two systems—aggressive revivalism and bureaucratic sectarianism—constantly came into conflict. The Booths and other English revivalists who bore an American stamp increasingly felt the dilemma. In working out that conflict, the Booths merged aggressive revivalism and Methodist polity into an ideology which in 1865 gave birth to a London home mission that was destined to become the Salvation Army.

In 1861, the Booths fled the New Connexion for freedom. To accept their version of events is to find that the Liverpool annual conference hounded William out of Methodism and that this expulsion led directly, four years later, to his founding a London home mission to the "heathen masses." Their son-in-law, Frederick Booth-Tucker, created that myth when he wrote Catherine's 1892 biography. Begbie upheld it in his 1920 biography of William, as did the Salvation Army's 1947 official history. Recent historians have embraced the myth, which holds that nineteenth-century sectarian bureaucrats forced the Booths out. But this one-sided tale is not persuasive. It alleges that, at the moment conference rejected his request for a revival ministry, a glance from William brought Catherine to her feet in the gallery, exclaiming, "Never!" They walked out arm-in-arm. In fact, conference had asked visitors, including Catherine, to leave the gallery, while William made his plea to become an evangelist, as he had been before 1857.

William's seminary mentor, Dr. William Cooke, presented a compromise which begged Booth to accept a circuit and request time away from pastoral duties to do evangelistic work. This motion carried by a large majority. According to an eyewitness, Thomas Scowby, Catherine, who was listening at the gallery door, heard the vote on Cooke's proposal and exclaimed, "No, never!" William sat pondering the situation, then picked up his hat, walked to the door, met his wife, and walked out together with her. But this was not the end. Booth's resignation came two months later, after he had tested the waters to see if he could succeed as an itinerant. Only then did he reject appointment to the prestigious Newcastle-upon-Tyne circuit. His departure was due less to the conference's push than to the pull of the Booths' desire for independent evangelism. It was not an impulsive act, but a calculated decision. Anti-revivalist Methodists did not reject him as much as he later wanted to believe. He was no martyr to the cause of revivalism among the poor.

Between 1854, when William began work as an evangelist for the New Connexion, and 1861, when he chafed under the heel of Methodist bureaucracy, he had found both success and frustration. His ability as a revivalist had impressed conference leaders in 1854, and they quickly had offered him opportunities. He had toured the Midlands, holding revivals at Stafford, Longton, Hanley, Burslem, Newcastle-under-Lyme, Fenton, and Stoke Newington, and had become evangelist for the entire Connexion in 1855. He preached in Bradford, Oldham, Mossley, Gateshead, Manchester, Jersey, York, Hull, Sheffield, Dewsbury, Hunslet, Leeds, Halifax, Macclesfield, Yarmouth, Birmingham, Nottingham, Chester, and Bristol. The Midlands and northern cities were the scenes of his 1860s success as an itinerant and were the base for his expanding home mission in the 1870s and for the Salvation Army in the 1880s.

But in 1857, conference had, by a 44–40 vote, curtailed his evangelistic perambulations and assigned him to "regular pastoral work." William wrote to Catherine's parents, "A party has been formed against me," chiefly ministers. The change was "a heavy blow to me and very much against my judgment. But I bowed to authority." He took Brighouse circuit for a year, then Gateshead for three, but all along pressed for his call to evangelize. A sympathizer advised him to follow Caughey out of denominational shackles: "The only way for such men as you and Caughey to escape the mental rack and handcuffs is to take out a license to hawk salvation from the great Magistrate above, and absolutely refuse to have any other master." In 1886, Booth looked back on 1861 as his "first step back again towards the simple plan of labour commenced at Nottingham fifteen years before," back to tenets of Finney and Caughey and Palmer, beyond the realm of sectarian Christianity. In 1861, however, his vision had not been so clear!

In June or July, as he contemplated resigning from the New Connexion, he visited London to find work in home missions. George Pearse, a member of the East London Special Services Committee, encouraged him to participate in the committee's services at the Garrick Theatre in Whitechapel. Booth found that his "sermonic address" was "of little service" with a small East End audience, a "different affair altogether to what I have ever taken part in." He wrote to John Stabb, another member of the committee, "I am still undecided how the Lord would have me act." He would "for the present moment at least watch and pray." In 1861, Booth did not hear Providence calling him to London's "heathen masses."[28]

William returned to Newcastle-upon-Tyne for a last attempt to reconcile with the New Connexion, but on July 18, eight weeks after conference, he submitted his resignation. The Booths were on their own. William sought Caughey's counsel, but Caughey did not respond. Rough treatment in 1846 had cowed him, and he could not face a scrap with the New Connexion, where he still had friends. Although ordained by the New Connexion, Booth now had been cut adrift from organized religion. One of his own converts, a young minister in Hayle, Cornwall, opened the "first door." Catherine accompanied him to witness "the most remarkable awakening" ever to occur in western Cornwall. From Hayle they went to preach at St. Ives, Lelant, and St. Just. By William's count, between three and four thousand professed salvation during the eighteen-month 1861–62 campaign.

When the Wesleyan conference met in Cornwall in 1862, the Booths felt that they might be "once more absorbed into the parent Methodist body." When this did not occur Catherine wrote later, "Our course out of the churches and downwards to the masses must be continued." Conference moved to close its chapels to the Booths and the Palmers, who were "not amenable to regular Conference discipline." *Minutes* referred to the disciplining of Caughey in 1847 and the banning of Lorenzo Dow in 1807. The two other main branches of British Methodism joined in this ban. English evangelists, by the late 1850s, were the leading element in British revivalism, but church leaders said they were "no better than religious charlatans, who make considerable sums by working in a violent and irrational manner on the physical and emotional susceptibilities of uneducated crowds." Booth's methods, like those of American itinerants, had drawn the ire of the "settled clergy."[29]

During their first two years of independent preaching, the Booths, working parallel to the Palmers, stayed in Cornwall at Penzance, Mousehole,
Redruth, and Camborne, and then left for Cardiff, Wales, to preach in a
large wooden circus. Nondenominational work was in vogue. Theoreti-
cally, such work would save people and bring them to churches to be
trained and cared for. But the Booths found at Walsall in the Black Country in mid-1863 that indoor services failed to charm sinners. Respectable
people were "too proud to enter, and the lower orders" were opposed
to such services. So William began speaking in the market square and
leading processions through dark slums to a Methodist chapel. Few followed, so he began a new kind of meeting—or so he thought—out of
which the hallelujah band movement grew. He invited notorious characters from Midland towns, who had been "remarkable in wickedness" but
now served God. He advertised a poacher, two prizefighters, and a "Birmingham jail-bird," and crowds followed a morning march to attend all-
day meetings. The movement succeeded, according to Ervine, because
Booth instinctively realized that "the damned could only be drawn from
hot sin by hot religion."[30]

In May 1864, Catherine began to hold her own services, in addition to
her chores as mother of four and chief domestic. She wondered why "it
never seems to occur to any of them that I cannot do two things at once."
But the family needed two incomes. The Booths were discovering that
itinerant evangelism was a hard way to make a living. They spent much of
1864 devising a plan for the future. In May they chose Leeds as their first
permanent residence in three years. After an illness, William retreated to
Smedley's spa in Matlock and then held revivals at Halifax, Bury, Hyde,
Stalybridge, and Sheffield, with a side trip to Gateshead. At Nottingham,
he asked his Congregationalist minister friend, J. B. Paton, for advice on
whether he could work with the independents. William was conscious
of the unstable nature of his work.

An additional burden was William's sensitivity in the face of his
wife's abilities, especially since the two were involved in the same type
of ministry. "You far exceed me in the influence you can command in a
service," he wrote to her. He wrote again after a journal had rejected an
article he had written, "You heard how they pitched into my writing and
praised yours. There, as elsewhere, I must decrease and you increase!"
Alas, his bombast covered an ego fragile indeed. Formidable in pulpit

and press, Catherine had talents that were greater than an insecure husband could cope with. In income as in talent, his wife threatened to outdo him. As soon as she recovered from giving birth to their sixth child, Marian, in mid-May, she was back on the preaching circuit. By June, she had held brief missions in Batley, Pudsey, and Woodhouse Carr. Five hundred adults and many children had been converted.

In spite of having two incomes, the Booths owed eighty-five pounds to the publisher of his hymnbook, which, to supplement their preaching fees, they sold along with Catherine's *Female Ministry.* Their annual income of three to four hundred pounds was much more than it had been with the New Connexion. As late as 1934, most nonconformist clergy earned less. Their income and lifestyle were troublesome issues throughout their lives. Critics questioned the extent to which they turned Salvation Army funds to personal use, but charges of misappropriation never were substantiated. In 1864, however, they were "on their own," without the parsonage, the baptismal and marriage fees, and other perquisites of settled clergy. It was the uncertainty of their income and not necessarily the amount, that kept them in turmoil. Financial insecurity, the nomadic nature of their lives, and the possibility that Catherine's ministry was more valued than William's—these made him miserable.

Their son Bramwell concluded that these years were "probably the darkest of [William's] whole life, at least from the time of his ordination onward." They were "wilderness years." Methodists in Bury treated him coldly, and he wrote to his depressed wife from Hyde, "I feel almost dead; powerless." Yet, at this time, biographer Ervine found William gaining "an autocratic manner that was often unpleasantly arrogant."[31] The Booths' departure from Methodist security had led to a life of anxiety, not the pleasurable independence they had craved.

With these anxieties, the Booths decided that neither Leeds nor Sheffield could offer the opportunities London could. In March 1865, in order to accommodate Catherine's engagements in London, to allow her to get home evenings after preaching, and to bring the family nearer to her parents in Brixton, William agreed to bring the family to a leased house in Hammersmith (London), between preaching at Louth, Lincolnshire, and Ripon in Yorkshire. It was Catherine's preaching in the dockside suburb of Rotherhithe that became William's "first step" toward London. That step had nothing to do with his career or with a desire to evangelize the poor. On February 26, she began services at Southwark's Free Methodist Circuit, which lasted until early May. Her success, he wrote, would dictate whether he would try to preach in a city which he feared was well beyond his intellectual powers. Catherine next preached in the squalid South London district of Bermondsey. Her last spring mission was at Deptford, as William ended his northern revivals.[32]

So the Booths' move to London had nothing to do with their reluctant exit from Methodism, nor did it arise from God's call to establish a mission in London's East End. Moving to London was a practical alternative to the depressing migrant lifestyle they had adopted in 1861. It was for her work, not his, that they came to London. In fact, the change was a first step *back* to denominationalism and *away from* itinerant freedom. And in fall 1865, William consummated his longing for discipline by founding a Christian Revival Association, forerunner of the Salvation Army, and by writing a Methodist discipline for its governance. While he sought freedom for himself, he soon would impose discipline on others, more severe than that which the 1861 conference had imposed on him. The man who would be free soon became the man who would be general. He would treat those who accepted discipline as "saints" and those who spurned his authority as "traitors."

Following his attraction to revivalism in 1846, William had been, in turn, an adolescent revivalist in Nottingham's slums, a local preacher in the Wesleyan conference, a Reform pastor, a seminarian, and an ordained minister whom the Methodist New Connexion assigned as an itinerant evangelist and then as a settled pastor. From 1861 to 1865, the Booths were itinerant revivalists. But the struggle between Methodist discipline and revivalism did not end in 1865. By then the Booths had fixed their ideological course. They followed the models of Caughey and Finney on revivalism and Phoebe Palmer on female ministry and holiness. They continued their Wesleyan lifestyle, which included teetotalism and plainness of dress and habit. Four years as nomads led them to decide, for the sake of Catherine's preaching, to live in London. This move started them down the road to the founding of the Salvation Army in 1878. Soon, in late summer 1865, William accepted an invitation from the East London Special Services Committee to preach to the East End's "heathen," while Catherine continued to preach in South and West London.

PART II.

Founding an Urban

Home Mission, 1865–79

When the Booths moved to London in 1865, they had no plan to found an urban mission. Yet, like other revivalists, they had weathered the uncertain income and family strain that were part of an itinerant life. The idea of a home lured them, but they did not want to become "settled ministers," an idea revivalists deplored. Consequently, for the next thirteen years, they experimented with ways to combine revivalism with an urban revival mission to save the unconverted "masses" in rapidly growing cities. Variously called Christian Revival Association, East London Revival Association, East London Christian Mission, and Christian Mission, Booth's experiments, by 1878, evolved into a "salvation army."

The experiment went through three phases. In the first phase, 1865–66, Booth operated a mission with financial support from two East London extradenominational evangelistic groups. Although not strictly under their control, in order to gain their support he had to conform to their notions of evangelism and frugality. The mission had trouble sustaining regular sites and building stable congregations. Its members were middle-class evangelicals, not the slum-dwellers who attended its meetings. The work involved making nightly forays into the streets, with a likelihood of physical abuse by roughs. This was the movement's charismatic stage, characterized by a dynamic leader, little structure or income, and no long-range goals. Most important, the mission was operated for, but not by, the East End poor.

A second phase began in 1867, when Booth formed a committee to advise him on financial and property matters as the mission acquired its first buildings. This phase ended when he ignored the committee's advice.

A third phase began in 1870, when Booth established a Methodist-style government. As general superintendent, he governed through conferences until 1878. District superintendents and lay speakers ran mission stations. Sources of income became more reliable, and membership grew, mainly outside of London after 1874. When the revival techniques learned from Caughey and Finney produced little success among the East End's "heathen" (a term the Booths used), the couple in 1878–79 wove those methods into a military jargon. This adaptability testifies to their unwillingness to give up on winning these masses and on broadening their appeal to the working class.

Thus the Booths' East End mission, indistinguishable from hundreds of others, became a salvation army. Numerous groups used the name "Christian Mission." The mission's doctrine was Wesleyan. It exhibited revival vigor in preaching, singing, house-to-house visiting, caring for the poor, distributing tracts, and temperance pledging. Its leaders were charismatic preachers who considered themselves to be spiritual heirs of the Apostles. All of these characteristics are common to the urban mission movement as a whole and illustrate Anglo-American missionary impulses at the time. Even before 1878, as it became apparent that London's masses were rejecting revivalism, the mission had begun to use militant language, popular music, and a Victorian delight in spectacle before the Booths renamed it "a salvation army."

3.

An East London

Home Mission, 1865–70

Practicality, not heavenly voices, dictated the Booths' move from Leeds to London in 1865. They sought a settled family life in a city familiar to them. Development of an urban home mission was an unintended result of the move. At least two contacts made by Catherine opened the doors to William's future. First, her "female preaching" came to the notice of the *Revival,* England's premier revival journal. In March, editors Richard Cope Morgan and Samuel Chase wrote to William that they wanted to hear Catherine preach. They agreed to female preaching in principle but doubted that a mother should forsake her home duties. They wanted William to read selected writings of Saint Paul. William called at the *Revival* office, eager to make friends with the influential editors. Shortly afterward, Morgan, a member of the East London Special Services Committee, invited William to preach in a tent in East London for a week because their regular revivalist was ill. This opportunity opened the way for him to find a sphere in which he would not be competing with his wife. Morgan, a member of the Plymouth Brethren and a Calvinist by training, continued as the Booths' good friend. Despite their theological differences, his paper became the Booths' publicist. In 1875 he broke with them over "holiness" doctrine, but he never lost contact with them.[1]

Catherine's second contact was with the Midnight Movement for Fallen Women,[2] one of many agencies in the 1860s that combined evangelism and social redemption. This contact previews the way in which the Booths later linked home mission work and social concerns—and especially concern for "fallen women"—in the Salvation Army. Since 1849, William's desire to be an ordained minister had drawn him away from the poor. Now he discovered what he came to see as his earlier calling through groups that regarded evangelism and social concern as

William Booth preaching in a tent on a disused burial ground in the Whitechapel district of East London in 1865. Courtesy of the Salvation Army National Archives and Research Center.

inseparable Christian duties. These agencies supported his mission from 1865 to 1868. They included the religious press, especially Morgan's *Revival* (*The Christian* after 1870). While the Wesleyan Conference press treated the Booths as schismatic brethren, the nonsectarian Nonconformist press took notice of any effort to affect East London's godless masses. Other journals reporting Booth's work included the *Wesleyan Times,* organ of the Free Methodists; the *Christian World,* begun in 1857 and growing to a circulation of one hundred thousand by 1867; the *Christian Times*; the *Nonconformist*; and the 1868 *Christian Year Book,* which listed Booth's mission under "Irregular Agencies."[3] Booth developed an instinct for getting the press's attention, which he used to advantage throughout his life.

In London, the Booths' ministries would be separate yet congruent. He would work in East London; her missions would be in West London and the provinces. Already she had scheduled her first West End services, to begin in June at the Polytechnic, Kensington Assembly Rooms, and the Myddleton Hall and Priory, Islington. Her West End contacts gained William access to extradenominational groups troubled by East London "heathenism." These agencies had interlocking directorates of wealthy London evangelicals. John Stabb and others linked the Midnight Movement and the *Revival* to the Christian Community, a group descended from seventeenth-century Huguenot settlers in East London's Spitalfields and Bethnal Green districts who had met at Wesley Chapel, City Road, in 1772. In 1849, the community had broken with Wesleyan Methodism to go with the Reformers. Later they chose to become nonsectarian. About twenty community members worked with Booth in his earliest East End open-air meetings at Mile End Waste in July 1865. From them he recruited two of his closest followers, John Eason and James Jermy (Jermy took Booth's mission ideas to America in 1872.) The Society of Friends, which had established the Open-Air Mission in 1853, also backed Booth's work by attending meetings and lending their Whitechapel Burial Ground for the tent in which Morgan and Chase invited Booth to preach. But Booth's main support came from two home mission groups founded in the 1850s and 1860s as a result of the American revivalist influence in England.[4]

The East London Special Services Committee officially asked William to work in East London; the Evangelisation Society supplied financial support. Both developed out of a nineteenth-century evangelical desire for united action beyond denominational borders. An 1846 London meeting formed an Evangelical Alliance to cement cooperation. Evangelicals formed voluntary agencies: tract societies, home and foreign mission societies, Sunday school associations, temperance and abolitionist unions, and Young Men's and Women's Christian Associations. Unlike later ecumenical agencies, these were not denominational creations. The 1846 alliance's agenda was "advancement of Evangelical Protestantism [and] the counteraction of infidelity, Popery, and other forms of superstition, error, and profaneness, especially the desecration of the Lord's Day."[5] These biases, identified with Manifest Destiny and Know-Nothingism in America, along with concern for social reform, produced imperial perfectionist-millennialist dreams of Anglo-American world redemption.

The Booths' mission roots were in this nonsectarian revival mentality. In the 1860s, revivalists expressed their inclusiveness and social concern in extradenominational voluntary agencies which constituted the soil in which Booth planted his mission in London's East End. Again it was an Anglo-American exchange of ideas that had led to the founding of agencies eager for religious and social reform. The East London Special Services Committee and the Evangelisation Society had grown out of the Evangelical Alliance. Reginald Radcliffe, when he came to London from Liverpool in 1861, had called "representatives and friends of all the agencies carrying on the Lord's work in the East End" to form an East London Special Services Committee. Morgan and Chase were members. Booth had met Radcliffe in 1857 at Chester. Radcliffe, who was a lawyer and lay-preacher, had organized preachers and tract-distributors to "attack" crowds at a public execution, a tactic Booth later used.[6] Two months earlier, when he was contemplating resignation from the New Connexion, Booth had visited London to discuss home mission work with committee member George Pearse. Now, in 1865, he found that the Special Services Committee was funding thirty mission halls from its Shoreditch headquarters and was eager to use his services in a tent in Whitechapel.[7]

A legal clash had triggered events which led the committee to place its tent in the Friends' Burial Ground where Booth first preached in 1865. In 1862 and 1863, the committee had set up the tent in Victoria Park, Hackney, as its summer mission. But early in 1864, the police commissioner prohibited meetings in public parks. The *Times* on July 2 reported that "metropolitan members and electors" had met at the House of Commons to protest the order.[8] This led the Society of Friends' trustees to lend their graveyard as a site for the tent on July 18, to conduct "services amongst the poorer classes not in the habit of attending any place of worship." John Stabb and Henry Thompson of the Special Services Committee and Samuel Hanson of the Evangelisation Society made the arrangements. The Evangelisation Society had been founded in 1864 to send evangelists "to preach the Lord Jesus to the unconverted." This group provided Booth with generous financial assistance until his mission was self-sufficient.[9]

In July, Booth had planned to go to Derby on an evangelistic tour. Just before he left, John Stabb and Samuel Chase of the East London Special Services Committee invited him to lead a week's services at their Quaker Burial Ground tent. Even with his vast experience, he later recalled, he worried about his "ability to deal with people of this class; I had made several efforts, but apparently failed, and the thought saddened and oppressed me beyond measure."[10] But it was not just the people's class that bothered him; he feared unstructured situations away from revival and Methodist practices with which he felt at home. The tent meetings went reasonably well, with large attendance and numerous converts. Christian friends who worked with him suggested that he devote his life to East London. This encouragement, plus the numbers of drunkards, blasphemers, thieves, gamblers, infidels, harlots, and pleasure seekers, in an area where so few ministered to eight hundred thousand who never entered a church or chapel, provided an irresistible pull. Booth asked himself, "Why go to Derby, or anywhere else, to find souls who need the gospel?" A voice promised, "I will help you—your need will be supplied." Later he recalled being "continually haunted with a desire to offer myself to Jesus Christ as an apostle for the heathen of East London."[11] But these were the reminiscences of fifty-seven-year-old General Booth, recalling his experiences for his Salvationist followers, not the thirty-six-year-old who in 1865 was trying to make up his mind what to do next.

For six weeks Booth held tent meetings nightly and three times on Sunday, preceded by open-air services on Mile End Waste opposite the Blind Beggar pub in Bethnal Green. The open-air congregation marched in procession to the tent, much as Booth had done four years earlier in Walsall. As many as fifteen penitents came forward each night, only about half the number to which he had been accustomed. The evangelical press thoroughly publicized his work. The *Revival* carried a letter from W. Jones Hayden, a member of the Special Services Committee, to John Stabb, commending "the labours of our dear Brother Booth."

Booth's decision to commit himself to the East End, at least for now, mixed anxiety with exuberance. His independence from bureaucracy's shackles produced glee, but a lack of ties to established religion heightened his insecurity. He gathered around him Christian Community members and others willing to work. Was he mastering a fear that he lacked the ability to deal with London's masses? He told his wife upon returning from a meeting, "Oh Kate, as I passed by the doors of the flaming gin-palaces tonight I seemed to hear a voice sounding in my ears, 'Where can you go and find such heathen as these,' . . . and I felt as though I ought at every cost to stop and preach to these East End multitudes." The sins of these "crowds had a fascination for me." But if these feelings lurked in Booth's mind in 1865, he did not reveal them until 1886. Kate responded with assurance, "Well, if you feel you ought to stay, stay." Her emotional and financial support were crucial, but now it was his organizational skill, his command of the principles of Finney and Caughey, that must produce results. Meanwhile, to support their family, Catherine, increasingly operating outside denominational boundaries, held meetings of three months' duration in some of London's largest halls. She informed her audiences of William's East End work and occasionally set up stations connected to his mission. William later recalled their nonsectarian state of mind in 1865: "I was strongly opposed to forming any separate organization." Sects created "divisions on the subject of practical Godliness and immediate results." His first inclination, in order to avert sectarianism, was his approach since 1861: "get the people saved, and send them to the churches." But he found this was "impracticable" because: "1st. They would not go when sent. 2nd. They are not wanted. 3rd. We wanted some of them at least ourselves, to help in the business of saving others." So he formed his own nonsectarian society. The *Revival* announced that he was forming a Christian Revival Association and in August 1865 published his first appeal for funds. He hoped to enroll a hundred persons immediately. He needed a central building in which to hold "our more private meetings, and in which to preach the Gospel when not engaged in special work elsewhere."[12] This last phrase indicates that Booth was not burning bridges to his earlier work. If the mission was unsuccessful, he could always return to itinerancy. When an August wind tore the tent to pieces, and costly repairs failed to mend it, the *Wesleyan Times* reported that Booth had engaged a large dancing hall. With an appeal for funds, a following of sorts, and support from lay revival committees and from his wife's West End work, William was about to organize his mission to bring the gospel to East London's "heathen."

The dancing room, available only on Sundays, seated 350. With friends, he moved benches into the hall early on Sunday mornings. The place was owned by a "godless" photographer who continued to ply his trade upstairs during services. After a morning open-air meeting at the end of the New Road, Whitechapel, Booth's address in the hall preceded the "breaking of bread." In the afternoon he preached on Commercial Road, followed by an "experience meeting" indoors. From 5:30 to 7:00, missioners conducted a service on Mile End Road, followed by a procession down Whitechapel Road to the hall, singing such hymns as "We're Bound for the Land of the Pure and the Holy," "There is a Fountain Filled with Blood," and "With a Turning from Sin, Let Repentance Begin." At the crowded hall's evening service, Booth and others went from seat to seat, inviting people to accept salvation—a "poor, painted, fallen female"; an "aged man and woman"; a "respectable looking young man"; sailors; a "troubled and trembling woman"; a "wanderer from the fold."[13]

Sometime in September, Booth received what he could only see as confirmation of his new work. Samuel Morley, Liberal member of Parliament for Nottingham, summoned him to his office. The summons was expected, since Morley was one of those to whom Booth had sent an account of his work, hoping for financial aid. Morley tendered a check for one hundred pounds toward family expenses; he hoped that other friends would raise the balance of Booth's support. Booth also had asked others for help. He went directly to Catherine at Horns Assembly Rooms, Kensington, with Morley's good news.[14] With one hundred pounds, proceeds from the sale of their books, and help from Cardiff friends Cory and Billups and from Booth's old sponsor Edward Rabbits, the Booths would have ample support for their large family and its middle-class lifestyle. But their most reliable asset still was Catherine's preaching in the West End, provincial towns, and summer resorts, where she found generous individuals willing to support the family and the mission. In November, the family moved from Hammersmith to South Hackney, two miles from Whitechapel, six miles closer to William's work. They lived in Hackney for twenty years, although two years later construction noise led them to move, at Catherine's request, to a house near Victoria Park. A seventh child, Eveline Cory, named for the Booths' Welsh benefactors, was born on December 25, 1865.

Catherine suffered from chronic diarrhea, and William took her to Tunbridge Wells to recuperate, a hard blow to their finances.[15] There they met Henry Reed, a wealthy retired Tasmanian sheep farmer and Wesleyan churchman who invited William to preach at his mission at Dunorlan, his palatial estate. William had East End commitments, but

Catherine preached so impressively at Dunorlan that Reed opened his pocketbook for them. So began a turbulent relationship that lasted until Reed's death in 1880.

Once established in Whitechapel, Booth received requests from friends in other East End districts—Bethnal Green, Limehouse, Poplar, and Canning Town—to establish mission stations in their areas. He responded, "Well, see if you can get any room suitable for services and let me know what it will cost, and I will come and see about it." This was the way the mission grew during the next thirteen years. In November, Booth reported that dancing-room offerings for thirteen weeks amounted to eleven pounds from the box placed at the door and twenty pounds from members' private offerings. Twenty pounds just covered rent. Other expenses included ten shillings to pay Brother Pye and the carman to remove the Quaker Burial ground tent. Rent of buildings for weeknight services, too much for missioners, was paid with money Booth raised from friends.[16]

Renting buildings was Booth's main concern. They used eleven different halls, mostly on weeknights, and the dancing room on Sundays. An old wool warehouse in Bethnal Green was their first long-term base. They also used a Free Church, termed a "ragged church" which catered to the poor, in Stepney. Holywell Mount Chapel in Shoreditch belonged to the Methodist New Connexion; the parish had declined when a railroad and factories replaced homes. In July 1866, two trustees offered the building for sixty pounds per year, with eighteen months left on the lease; Booth signed. He briefly used a stable in a court off Whitechapel Road, but the mission was not congenial with a sparring club next door. Other buildings were a "covered skittle alley" attached to a pub in Whitechapel; a mission room at Reverend Tyler's church on Church (now Hanbury) Street; a carpenter's shop in Old Ford; a wooden pigsty where "stench oozed" through the wall in Poplar; and a room behind a pigeon shop in Shoreditch. Stations moved from rented hall to rented hall until they raised funds sufficient to purchase their own building. Many halls stood near back courts inhabited by Irish immigrants, where clashes between the mission intruders and Catholic inhabitants were inevitable.

In a September 1866 report, published while a cholera epidemic swept London, Booth reported three sites at which the mission held seventeen open-air and twenty indoor meetings a week. "Men who delight in evangelistic work, and sisters also" spoke outdoors and in. The cost of rent, free teas, tracts, and other expenses caused Booth to close his report with an appeal—"We want funds." He also expressed need for "a Pentecostal baptism of the Holy Ghost."[17] Catherine continued to preach, but after her 1866–67 illness, she never completely regained health.

Between 1867 and 1870, the mission grew by adding stations and members, absorbing other missions, and renting larger halls. The year 1867 was the turning point; the mission matured from a dependent home mission with Evangelisation Society support into a society with its own committee to advise Booth and raise money. All the while, Booth took only as much advice from anyone as was absolutely necessary in order to continue his work. Yet, overall, the mission differed little from other home missions, with a mixed program of religion and poor relief. If it was more successful, it was due to the energy of Booth and his lay associates and not to the originality of its organization or program.

After his hesitant acceptance of the request to preach in the tent, Booth had slowly grasped the prospect of an independent mission to the "heathen" of London's East End, backed by a mix of individuals and voluntary agencies. The man who once had resisted Methodist discipline now manipulated committeemen, supporting agencies, and missioners. Those who deserted him he treated as God's foes, and those who aided him he saw as saints. The mission's spirit blunted Booth's heavy-handed exercise of authority. Only time would tell whether this would be another short-lived mission or a lasting entity destined to develop its own traditions. Booth's fervor made him think of himself as God's chosen instrument, virtually to the exclusion of evangelists and missions doing the same work or laymen whose mature advice he might profitably have accepted. While such traits may be seen as defects, they proved essential to Booth's success. As God's Englishman, anxiety concerning church and nation drove him toward extradenominational revivalism and later toward social reform.

The chief concern of the East London Christian Mission from 1867 to 1870 was survival. First, as the Evangelisation Society gradually withdrew its support, the mission became increasingly self-sufficient. Booth collected donations from subscribers, many of whom Catherine recruited through missions among the wealthy. Second, by 1870, Booth had a committee of "gentlemen" to advise him in management, their names lending credibility to his operations. Third, by producing his own lay leadership, he slowly expanded his East End following and the number of halls he rented for services. Growth came primarily from laymen who moved from the neighborhood of an East End station to the suburbs, taking the mission with them. A less fruitful means of growth came from absorbing other missions. Extension beyond East London by this means—to Upper Norwood, Croydon, Brighton, Hastings, Edinburgh—was unsuccessful, often ending in schisms led by missioners who preferred to be independent of Booth's control.

As the mission moved beyond London, Booth changed its name from the East London Christian Mission to simply the Christian Mission, and its monthly magazine, begun in 1868 as the *East London Evangelist,* became the *Christian Mission Magazine.* By 1870, Booth had no intention of limiting himself to East London, although that remained his key field. In spite of his minimal success, the press used his mission to hail what could happen among the "masses" if missions employed effective methods.

From 1867 to 1870, the number of stations, leaders, and members increased, all due to the work of lay members. The one Whitechapel Station grew to nine stations by March 1867. A "Biblewoman," Eliza Collingridge, became Booth's first paid employee. She visited house-to-house, distributed tracts, and led women's Bible study–prayer groups. She also became a forceful preacher, and by 1868, Booth assigned her to superintend a station, the first woman to hold such a post. Six years later Annie Davis became the first woman to lead a station full-time. In 1867, the mission's seating capacity reached eight thousand, but membership was only three hundred. Still *for,* but not *by* the East End masses, only subscribers who met its high doctrinal standards would become members. Booth made no membership statistics available until 1871, when he claimed 998 members. By late 1867, he had ten workers "wholly given up to the work." In 1868, the *Christian Year Book* identified Booth as "carrying on evangelistic work on a large scale." In January 1868, Booth spoke on "The Evangelization of London" at an Evangelical Alliance meeting. In February, the *Revival* carried a report, "The Heathen of Our Own Land," which stated that Booth employed twenty persons "assisted by a large band of devoted helpers." Since Booth had said "not a single official salary is paid," the *Revival* assumed that he meant "office staff" salaries, since at least nine workers were "sustained" by the mission. They held 120 outdoor services weekly with an estimated fourteen thousand in attendance.[18]

In 1868, Booth reported 140 weekly services and four thousand eager enquirers seeking salvation since 1865. But less than a tenth of the enquirers had become members. Members' offerings of thirty to forty pounds a week did not meet expenses at the thirteen stations. The *Nonconformist* called the membership "working-class." An article in the *Revival,* by Gawin Kirkham, head of the Open-Air Mission and a member of Booth's council, described a Sunday afternoon meeting at which Booth told the audience that the working class had an aversion to churches but would "eagerly listen to any speaker who, with ordinary ability, in an earnest and loving manner, could set before them the truths of the Bible in the open air."[19]

In 1869, Booth opened stations at Limehouse and Canning Town. Eliza Collingridge and James Dowdle, the first paid evangelist, continued to be busy. East London Theatre congregations averaged nearly two thousand on four Sunday evenings in July, with over sixty enquirers, and the mission held camp meetings in London Fields. On Sunday, July 18, Henry Reed led a meeting of the whole mission at Wesley Chapel, Bethnal Green, with about 1,800 present. The next day 1,420 went to Reed's Tunbridge Wells estate for an excursion on two special trains. They held morning and afternoon meetings and then walked in procession back to the trains. They prayed and sang hymns in the carriages until eleven o'clock, when they arrived back in London. Such was a missioner's recreation. Laymen opened stations at Bow Common and Old Ford. Two missioners moved to Old Ford and asked Booth to take over "two rooms they could knock into one." Likewise, three or four men who attended meetings at Poplar asked to "take the financial responsibility" for renting rooms at Canning Town. But about the same time, trouble erupted at Stratford, when a long "misunderstanding" caused the brother in charge to leave and take most of the people with him.[20]

The mission also grew by absorbing existing missions whose organizers asked Booth to take over. In 1868, a gentleman in Upper Norwood asked Booth to run a mission he had built for a Gypsy Hill colony. Gentlemen were willing to support mission halls in order to dictate the manner of their operations. Booth had no use for such missions, even when run by his friends Edward Rabbits and Henry Reed. The paternal-

Christian Mission Headquarters on
Whitechapel Road, East London,
formerly a beerhouse known as
"The Eastern Star." Courtesy of the
Salvation Army National Archives
and Research Center.

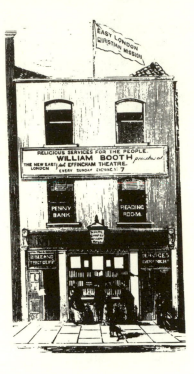

istic benefactor held sway over preacher and members. In the Upper
Norwood instance, the gentleman resumed possession of his mission
once conditions improved.[21]

In July 1869, the Booths made their first visit to Scotland, with their
sickly son Bramwell. They stayed with John Melrose, a wealthy, child-
less merchant, who offered to subsidize Bramwell's education. A "gentleman" who had visited East London and become inspired by Booth's work
was copying it in a "dull, dingy-looking loft" in an Edinburgh slum. William felt that he and Catherine had "gone out of our parish"; they had
left London and England. Still, this was a moving outing for the Booths,
who had read of Wesley's and Finney's poor reception by the clannish,
Calvinist Scots. On July 25, four hundred attended a free breakfast at which
William preached. Catherine spoke to a packed chapel that evening. At a
tea held in their honor on August 16, their last day in Scotland, they
disclosed Edinburgh's amalgamation into the Christian Mission. The union
lasted until 1870, when Booth cut it off for financial reasons. East London's
funds were inadequate to support Edinburgh.[22]

Booth continued to have problems finding buildings large enough to permit growth but not so large as to be a financial burden. In 1867, he opened his first headquarters at the Eastern Star, formerly a "low beerhouse, notorious for immorality," which soon burned. He rebuilt it with a bookstore in front and a hall in back. This Whitechapel Road building provided rooms for classes upstairs: a reading room with cheap refreshments, mothers' meetings, Bible classes, believers' meetings, and a residence for the Biblewoman and her husband. This division of space was ideal for a mission operation. Booth continued to rent music halls for large Sunday services and storefronts along main thoroughfares for weeknights. For example, Shoreditch station occupied the drafty City of London Theatre, then the Cambridge and Apollo Music Halls on Sundays. Until 1870, 250 Shoreditch missioners gathered for weeknight meetings in a coffee house, with a shop for religious literature, rooms upstairs for private meetings, and a small refuge for "friendless penniless girls." When brewers Hanbury, Truman, and Brixton purchased the Apollo and adjoining pub, they allowed Booth to use the hall free of rent until 1875. Booth took largess from brewers when it benefited his mission. He also recommenced services at the renovated Effingham Theatre, now called the New East London Theatre.[23]

The Evangelisation Society, which had supported the mission financially over the winter, expected that spring weather would permit outdoor services to reduce expenses. When the mission continued services indoors, the society continued to pay its rent. In a letter to the *East London Observer,* "Anti-Humbug" indicated that he did not share the Evangelisation Society's desire to see the mission move outdoors. He opposed the noise. In the fall, the Bethnal Green station had occupied a Three Colts' Lane wool shed where "petty persecution" included "trains of gunpowder" and harassment of open-air services by police, publicans, and pub customers. In February, the station moved to an old tin-plate factory. When a railway company demolished this hall, the station moved to Thomas Passage Hall, then to a chapel in Hart's Lane, and finally to a Railway Arch. At the time, the mission also held services at the Free Church, Mile End New Town; at Alfred Street Chapel, Stepney; and at Satchwell Street, Bethnal Green. The Limehouse station completed a year-long project to lease a penny gaff (cheap music hall) called the Eastern Alhambra in 1868. The gaff's three main qualifications for mission work were that it

was well located on a busy street, was near good open-air meeting locations, and was surrounded by a heathen population. Dr. Thomas Bernardo,
then a student at London Hospital and later a founder of children's
homes, assisted at this station.[24]

Catherine seldom preached in the East End, and William seldom left
it. For three months in early 1867, she preached at the Eyre Arms Assembly Rooms in Saint John's Wood, and weeknights in Baptist and independent churches. Most astounding, her audiences were over 75 percent
"gentlemen," a wonder considering the alleged opposition to female
preaching. At the end of these meetings, several men offered to build
her a permanent hall. She declined, possibly to avoid unwanted rivalry
with William, although a regular platform would have been more to her
liking than the peripatetic life she engaged in. A young man who attended
her meetings asked the Evangelisation Society to increase William's grant
to between twelve and fourteen pounds per week, as William already had
requested. As the society had received a five-thousand-pound donation for
just the kind of work William was doing, this young man's testimonial to
Catherine's work turned the tide in William's favor with the society.

At a lady's suggestion, Catherine in 1867 began preaching at seaside
resorts, accompanying her West End following to its summer retreats. At
Ramsgate, she overfilled the hall. She moved to Margate's Royal Assembly Rooms for Sundays during the season and rented a house into which
she moved her children, a servant, and a friend. William remained in
London with the other two servants, a cook and a housemaid. Mrs.
Billups of Cardiff was at Margate with her family, including her daughter, Mary Coutts Billups, whom Catherine's preaching converted. Mary
became Booth's chief aid in producing the mission's first tune book to
accompany his hymnal, which included only words. At Margate, Mr.
Knight, a publisher, offered to print Catherine's sermons. She refused,
again fearing that her preaching might be praised more highly than
William's. Another reason might have been the messy condition of her
notes. Publication could have raised additional income for the family, an
opportunity she seldom missed. That fall she spoke for the first time in
the East End, at the Oriental Music Hall, Poplar, where she attacked Plymouth Brethrenism, a hard-line Calvinist sect whose theology and opposition to female preaching raised her ire.

In October, illness reduced her to the task of writing the mission's "begging letters." She raised funds to purchase the People's Hall by managing a sale of "gold and silver ornaments, jewelry," items she preached against as "worldly." She wrote to Mrs. Billups after rereading Finney, "you need no human ordination, no long and tedious preparation, no high-flown language, no towering eloquence; all you want is the full baptism of the Spirit on your heart, the Bible in your hand, and humility and simplicity in your manner." She expounded on health and joined those who attacked Jenner's vaccination. Depression caused her to brood over England's "going down hill at an awful rate." At the time of her last child's (Lucy) birth in April 1868, she began a three-month campaign at Croydon, which led to the opening of another mission station. When she returned from Edinburgh, the Evangelisation Society asked her to preach at Brighton, known as "London by the sea," her second summer at resorts. Her first two Sundays were in the Grand Concert Hall. When the owner saw the crowds, he raised the rent. Outraged, she moved to the three-thousand-seat Dome. This building, built by George IV in 1782, had a Chinese interior and an onion-shaped dome and minarets in the style of an Indian palace. One of the most impressive halls in England, it was a great challenge to Catherine's voice. She succeeded in being heard while preaching a gospel which provided no easy balm to the consciences of the rich.

Here she met Father Ignatius, who had revived the Church of England's Benedictine Order. He wrote to her expressing a desire that she be "led into 'all truth.'" She shared his hope and in turn prayed that God would "enable you to lead hundreds of poor deluded souls, who are seeking rest in 'washings and carnal rites,' to find this blest inward kingdom." She hoped to meet him in that day when "all the saints will see eye to eye." He respected her refusal to lower her colors when pressed by an Anglican version of truth. She expressed her creed that it was not ceremonial religion or priestly sacrament, but the experience of rebirth that brought salvation. He wrote to a friend at her death in 1890, "What a glorious woman! What a 'mother of giants in Israel!' What an astonishing Fact is The Salvation Army! What a shame, and what a glory to the churches! . . . Newman, Liddon, Booth—true saints 'promoted' almost together."[25]

While Catherine preached at Brighton, her mother was dying of cancer, a horrendous death similar to Catherine's twenty-one years later. The Mumfords had moved to the house next to the Booths'. Catherine had injected morphine when her mother suffered extreme depression. Mrs. Mumford's death on December 16, 1868, at age sixty-seven, was Catherine's first experience with the death of a close relative. The death certificate listed her as a "widow," although in fact Mr. Mumford was alive, possibly on a drunken spree. The attending nurse who notified the authorities likely never had heard his name spoken. He died on April 10, 1879.

In March 1867, William set up his first organization, a council of gentlemen to advise him and provide financial backing. The council included ten well-known philanthropists serving as referees (advisors), and a committee to monitor mission operations. Booth-Tucker later claimed that Booth worked with the council in "perfect harmony" until he dissolved it in a "friendly manner." If that is true, then they must have been, as Ervine concluded, "a respectable Council and a submissive Committee." In the previous two years, Booth had acted on his own in fundraising and acquiring halls. Now he hoped that these gentlemen, committed to reaching the East End's masses with the gospel, would help him increase his support from the Evangelisation Society, other groups, and individuals. Booth's honorary legal advisor, Frederick Whittaker of Gray's Inn, announced the new committee, with himself as secretary.[26]

The Evangelisation Society gave 3 pounds a week for each of five stations *where no church was formed,* beginning in February. In March, the society voted 12 pounds for a month's rent of Easton Hall, 4 for an evangelist's salary, and 1 for printing. For opening Oriental Music Hall, Poplar, the society granted 7 pounds. Mission collections amounted to 3 pounds per week, less than a tenth of the mission's needs; another 20 pounds came from donors. In July, after reporting to his committee that there had been one thousand converts and that he had nearly three hundred helpers, Booth made a brash request that the society provide 112 pounds per year to erect a hall in Poplar. In response to his escalating costs, the society refused this request. In August, Charles Owen, a Millwall factory owner, became mission secretary. Booth reported a balance of nearly 33 pounds in September's financial statement, although the mission had overspent on poor relief. Not a penny of the funds went to his own support, Booth claimed.

Although the Evangelisation Society granted Booth another 100 pounds by November, his October request had led to an inquiry. It found that his accounts differed from the society's own by 114 pounds, due to continuation at Oriental Music Hall and Pavilion Theatre without Booth's requesting an extension of previous grants. After the society sent 50 pounds in partial payment, it directed its secretary to tell Booth of the group's alarm at seeing circulars stating that the mission needed 40 pounds per week. They feared that their "connection with him would bring them into discredit." This experience with the Evangelisation Society epitomizes Booth's stormy relations with committees.

At the end of 1867, the society warned that it would fund Booth at four pounds per week for only one more quarter; his fiscally conservative patrons were alarmed at a torrent of expenditures which menaced both his organization and theirs. In January, the society granted eight pounds per week to rent two theaters through March, double what they had promised. In April they hoped that Booth would move to the streets and give up costly theaters, but the minutes from April to August show that the weekly grant continued. By June, expenses had reached fifty pounds per week. Booth appealed to the *Revival* for his "unsectarian" work. By September, he was leasing the Limehouse penny gaff for fifty-two pounds, with ninety pounds spent for refurbishing. Requests that he think conservatively had no effect, and the society made its last grant to Booth: fifty pounds for January to March 1869. On April 7, the society's minutes read, "The honorary secretary was requested to inform Mr. Booth that the committee find themselves compelled to relinquish the pecuniary grant hitherto made to him [since the mission was now] a permanent, organized institution."[27] Booth was on his own. His mission was no longer a grant-supported experiment; it had become a "permanent mission."

Purchase of the People's Market for transformation into a People's Mission Hall proves that Booth's committee had no more control over his fiscal adventures than did the Evangelisation Society. It was no board of trustees with power to make policy and authorize expenditures, although at times that appeared to be its role. The purchase also indicates that Booth's style was autocratic long before he invented the Salvation Army in 1878. Tabernacles were the evangelists' dream. Baptist Charles H. Spurgeon built Metropolitan Tabernacle in South London, and Congregationalists John Campbell and Joseph Parker built Moorfields Tabernacle and City Temple to draw crowds of working-class Londoners.[28] Success at the Effingham Theatre gave Booth a taste for tabernacles. And if he purchased the market, which had a large shop in front, a soup kitchen, and seating for nearly two thousand, the mission could save the five-hundred-pound annual cost of the East London Theatre, which seated crowds in dreary comfortlessness, and rent for weeknight meeting rooms. To assure contributors that he would honor the purpose for which the property was acquired, he would place it in trust. Some were saying that he constantly appealed for funds—first a beer-house, then a Unitarian chapel, then a penny gaff, now a People's Market—but, he asked them, had he not shown "a rich harvest of souls" in return for these gifts?

In August 1868, Booth began amassing funds to buy People's Market. Subscribers sent donations—250 pounds from "a Friend," 200 from Samuel Morley. The owner, ham and beef dealer John McAll, a member of Booth's committee, had opened the market in February. It had failed, and McAll was looking for a buyer. After McAll resigned from the committee pending a sale, his financial position worsened, and Booth's object came closer. On October 3, Booth told the *East End Observer* that the deal would be closed soon, but McAll refused Booth's offer of 2,500 pounds. The matter was in this confused state when Henry Reed offered Booth a proposal on New Year's Eve. Reed would build a two-thousand-seat hall with "every possible requisite for the carrying on of the work," and would provide "a generous sum" for the family, if Booth would accept Reed's conditions. If Reed ever disapproved of Booth's behavior, he could repossess the hall. Refusing conditions that would have made him Reed's slave, Booth wrote, "Your views and ours differ so much that to attempt together such a work would be unwise."

Contributions of 1,300 pounds were garnered at the Temperance Permanent Land and Building Society, with another 1,750 promised. It would take another thousand pounds to refurbish the hall. In October 1869, McAll dropped his price to 1,750 pounds, 750 lower than the original price. Booth purchased the hall and began refurbishing. The tabernacle opened on April 10, 1870, his forty-first birthday. With a front like a chapel, the inside resembled "a music hall minus ornament." Booth would run a soup kitchen at 188 Whitechapel Road to feed the poor and at the same time aid the mission's income. But trouble was brewing.

Four days after the opening, the committee informed Habershon and Pite, Architects, that their bill for 1,411 pounds, plus 95 pounds to move the soup kitchen to Whitechapel, was much more than Booth had told them the mission could afford. But they learned that the 500-pound over-age was due to Booth's mismanagement. He had failed to accept low bids for foundation and excavation work and had paid nearly double for seats. He was loathe to depend on the philanthropic committee's exper-tise. While the frugal religious conservatives found his theology accept-able, they found his spending wasteful. Booth asked Henry Reed to bail him out, but instead received a stinging rebuke. Going into debt by 500 pounds for a hall that Reed from the first had opposed buying was "a violation of your word." Reed gave his advice: sell your home, move your family to a small house—"clerks live upon £100 per year"—and ask your wife and daughters to "keep the house." Catherine must stop preaching; Reed never had approved of her doing so. He chided Booth for not consulting his committee, of which Reed was not a member. Booth re-jected the advice.

In late April, the committee heard Booth's version of his correspon-dence with the architects, who were demanding money to pay contrac-tors. He had paid them all he had available, but they threatened to sue. He was refusing to make an appeal for funds until he had seen their accounts. The committee did not want to become involved in Booth's dealings, since he had not consulted them. Instead, they agreed that he personally should assume management of the Whitechapel soup con-cession, which he would lease from the mission for 140 pounds a year. In return, they would pay his thousand-pound life insurance policy out of mission funds.[29]

This venture signals Booth's changed attitude toward property. Where before he had rented buildings, now he was an owner. Renters are mobile and liable only for rent. Owners are stable and liable for long-term obli-gations. He had gone from secular halls to a building employed for mis-sion purposes alone. Such permanency has a settling effect; mortgages cause missioners to be more concerned with upkeep than outreach.[30] The Evangelisation Society having decided to cut off grants since the mission had become a "permanent institution," Booth's mission could now add "settled" and "mortgaged" to its self-definition.

Between 1867 and 1870, Booth developed an impressive urban home mission program which emphasized "outdoor relief," that is, hand-outs of food and clothing, soup kitchens and free teas, maternal societies, and a Biblewoman's door-to-door survey of spiritual and physical needs. Booth used physical need as an entree to conversion. There was potential for "breakfast and coal Christians"—or, as the Irish termed them, "soupers"—to take unfair benefit of the mission's assistance. But, for Booth, meeting physical need without delivering a message of spiritual hope was unconscionable. Economic panic and cholera during the winter of 1866–67 caused the mission to increase handouts. On one occasion it fed one thousand at the Cambridge Music Hall, before T. B. Smithies, editor of the *British Workman* spoke. This aid elicited support from the Society of Friends. On Good Friday, three hundred persons attended a tea at Poplar and one thousand a similar event at the East London Theatre, as missioners held open-air services aimed at producing a crowd for an indoor evangelistic service. In early 1868, the *Saturday Review* indicted the mission for inducing "the poor to worship by the bait of a breakfast and coal ticket," the same lure used by political machines to entice the poor to give their votes.

The Charity Organisation Society, formed in 1869, favored case inquiries and opposed handouts. But urban missions, poor-law committees, trade unions, and political parties continued handouts to the needy from motives viewed as either exploitive or noble. Booth hoped to win converts at free teas and Christmas dinners; charity, after all, diverted income from tract printing, Bible carriages, and hall rentals. W. T. Stead held that it was Booth's genius to use converts to win converts. A missioner rebutted the *Saturday Review's* charge: "Would they not call it a mockery to talk about their souls whilst their bodies were perishing with hunger?" Booth reported in September 1867 that he spent three hundred pounds for two hundred weekly meat and bread tickets, gave or lent money, and ran maternal societies and a Poplar soup kitchen. The mission found work for the unemployed and assisted emigrants. Its first Christmas appeal in 1869 was for one hundred pounds to distribute three hundred dinners of four pounds of beef, a plum pudding, and an ounce of tea. Booth asserted that inquiries were made as to need, but the recipient did not have to attend the mission to be assisted.[31]

Saving souls was Booth's focus. He employed open-air services, door-to-door visitation, tract distribution, cottage meetings, and the dole to bring people to meetings at which their spiritual condition could be altered. Indoor meetings combined American revivalism with English music-hall entertainment. A *Christian World* article distinguished mission services on Sundays at the Apollo Music Hall from events there on week-days, when young people crowded in to mimic popular comic songs, accompanied by a three-piece orchestra. On Sunday evenings, instead of "noisy choruses of popular songs," those present raised their voices in "gladsome notes of praise" which touched "the unwashed, grimy look-ing idlers who lounge[d] at the public-house bar." They "slowly put out their pipes, [left] off drinking their beer, and either enter[ed] the hall from the bar or else [betook] themselves to the tap-room."

Sympathizers drew distinctions, but critics saw similarities between music-hall and gospel-hall formats. Both sang lively songs to popular British or American tunes. American camp meetings and revivals used popular tunes adapted to religious lyrics, as had Wesley and other eigh-teenth-century preachers. As an itinerant preacher in the 1850s, Booth had turned over piles of music at a bookseller's to find tunes Catherine could put to religious words. When he found the "Bridal Waltz," he hesi-tated paying "so much for the Devil's music." He used Whitefield's re-sponse to an Episcopal cleric who accused him of using ungodly tunes: "Can you assign a good reason why the devil should always have the best tunes?" Catherine once wrote to William that a postboy had passed her window humming, "Why did my master sell me," an American abo-litionist melody to which William put religious words. Booth, like most revivalists, published a book of hymns in 1864, but there is no evidence that he included his own work.

Speeches in interludes between songs were kept brief, a technique Booth had learned from Caughey and used with hallelujah bands. Restless audiences would not abide orations. Humor was essential. Catherine's in-tense logic was less suited to a music-hall setting than William's terse points sprinkled with often self-deprecating anecdotes. Not all services were alike. The converts' experience meeting with testimonies, on Sun-day afternoons, came closest to the music-hall format and, Salvationist historian Robert Sandall noted, served as "the mission's counter attrac-tion to the public-house 'sing song.'"[32] In fact, the mission adopted terms like "sing-song" and "free-and-easy" from the music-hall bill. Speakers' testimonies told of how they had met the mission and how their lives had changed following conversion from sin to salvation. These talks of-ten were humorous and told of experiences that others in the hall could identify with. Hand-clapping to choruses was common, along with other physical movement.

Services following free breakfasts, attended by the poorest of the poor, were a particular challenge to leaders who wanted to hold attention and get a message across. The *Morning Advertiser* described an East London Theatre crowd of over eight hundred at a breakfast meeting. From "foetid courts and alleys, from the casual wards, from registered lodging houses, from sleep on doorsteps and in railway arches" came a "mixed multitude," Negroes, mulattos, and "denizens of distant countries," clad "in rags and tatters."[33] Critics aimed barbs at this raucous example of mission services; they found elements of music-hall ribaldry in bad taste in a church, but Booth had discovered in 1854 that "nothing moves the people like the terrific." This was even more true among East London's poor than among the Midlands' working class.

Booth launched the *East London Evangelist* in October 1868, "partly because editors of other religious papers insisted on altering his reports," according to Ervine, but the idea went back to the 1850s. William had written to Catherine in 1855 regarding the New Connexion magazine, "What a poor magazine your letter is in. I am literally ashamed of it as the organ of our denomination." The editor had rejected William's "Apostolic Ministry" essay, so his judgment was clouded. Nevertheless, William vowed that some day the "revival movement shall have an organ." A first edition stated goals: to advocate "earnest Christianity" and ignore "minor points of doctrine"; to report "Revival Facts and Incidents" from around the world, as even secular newspapers did in America; to cull effective revival methods from history and print life-sketches of devout Christians; to publish sermon outlines suitable for open-air, mission hall, or village pulpit, and examples that would arrest attention and explain biblical truths; and to devote ample space to the subject of holiness, "the great want of the age." This publication would "break up the slumbers of the professing church, arrest the attention of a dying world, and clothe the religion of Jesus with its primitive simplicity, fervour, and energy," and support a "mighty outpouring of the Holy Ghost to stem the rising tide of error and superstition." Booth reprinted a mission history he had prepared for his 1867 annual report. In this first account of the mission's origins, its founder invented a past for a society which, he was beginning to see, had a future. It was more factual than histories created in the 1880s when millennialist visions had begun to take over.[34]

With outdoor and indoor services; a magazine; visitation; tract sales; mothers', temperance, and believers' meetings; bands of hope for junior abstinence pledgers; Bible classes; classes in reading, writing, and arithmetic; reading rooms; penny banks; food distribution to the destitute and sick; and soup kitchens, Booth's program was like those of other Anglo-American urban home missions. In addition, his mission had shops at Shoreditch and Whitechapel to sell "goods sent for the benefit of the Mission."

Booth believed that God worked miracles of conversion in ways other than gospel preaching in large revival meetings. The mission's program could best be viewed as arranged in concentric circles. At the outer rim, the organization used retail shops and poor relief. Moving inward, missioners operated educational programs to draw the "heathen" within reach. Classes taught the gospel in minor doses along with temperance, maternal advice, and reading. Booth ruthlessly canceled programs which did not move the masses closer to the central point of conversion. Closest to the center were nightly open-air and indoor services, visitation, and literature sales. Conversion was most likely to happen at a penitent form at the end of a hot revival sermon at one of the mission stations. At the inner circle, the believers' meeting made converts into "helpers" in the work. Training lay members as speakers, teachers, and visitors was, above all, Booth's genius. Summing up, Booth observed that his East London mission was a true home mission to the "heathen of London." It sympathized with man as man, body and soul, for time and eternity. Like all missions, his was "evangelistic and unsectarian."[35] Viewing London's masses as "heathen" was no Boothian novelty; it was a Victorian mindset. A combined soul and body ministry in a nonsectarian voluntary approach was popular at the time. Therefore, the reason for Booth's persistence after other missions had died out must be found elsewhere than in the novelty of his program.

Although the Booths were Wesleyan-Arminian doctrinally, in 1865 they merged articles of faith from broad creeds of the Evangelical Alliance and the Methodist New Connexion.[36] Their brief new creed, with the addition of three articles in 1870 and one more in 1876, remains

Salvation Army doctrine today. The alliance had blended standard creeds in 1846, in order to attain unity to oppose the forces of infidelity and popery. Historian J. Edwin Orr found that, after 1859, a year of massive revivals in England and the U.S., the 1846 dogma was "so widely adopted that it led to a practice of fraternal fellowship having the force of a major doctrine."[37] The Booths were not the only ones to borrow from the 1846 creed. To attract broad support for their mission, they found that an ecumenical creed met their purpose. Only in 1875–76 did they adopt doctrines with a purely Wesleyan cast. Then the mission added an article which dealt with holiness and the perseverance of the saints.[38] Calvinists, who until 1876 had served as mission evangelists, emphasized a sovereign God who did not permit human participation in the act of salvation. At first broad in its scope, the mission became narrow and sectarian by 1876.

If they copied existing creeds, the Booths had reason to delete points that discussed a person's right to interpret Scripture,[39] and the divine institution of an ordained ministry and sacraments. These deletions in 1865–66 may have been made in deference to the mission's Quaker supporters. The 1846 Evangelical Alliance conference also had considered the Quakers when it adopted its stand on sacraments and on ordained ministry, but it had determined that a larger constituency would be offended if they were left out. Booth retained baptism and communion as Salvation Army practice as late as 1883, but he did not include them in his creed. When the army ceased practicing sacraments, Booth invented rites performed only by officer-clergy, thus perpetuating a sacramental tradition after he had set aside the historical rites of baptism and the Lord's Supper. This early, pragmatic deletion of sacraments then became dogma. While Booth blurred the line between laity and clergy among mission preachers, he still clung to his own ministerial authority and used the title "Reverend" while denying its use to others.[40]

Booth's *Christian Mission Magazine* shared the Evangelical Alliance's view that high-church ritualism was a prime enemy of evangelicals. In an editorial response to a Church of England congress declaration that "the day of 'Evangelicalism' was past, and that 'the masses are not to be taken so much by the ear as by the eye,'" Booth argued that "a living Church—a Church which enjoys constant displays of God's saving grace—can attract the masses, and can hold them; but no other Church can."

Catherine told a Chatham audience that Church of England ritualists were above the level of the East End masses who "never attend a place of worship." Churchmen did not hold unsectarian services in mission halls, theaters, music halls, and penny gaffs, where thousands heard the gospel. Volunteer laymen and only sixteen paid missionaries were proving the Christian Mission's reputation as the church's only hope for converting the heathen masses.[41]

In the 1870s, American Wesleyan revivalists Phoebe Palmer and Robert and Hannah Smith inspired the Booths' renewed interest in the doctrine of holiness. In 1870, two new articles expressed this Wesleyan-Arminian position. One added an Arminian clause to an earlier statement on the atonement: "We believe that we are justified by grace through faith in our Lord Jesus Christ and that *he that believeth hath the witness in himself*" (emphasis added). A believer could receive grace by placing faith in Christ and could have personal knowledge of salvation. This belief was not new to the Wesleyan Booths, but it excluded Calvinists from their fellowship. Calvinists, who hitherto had served as mission evangelists, held that God would not permit a human role in salvation. To enforce adherence to the new doctrine, Bramwell Booth proposed to the 1873 Christian Mission conference that "no person shall be allowed to teach . . . the doctrine of final perseverance in Holiness" (that the "elect" of God could not sin or fall from grace). He hoped to root out confirmed Calvinists still in the mission. This position took doctrinal form in 1876: "We believe that the Scriptures teach that not only does continuance in the favor of God depend upon continued faith in and obedience to Christ but that it is possible for those who have been truly converted to fall away and be eternally lost."

The 1876 conference also adopted this article: "We believe that it is the privilege of all believers to be 'wholly sanctified' and that their 'whole spirit and soul and body' may 'be preserved blameless unto the coming of our Lord Jesus Christ.' 1 Thess. 5:23." This reveals growing Anglo-American interest in a doctrine of holiness. It also indicated a growing trend toward sectarian exclusiveness. The mission became less ecumenical as it became independent of the need to recruit evangelists and solicit funds from evangelical societies. The primacy of this Wesleyan doctrine of entire sanctification, or holiness, can be seen in the *Christian Mission Magazine*, which in September 1870 began a new column, "Flame of Fire," to explain the doctrine. The column carried a biography of William Bramwell, a Methodist contemporary of John Wesley's, for whom the Booths had named their first child. There were also articles by Phoebe Palmer and James Caughey. The Booths followed Caughey and Palmer in preaching an instantaneous holiness experience in which God places purity in the individual character when the individual places himself wholly in God's control through an act of total consecration.

Between the time Caughey and the Palmers left England in the late 1860s, and the time Robert and Hannah Smith came from Philadelphia in 1875, the Booths had slighted holiness teaching. In 1873, Robert Pearsall Smith stimulated acceptance of holiness across sectarian lines. In 1875, Hannah Whitall Smith published her classic, *The Christian's Secret of a Happy Life,* and the Smiths spoke at Brighton to evangelicals from all denominations. The conference also heard Theodore Monod, a French Reformed pastor who had attended seminary in Pennsylvania; in 1881, he supported the Salvation Army's invasion of France. Before the Smiths left England in 1875, they contacted the Booths. Historian John Kent observes, "American Methodism has never been identified as a formative influence on the Salvation Army but in fact links were very close." Bramwell Booth told why the army scorned this link: "Some of the opposition which developed in the long run against the Booths was originally due to a prejudice against 'foreigners,' particularly these evangelists from the United States."[42] American revivalists still were unpopular in the 1870s, in spite of the success of Moody and Sankey in England.

Each of the mission's four leaders—William and Catherine Booth, their son Bramwell, and George Scott Railton, who became mission secretary in 1872—claimed a holiness experience, and all four believed that holiness was the mission's distinctive doctrine. Catherine's biographer wrote that "she had not claimed it until she was 32," although she had craved the experience since she was eighteen. She had read the life of an early Methodist, William Carvosso. She said that she lacked the assent of reason. She wrote to William in August 1860, "Oh, why could I not believe for the blessing of holiness?" After reading the book, *The Higher Life,* she pursued holiness in prayer. William asked, "Don't you lay all on the altar?" a phrase Palmer and Caughey used for consecration. She responded: "I am sure I do, [and] immediately the word was given to me to confirm my faith. . . . I held fast the beginning of my confidence and it grew stronger. . . . I did not feel much rapturous joy, but 'perfect peace.'"[43]

Bramwell's experience, according to his daughter, came "almost abruptly." It must have been in the mid-1870s, when the holiness emphasis revived in England. One Sunday, as he was walking from one mission station to another, pondering his lack of faith in a holy life, he suddenly understood that faith was a matter of the will. He knelt in a field and submitted himself to Christ. In October 1874, Bramwell wrote to Railton that William, who had had the experience after much family prayer, was "strongly inclined to make an effort at the country on the question; so far as I can see the present plan is to establish a weekly holiness prayer meeting in London."[44] Here was Phoebe Palmer's weekly Tuesday Meeting influence.

Although his biographer, Bernard Watson, claims that Railton and Catherine Booth were "the first of the Army's theologians and played a vital part in making the Salvation Army to some extent a holiness movement," he did not describe Railton's experience. It was Railton who moved acceptance of the holiness doctrine in the 1876 Christian Mission conference, holding that a believer's heart still had evil inclinations or "roots of bitterness" after conversion. These must be taken out by God's Spirit. An "entirely sanctified" believer produces only fruits of the Spirit.[45]

At the 1877 mission conference, William Booth said: "Any Evangelist who did not hold and proclaim the ability of Jesus Christ to save His people to the uttermost from sin [conversion] and from sinning [sanctification] I should consider out of place amongst us." Holiness meant separation from sin and consecration to God, doing God's will constantly. For most Christians, early deliverance from sin is partial; "roots of bitterness" remain in the heart. But, Booth claimed, God delivers from sin's mastery those who submit to grace. Holiness does not deliver from mental or physical imperfection, from temptation, from making mistakes, or even from a fall. But the sanctified are not "merely without deliberate sin," for any sinning places the individual at odds with God. Love fulfills the law, and a heart full of love for God and everyone else is not conscious of sin. Finally, Booth held that holiness was all-important to leaders of God's Israel, because it produces a gentle yet fearless spirit.[46]

Whether or not it was a "turning point," 1867–70 at least began a shift for the Booths, although their maturing mission was indistinguish-able from other urban home missions. True, W. T. Stead remarked about its goal: "No one can keep saved who does not try to save other people."[47] Even this, however, was not an original idea, it was the genius of apos-tolic Christianity. The era prescribed the Booths' methods, including American revivalist methods they applied in East London. They had en-listed untutored working men and women of evangelical background, along with a few refined "gentlemen" and "ladies," to take leading roles. They had moved beyond London, although with only mild success by 1870. They had split from outside authority, even from their own hand-picked committee. They had rejected offers to subsidize their work that had strings attached. Yet the mission was not self-sustaining; fundraising took a large part of the couple's time. They had abandoned mission sta-tions which they did not control totally or which had become schismatic. By 1870, however, the Booths alone determined the mission's doctrine, method, and organization.

4.

Failure in East London,

1870–77

One Sunday evening in 1869, William Booth led his thirteen-year-old son Bramwell down East London's filthy streets and into a crowded pub: "These are the people I want you to live and labour for." Earlier he had told Bramwell that "the poor have nothing but the public-house—nothing but the public-house."[1] Here is a clearer statement of a call from God than we have heard about in Booth's entry into the "regular" preaching ministry, in his conversion, or in any of his previous crises. It is the best avowal we have that Booth felt that work among the poor was his life's work.

Booth was not naïve concerning his talent for reaching these masses. He had had little success when he preached in the East End in 1849–50 and in 1861. The masses were "heathen" in that they were not from his cultural setting; they were Irish Roman Catholics, Turks, Armenians, and other ethnic groups unfamiliar with Booth's revivalist Methodism. Alien to English society, the newcomers had established their own cultural identity in the East End. They met at pubs, churches, and ethnic societies; opened businesses and lending institutions; clung to the traditional values of the cultures they had left due to famine or persecution; and defied Booth's well-intentioned religious aggression. They violently told the mission that they disliked its religious imperialism and its rejection of their values. Christianity has never evangelized beyond its own cultural borders except when a "heathen" culture was already crumbling. And when it succeeded, it embraced the culture it evangelized and rebaptized pagan practices as Christian.[2] Booth did not want to rebaptize habits he intensely disliked. Booth's inability to reach across cultures led to the failure of his mission in East London and in other immigrant enclaves where his mission did not embrace non-Protestant values characteristic of the home culture.[3] Mission statistics indicate that the mission failed in ethnically diverse cities, while it grew in England's Midlands and North, the evangelized "Burned-Over" districts. Yet, through the use of unsupported facts perpetuated in part by historians, the Booths sustained their reputations as successful urban evangelists. They told supporters that they stood in the gap between the status quo and slum chaos bred by socialism and anarchy, a manifest threat to comfortable middle-class entrepreneurs with evangelical sentiments. But the Booths did not solve the slum problem with revivalism either in the 1870s or in the 1880s. Finally, in the late 1880s, they turned away from reliance on revivalism and toward a social reform program. In the process, of course, they gave the gospel a more social and less individual definition.

The Booths knew London. Catherine had moved to its Brixton suburb with her parents in 1844, at age sixteen, and she lived there till her marriage in 1855. She frequently returned to the city when she was not touring with William or on her own. William had come to London in 1849 and found employment as a pawnbroker's assistant.[4] Before their marriage, William had spent six months there in 1854, studying with Dr. Cooke, after which time the Methodist New Connexion appointed him to a London circuit, although he spent much of his time evangelizing elsewhere. In 1855, William visited a chapel at Wapping, east of the Tower, and felt "sympathy for the poor" as he walked "their filthy streets." Beyond this, his diary made no reference to the East End. He turned away from London in 1861, when the Evangelisation Society offered him an opportunity to be a home missionary there; he felt that the East End was not his calling. Only in 1865, after a year of "wilderness" wanderings, did he and Catherine return, and then not for the sake of his vocation, but of hers. A "voice" did not call him to London. Only because another preacher was unavailable was he prevailed upon to try his hand at preaching to the East End's "heathen."

By 1870, William felt confident in his new parish. He issued his first and most important work on revivalism, *How to Reach the Masses with the Gospel,* in which he described God's call to go into highways and hedges and bring in the thousands who seemed to be beyond all religious influence; who, if not "bitterly opposed to Christianity, are totally indifferent to it." He portrayed the East End as his evangelical readers saw it: "multitudes in the grossest heathen darkness"—drunkards, blasphemers, harlots, infidels, thieves, gamblers, and pleasure seekers. Gamblers, using terrible language, gathered on small lots. Public-houses were "nests for the habits of the poor." The Sabbath was a day of pleasure, idleness, or business. Evangelicals had to win these "multitudes" from gin-palaces, theaters, concert halls, and infidel lectures, "to Christ and usefulness and heaven." East London demanded "our most strenuous efforts."[5] Booth had found a malady at the center of England's Christian capital. He urged evangelicals to help him apply the remedy of revivalism that he had learned from Caughey.

London was the world's largest city, with twice the population of Paris and three-fifths of Britain's employed workers. While the name "East End" was not used extensively until the 1880s, the area already was well defined. Larger than Berlin, East London was isolated by an invisible barricade of poverty. In the early 1880s, an analyst of the East End, Andrew Mearns, saw himself as "a traveller in the undiscovered country of the poor." In 1865, East London already was the place described later in dramatic studies that caught the public's attention. Among these were Mearns's *The Bitter Cry of Outcast London* (1883); G. R. Sims's *How the Poor Live* (1889); and the first of seventeen volumes of *Life and Labour of the People of London* (1889), by Charles Booth (no relation to William). C. F. G. Masterman anonymously issued *From the Abyss* in 1902; and Jack London's *People of the Abyss,* describing his seven weeks in East London, followed in 1903. These last works, examples of the literary genre of travelers' tales, described the social pathology that Booth saw in the 1870s, although he viewed it strictly as being the result of a spiritual plague that must be removed from Christian England.

Benjamin Disraeli had detected "two nations" in his 1847 novel, *Sybil,* with "no intercourse and no sympathy" between them. Andrew Mearns discerned London's extremes, "the icy form and fashion of Belgravia" and "the perpetual icy water of poverty in Bethnal Green." Benjamin Jowett contended in 1865 that "what is wanted just now is not preaching for the poor, but teaching in schools, better and more of it, and preaching to the clergy and educated classes." The Booths were preaching on both sides of the wall that, in Carlyle's terms, divided "drudges from dandies." A bridge over the wall could carry financial and spiritual assets to turn East London's heathen into Christian Englishmen. Catherine sought help in the west, and William dispensed it in the east. Therefore, of the two, it was mainly she who threatened that the masses might break down the wall and engulf all England in social and political chaos.

As the Booths arrived in London in 1865, Methodists had begun vacating their East End chapels in Spitalfields, Saint Georges, Seaman's Grove, and Limehouse. Construction of railroads, the underground, and factories had devastated neighborhoods, but a greater threat was the "low Irish" population. Booth's mission inherited some vacated Methodist chapels, but slum-dwellers found them unattractive, preferring pubs and music halls. By 1875, however, Booth had found that even moving his Methodist message to secular halls was no solution to "reaching the masses with the gospel." As attendance dropped, Booth's Christian Mission, like the missions of the Methodists, Baptists, and Congregationalists before it, moved outside London's East End, to locations where evangelists found it easier to gather congregations and financial resources. Booth's associates culled converts from the "better sort," from tradesmen—those few with a Methodist or evangelical background—whose houses lined principal streets, to form an "organization of converted people."[6] That Booth raised a mere handful from London's slums to working-class stability is the tragedy of his failure.

Trade disruption during America's Civil War increased East End unemployment. Famine stalked back streets. While twenty-five thousand obtained handouts, the unemployed lived in East End warehouses. In 1867, as shipyards closed, unemployment in Poplar and Bromley was up nine thousand over the previous year. After a bad harvest, Booth wrote, "Only the government can give effectual assistance, but it is to be feared that, in the coming short session, too many things of national importance will crowd on the attention of Parliament for the East of London to get even a passing notice."

As many as one hundred thousand unemployed, uneducated children became petty thieves. Girls and some boys became prostitutes. Lack of sanitation bred cholera; London's sewerage emptied into the Thames, from which inhabitants drew drinking water. In the summer epidemic of 1866, eight thousand died, four thousand of them in the East End districts of Bethnal Green, Poplar, Stepney, and Whitechapel, where Booth's mission was located. Smallpox was common, and Bethnal Green matchbox makers suffered from the industrial illness of phossy jaw. Nor did the habits of the poor improve their health. Cheap licenses permitted the sale of untaxed beer, cider, and perry. There were 49,130 licensed beer-shops by 1869. Sydney Smith, a fortnight after the Beer Act became law, wrote: "Everybody is drunk. Those who are not singing are sprawling. The sovereign people are in a beastly state." The *Nonconformist* reported that on "Whitechapel Road, within a distance of half a mile, nearly 19,000 persons may be seen to enter the public houses on the Sabbath Day while on Saturday evenings the number is even larger. This place is surrounded by the most hideous vice, the most dreadful crime, the most abject misery." Pubs and gin shops "explain why poverty and misery reign supreme." One report advised, "Gin, not religion, was the opiate of the people."[7]

Changes were under way. Edwin Chadwick described the city's meager capacity for clean water, drainage, and refuse disposal. Attitudes toward criminals changed, as Parliament abolished imprisonment for debt; public executions ended in 1868. Florence Nightingale provided care, as nursing became a calling for ladies. The Corn Act removed the duty on wheat, reducing the price of bread. Parliament passed laws regulating factories and mines, unemployment, and child labor. By 1870, East London conditions had improved from what they had been in 1855, but England soon became aware that the area contained germs which endangered the social health of the nation.

Booth's *East London Evangelist* began 1869 by voicing concern for the East End poor. The area was a prime recruiting ground for criminals, due to "chronic pauperism." In its most vivid attack on the problem, the paper argued that the public did not grasp the implications of this "canker in the rose."[8] Provincial poverty gravitated toward London. London "divided into two great [west-east] poles." Disraeli, from whom Booth had adopted the two-nation idea, became prime minister in 1868. Booth was Disraelian in his belief that, out of a deep concern for society, not to mention their own safety, the rich must help the poor; "legislation may do much to counteract the mischief," but "the spread of religious feeling will do more." To spread religion, his mission needed "more stations, more workers, more resources," and, always, more "funds." The Booths' primary appeal was to compassion for the starving, but they also brandished the threat that, if religion failed to ameliorate poverty and crime, all society would suffer. In July, the magazine reasoned that the principal enemies of East End inhabitants were poverty, sickness, and unemployment. Booth's poor relief program was his only line of access to this culture, which resisted his evangelical religion.[9]

Booth would avert social disaster by attacking the dark forces of heathenism. When he spoke of the "heathen," he meant more than those who were not yet redeemed by faith through grace. Like other evangelists, he always fleshed out the definition by referring to behavior: drunkenness, Sabbath-breaking, prostitution, and other evidence of the collapse of the Anglo-Christian ethic. These vices pointed to radical change in England's "Christian" culture in the wake of urbanization, industrialization, and rootlessness due to migration. These latter trends were the same targets revivalists from the 1820s to the 1850s had chosen; this undoubtedly was why Booth continued to argue that Finney's methods were appropriate. The battlefield had changed and enlarged. It was no longer the homogeneous Midlands where Caughey had preached. England had become quite diverse and contained cultures which were not responsive to revival preaching.

Heathenism was the best term Booth could find for London's problems. What he saw was as distinct from the England he craved as was Hottentot culture in South Africa. Booth and others often characterized the "low Irish" as Hottentots, when better judgment failed and they expressed their true feelings. He used the term *heathenism* in 1890, when he published a social manifesto, *In Darkest England and the Way Out*, which adopted the metaphor of darkness from Henry M. Stanley's *In Darkest Africa* (1890). Heathen behavior posed the threat of incipient radicalism on England's doorstep, malignancy in a culture risking decay. Traditional values could not be restored by education, Booth argued. Only aggressive Christianity could dam the flood of alien ideology—infidelity, intemperance, popery—and the new political threats of socialism and anarchy. But revivalism also was proving to be futile against these perils.

Booth's associate Railton plunged into the debate over East London's malaise in December 1873. Reacting to the social criticism in Matthew Arnold's *Culture and Anarchy* (1869), Railton could not agree that the English might rid themselves of roughness, deformity, inequality, and inconsistency by improving their culture. If improvement came from having a superior culture, Railton argued, Italy, with "more culture than any other nation in Europe, would have perfected men through culture." Instead, law and order there were in disarray, "assassination is common, and its people are distinguished for cruelty to animals." And if culture failed with individuals, it failed with the mass. "How many Bethnal Green Museums, how many National Galleries, how many conversations and lectures would be necessary to culture the people of East London?" Education, employment, and good humor simply create comfort "in a perishing world" for those "content only to dream about eternity." If you wanted a lesson in how to make gentlemen, Railton advised, you should see the wildest East London character "born again of the Holy Ghost"; the most intelligent Belgravian could not rise a step nearer God.[10] While Railton's solution worked miracles with individuals, it did not succeed when Booth's mission applied it to the East End masses.

Characteristics of the "casual poor" account for some problems faced by the Christian Mission. First, casuals proved inept at organizing a radical response to their condition. Mid-Victorian London was a unique part of industrial England. Unlike the thriving Midlands cities, London's enterprise was commercial. There was no factory working class, which in other places had begun to define itself as a discrete social unit in opposition to hostile factory owners. Instead, London's society was divided into aristocracy, artisans, shopkeepers, and, the bottom group, the casual poor. This last group, which Booth intended to save, did not form a unified whole, and thus did not organize to respond to its oppressed state. Instead of joining the rising trades union movement, it resorted to mindless rioting, purposeless looting, and meaningless fighting. It was not a class in the classical sense. The casuals were easily appeased by a meal, a lodging, a handout. Temporary employment permitted them to continue their day-to-day existence. They did not ask for more.

Christian Mission membership, initially drawn from middle-class evangelical subscribers to its funds, never effectively shifted to East End casuals. Irregular attendance at mission meetings and uncertain income led to frequent changes in meeting places. Booth drew leadership from outside the area, seldom from East End converts. By the mid-1870s, Booth realized this was not a locale for a permanent organization. Every other Protestant sect had given up on the East End as an area for effective evangelization. The Social Democratic Federation's Marxists could not organize the residents, nor could the Liberals. The East Enders were amenable to Tory political machines which gained their affection through temporary handouts, just as American political bosses were winning immigrant support. Even the Trade Union Council found that East End casual workers refused long-term commitment to a cause.

Sidney Webb and Beatrice Webb found that, unlike London's radical artisans, unskilled casuals saw society as "'divided vertically by trade,' instead of horizontally between employers and wage earners." Yet historian Gareth Steadman Jones detected a primitive hostility toward the rich, "hatred of the forces of law and order," dislike of preachers, and willingness to riot. Street traders, porters, dock workers, casual laborers, vagrants, beggars, and petty criminals shared these attitudes. Of dustmen (garbagemen), Henry Mayhew wrote, "I cannot say that they are Chartists, for they have no very clear knowledge of what the charter requires." They have a notion that it is opposed to the government, and that its enactment "would make them all right"; but they have no idea "in what manner it would be likely to operate upon their interests." Jones noted that the poor's aims were short-term and that their occasional rioting came when they saw their chance "to settle accounts with the rich and respectable—if only for a day."[11]

They did not form a stable class consciousness because of fatalism induced by near-starvation, chronic unemployment, the struggle for a day's wage at the dock gate, and erratic charity. They spurned the Charity Organisation Society's Victorian self-help ethic. And London socialists found no point at which to connect with their lack of class consciousness. Friedrich Engels censured the Social Democratic Federation for recruiting "masses of the poor devils of the East End who vegetate in the borderland between working class and *lumpenproletariat,* and a sufficient admixture of roughs and 'Arrays' to leaven the whole into a mass ready for any 'lark' up to a wild *riot a propos de rien.*" George Bernard Shaw wrote: "Angry as they are, they do not want revolution, they want a job. If they be left too long without it, they may turn out and run amuck through the streets until they are destroyed like so many mad dogs. But a job or even a meal will stop them at any time." In this atmosphere, both the rich and the upper working class barricaded their homes against the poor.[12]

By the time of the 1889 East End Dock Strike, Engels hoped that the labor movement would finally absorb "the lowest of the outcast, the dock labourers." But the 1889–91 expansion in Ben Tillet's dock union was temporary. They resisted regimentation and ebbed away when depression returned in 1891. Dockers were not drawn by the radicalism of strike organizers John Burns and Tom Mann. They had no interest in theory, only in food. Socialist H. H. Champion found that while socialism grew in outlying industrial districts like Bow, West Ham, and Woolwich, "poverty-stricken areas of inner South and East London renewed support of the more 'generous' and xenophobic Conservative candidates" until the twentieth century.[13]

The second obstacle to Christian Mission growth was the East End's predominantly Irish Roman Catholic populace. Booth's call was to impose an Anglo-Wesleyan culture on East Enders. But the Irish resisted this imposition. Large cities contained ethnic social institutions, and London held England's largest Irish community. By 1861, its 107,000 Irish immigrants had established a mix of social and political customs. Whitechapel, London's traditional home of foreign inhabitants, drew the Irish into dockside lodging houses, brothels, and taverns; some areas were 75 percent Irish. Transit costs kept the poorest there until the 1880s, when fewer than half as many Irish lived in Saint Giles, Whitechapel, and Southwark as in 1861; East European Jews had replaced them.

Probably due to lack of funds to rent halls on English-controlled boulevards, Booth sought his meeting places in Irish-dominated side streets and back alleys, where social integration with the host culture was keenly resented. In back streets tucked away behind railroad viaducts, the Irish lived separate lives. There, in a "chain of Irish islands," Booth, with his aggressive evangelism, evoked animosity. Pubs were centers of songfest and politics. Eric J. Hobsbaum found that, while "all that lay beyond a tiny circle of personal acquaintance or walking distance was darkness," the Irish community was not culturally impoverished. Above all, Roman Catholicism provided it with an alternative to the secular ideology of London workers and to Protestant theology, an "alternative to assimilation."[14]

The mission found transient quarters in these repugnant back streets until a proprietor or street gang decided the assertive Protestants in their midst would no longer be accepted. "Street Arabs" who attacked the mission's processions were mostly "low Irish" Catholics. On occasion, it was publicans, quite possibly also Irish Catholics, who paid for muscle to be used against the mission.[15] It is virtually certain that "mobs" were not acting entirely for sport or ideology. The mission, viewed as a threat

to their religion and lifestyle, gave the Irish every reason to oppose intrusion into their neighborhood. That it was also sport to attack earnest
marchers made it all the more blessed to remove the menace. Sanctimo-
nious sermonizing and loud singing provided occasion for sport for boys
inclined to engage in mock battles or molestation. Booth seldom referred
to the Irish by name, although he knew who they were. Instead he described them as "heathen" or "devilish." He intended to bring everyone
to Christ in ways revivalism decreed. With no respect for Irish Catholic
culture or "popery," Booth ignored it and waged war against hell, hoping to pluck individual "brands from the burning."

The Catholic Irish had arrived in England's urban slums long before
Booth set up his East London mission in 1865. These aliens in English
cities needed an alternative to London's secularism, so they established
what historian Lynn Hollen Lees calls "a Catholic workers' culture." With
the help of priests, Irish migrants made their Gaelic culture into an Irish
loyalty roughly congruous with Roman Catholic orthodoxy. They replaced
staid English evening prayers with the sale of food, drink, and relics in a
carnival milieu which combined pre-Christian folk beliefs and recreation
with religious ritual. Of course it was just these practices that caused the
Booths and other evangelicals to refer to Irish slum-dwellers as "heathen."

To cope with the Irish, the English Catholic church employed methods the Booths had learned from American revivalists in the 1840s. Priests
preached in East End sheds, attics, stables, and factories before the
Booths arrived in 1865. People came to chapel every evening to say
prayers and learn catechism. To increase popular interest, preachers conducted Methodist-style missions, with sermons, candlelight processions,
and calls to repentance. Afterwards, priests rented back-street rooms and
held meetings nightly to teach doctrine, sing hymns, and say the rosary.
Medals, banners, and scarves identified confraternity groups. Still, such
missions had minimal success. In London, most Irish took part only in
major Catholic rituals marking birth and death. But disinterest in Catholic ritual must not be taken to indicate apathy toward the church. Henry
Mayhew found that the Irish rushed to a priest as he passed by, boys
saluted by touching their hair, women curtsied. Charles Booth's survey
found the Irish "almost universally submissive" to the church. A Protestant visitor in Saint Giles found that Irish Catholics slammed doors, cursed
him, and rejected his pleas for their salvation.

Catholic parishes in "urban villages" looked like Protestant missions. In 1861, Saint Patrick's, Soho, had a mothers' meeting, an annual tea, charities, and boys' and girl's clubs, all common in Booth's mission by 1870. Priests visited door-to-door. In 1849, an Irish priest formed a Society of Saint Patrick with a badge and wand of office. The society's "special constables" held marches, engaged in visitation, quieted gin palaces and dancing halls, and replaced the rowdy wake with the rosary and prayers for the dead. They formed relief agencies and schools, an emigration society, an employment bureau for unemployed servants, and excursions to resorts outside London. Six years before Booth's mission took its military title in 1878, Henry Manning, Roman Catholic primate of England, founded a League of the Cross with "brigades, captains, and honor guards dressed in scarlet sashes." By 1874, twenty-eight thousand had joined the league, which held outdoor rallies for workers and annual processions at the Crystal Palace where "temperance soldiers" marched with brass bands. By 1890, priests headed at least forty-two branches in Westminster and Southwark.[16]

Late-nineteenth-century Catholics feared "leakage" in the hostile Anglo-American urban milieu through proselytizing carried on by missions like Booth's. To resist this and to create a strong Catholic church in England, Manning set three goals: educate Catholic youth; promote temperance; and improve the clergy. His primary concern was Irish immigrants, England's Catholic majority. Cardinal Vaughan's 1894 census showed that many aged between fourteen and twenty-one were lost to the church through non-Catholic benevolent enterprises, so he sent Catholic agents to police courts, where Booth's missioners had been at work for a decade, and provided children's homes.[17] In the 1880s, Manning, like Booth, turned away from purely sectarian evangelism to a concern for the social and spiritual needs of England's poor. He commended the Salvation Army, which, he wrote in 1892, "could never have existed but for the spiritual desolation of England." Even though the army was outside the church, it sowed "good seed" in calling mankind to repent. Manning felt, however, that the army's use of military titles caused "needless provocation." Overall, his fears about the army outweighed his hopes. The *War Cry,* Booth's weekly, exulted that, although Manning saw salvationists as heretics, he still provided a "wonderful contrast with the strange and often groundless attacks of Protestant divines and editors."[18]

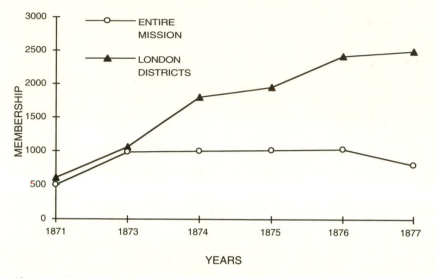

Christian Mission Membership in London Districts, 1871–77.

Salvationist sectarianism also diminished in the 1880s. Although Booth had warned salvationists not to bait Catholics, their militant rhetoric continued to lead to clashes in Irish-dominated slums of England and America. Booth himself had argued that popery and superstition were spreading, and his *War Cry,* as late as 1887, called for the salvation of "Mad Julia," "Brigit," and "Nell Cavanaugh." Mrs. Commissioner Carleton, from northern Ireland, was the author of most of these articles aimed at saving the "devout Romanist." Brigit did not need priests or confession, but Jesus. Carleton reasoned, if the army could convince Briget of this, opponents would stop reproaching its rough methods which had saved thousands that were worse than "Brigit, the Irish Roman Catholic." Carleton wrote of good Catholic "Nell" who had observed the church's rites. When mass and penance brought no joy, Nell turned to dance, theater, concert hall, and ball room. Engulfed by drink and freethinking, she became an atheist. Then Captain Maybee, a London slum officer, came to her door with the *War Cry* and asked Nell, "Are you right for Heaven?" This sort of article ceased in 1887; the army had begun to move toward a social program for the slums. In the future, it resisted harsh sectarian clashes which would injure its social program.

It is no surprise that Booth failed to establish a self-sustaining mission in East London, given Irish Catholic hostility to the English Protes-

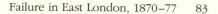

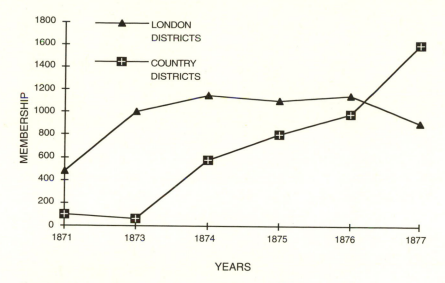

Christian Mission Membership in the provinces, 1871–77.

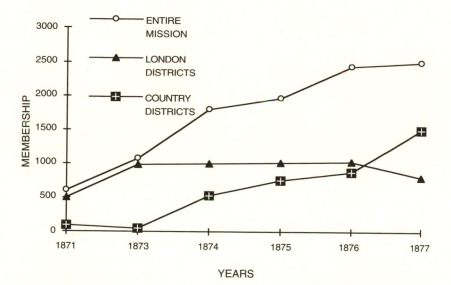

Entire Christian Mission Membership: Decline in London and growth in the provinces, 1871–77.

tant home culture and the disinclination of casual workers to join any organized group. What is remarkable is that the Christian Mission, named Salvation Army after 1878, gained fame for its success despite proof to the contrary. Perhaps belief in its conquest of the heathen masses derived from a need to affirm that the English Protestant home culture could absorb all foreign elements. To rule the heathen overseas and not dominate them at home was unthinkable. The English and Americans yearned to credit Booth with success. This wish gave birth to Booth's reputation as the preeminent acculturation agent of the "heathen" in Anglo-American society. Of course, there were those who pointed to Booth's failures, but their voices were drowned in protests from Booth and others who elected to assert that he was converting the heathen to the gospel. Booth presented statistics which showed that thousands attended mission meetings, many were converted, and some became members.

But the Christian Mission failed in East London. The most telling rebuttal to Booth's claims were his own statistics. Previously unanalyzed figures appear in the conference *Minutes* and the *Christian Mission Magazine* from 1870 to 1877. They show minimal growth in the East End from 1865 to 1875, followed by stagnation and decline. Such figures are not altogether reliable in detail, as Booth himself found when he read inflated membership figures during a period of "stagnation" in 1877, but they do point to patterns of growth and decline in the mission. Booth inherited from Methodism Wesleyan scruples alive to the sin of falsification and a system of generating meticulous monthly reports from each station. Reports included the number attending meetings and a financial statement. William and Railton closely studied these reports (still used in the army) to rate evangelists on increases or declines. If numbers of members or attendance declined, a preacher might expect to receive a new, less important station at the next annual conference. Since much of the mission's income came from the sale of its magazine, which gradually replaced tract distribution, evangelists also reported these sales.

In 1871, nearly all mission members belonged to four East End stations—Whitechapel, Poplar, Limehouse, and Shoreditch—with a few at the South London Croydon station. Hastings was the only station outside London. From 1874 to 1877 (the last year for which the mission published membership statistics), the mission suffered a terrible decline in East London. For over a hundred years, the Salvation Army has made extensive statistics available to the public but has not publicized its membership. By 1877, the Shoreditch station, which, with 325 members in 1871, was one of the mission's largest, had ceased to exist. Poplar, with 199 members in 1874, had only 34 in 1877; Limehouse had 183 in 1874, but 75 in 1877; and Whitechapel, the "mother" station, had fallen from 372 to 221. Canning Town (30) and Plaistow (12) were on the verge of collapse. In 1877, total East End membership (six stations) was 370, under half the 1871 membership of 818 at four stations.[19]

But from 1871 to 1877, overall mission membership more than doubled, as participation declined in East London. By 1877, just before Booth renamed his mission "a salvation army," total membership stood at 2,516. But "city districts" had dropped to 925 members after climbing to 1,146 in 1874. Provincial working-class towns counted 1,651 members, compared to just 61 in 1873. As a notable mark of mission decline, sales of the *Christian Mission Magazine,* a major source of self-support, fell in East London after 1873, while total sales increased. "Self-support" meant that a station no longer depended on general fund grants; it did not mean that the members' donations covered the station's costs.

Later analysts of the Salvation Army's trouble in sustaining a religious ministry in the "inner city" assume that Booth had prospered in East London and blame the army's failure on an inability to capture Booth's zeal. But Christian Mission statistics point to Booth's failure within a decade of opening his mission. The "stagnation" Booth acknowledged in 1877 had set in by 1874–75 in the East End and was offset only by growth in provincial towns.

The best evidence that Booth realized that the mission was shrinking in London was his 1875 reclassification of districts to give the fastest growing ones a larger voice at conference. He allowed two lay delegates to attend from large districts. Weak districts sent only one lay delegate, and they were all in London. By 1877, stations outside London numbered seventeen, compared to just one in 1871. Increased membership in provincial stations contrasted sharply with the decline in city districts by 1877.[20]

The mission by 1877 had become something quite different than it had been in 1870. It had grown at the periphery, but it was dying at the center. Of course, this was not intentional; the mission still preached to East London's heathen. Since appeals to save the city's masses produced considerable mission income from evangelical donors, Booth could only hope that his East End failure was only temporary and would go unnoticed. Was this the reason he issued no membership statistics in conference *Minutes* or the *Christian Mission Magazine* after 1877? Even his Methodist urge to record success had to be stifled when numbers pointed to failure in this area of primary concern. Although the mission's overall growth rate had not altered since the last major spurt in 1874, Booth realized that new growth had come from opening stations outside London. Nine "country" stations had one hundred or more members. Stockton had surpassed Whitechapel. Of the £4,252 in receipts for 1877, £2,731 came from provincial stations. Of 5,526 monthly magazines sold, country stations sold 3,936 (71 percent). Declines in London pointed to a need for organizational change.[21]

When Booth discussed untruthful statistical reports at the 1877 annual conference he had "reason to complain of the returns made last year." Some preachers inflated tallies so as to appear better than they were, and Booth fretted, "We had better state the number of members under than over the mark." When conference had appointed a preacher to a station, he could not find the members his predecessor had listed. Then he deleted those members names so as to diminish his predecessor's work; he now had a lower base upon which to build. Booth found that average attendance at weekly class meetings varied greatly. Some stations admitted "strangers," which made comparison impossible. As for lay speakers, figures were "very irregular." Some listed those who rarely spoke. One-fourth of all missioners were lay speakers. Booth wanted the low number of female speakers to be given "special attention." As for enquirers, Booth argued, "we have no business to report persons unless we really believe them to have been converted." He felt the Sunday morning seven o'clock prayer meeting attendance was too small and the number of weeknight services must increase. Some stations held no public experience meetings because some members used all the time to say the same things over and over. In some places, small private believers' meetings took up a hall that could have been used for public meetings. Sales of the mission *Magazine* were inadequate. Booth pleaded for "a great deal more open-air work." These statistics were a harbinger of radical changes to come.

Booth's last address to the 1877 conference struck the most disparaging note heard at any conference in the mission's twelve-year history; the address had special implications for London. "In many of our old stations we appear, from the returns, to have had something very like *stagnation* during the year. We have only got a net increase of 200 members." Since old stations were in London, the statement indicates that Booth realized that there was serious decline at the mission's heart. It may also indicate that sustained growth after the first spurt at any station was unlikely—an ominous sign.[22]

London, more than other English cities, had amassed a diverse ethnic population, primarily in its East End. In 1865, when the Booths arrived, the dominant Irish Roman Catholic casual workers had instituted cultural norms to shield them against assimilation into English culture. The Irish resisted joining organizations which would draw them into the dominant culture; they particularly opposed Protestant revivalists. Booth the Methodist abhorred Irish culture. He opposed intemperance, popery, Sabbath-breaking, and gambling, all vices associated with the Irish. His intolerance of their lifestyle ill equipped him to win them to his views.

Rancor between Booth's home mission and East London's Irish Catholics, whom he viewed as heathens, had a predictable result. By 1874, Christian Mission statistics show, it had failed in the East End. Its few successes were in a part of the populace drawn to the city from rural areas where evangelicals prevailed. Mission converts' biographies indicate that they came from Midlands and northern village settings where they had been raised by "godly parents." A praying mother or fortuitous meeting with a mission had allowed them to survive "narrow escapes" and the company of "evil companions." These were not the testimonies of Irish Roman Catholics, but of the English raised as evangelicals.

5.

Forming a "Salvation Army,"

1877–79

From 1877 to 1879, Booth recast the Christian Mission, formed with a Methodist conference polity, into a military system. The general superintendent and the conference became a general and a war council. If one ignores the military speech, there was little change from the Methodist structure, but a new military language stressed Booth's idea of his divine right to absolute control. At the 1877 annual mission conference, the last time there would be a free exchange of ideas, he made it clear that he was creating a system modeled after Queen Victoria's imperial command. Since militarism had caught the Victorian imagination, Booth rechristened his mission a "salvation army" to capture the new mood.

Although no minutes record the fact, it had been a special 1876 Christmas meeting of leaders that precipitated changes in the mission, which the Booths instigated at the seventh annual mission conference on June 11–14, 1877. The mission's headquarters staff was made up of the conference president, the Reverend W. Booth and Catherine Booth, listed together; Nathaniel J. Powell, Esq., treasurer; Robert Paton, honorary secretary; George Scott Railton, general secretary; and Bramwell Booth, traveling secretary. Catherine Booth, the Booths' eldest daughter, performed evangelistic work. The 1877 conference counted twenty-two evangelists, thirty-three lay delegates, and eleven persons specially invited by the general superintendent.

Following the president's address, Railton and Dr. John Reid Morrison moved to overturn a rule which prevented organizational changes for ten years. They reasoned that previous rules "should not be allowed to interfere with the adoption of the program [Booth] has set forth for the conduct of the present and future conferences." The mission magazine's 1877 conference issue revealed that "the days of debate are over." Henceforth they would meet "to confer with God." Parliamentary debates Booth once had seen as invigorating he now found to be diversions. Future councils would focus on spiritual exhilaration and leave management to the Booths. What came to an end was the Wesleyan conference system; Wesleyan discipline and doctrine remained. Soon Booth adopted a military system from the increasingly popular British Army.

Supporters of the new system agreed that Booth's autocratic control, without the annual intrusion of conference, would leave missioners free to concentrate on aggressive spiritual warfare. Booth insisted that, whereas in former conferences delegates had taken ten minutes to get "down on our knees to talk with God," they now would spend fifteen or thirty minutes in prayer. The mission was on a "higher path." Tuesday evening's Holiness Meeting was "a far richer feasting time," and Wednesday's love feast "surpassed all that had gone before it for mighty spiritual power."

Booth packed his presidential address with military idiom. He had told delegates that this 1877 meeting was a turning point for "officers and leaders in [God's] army," as they pondered "how we can best advance the interests of that army." They had been "brayed" the past year; "God has been bruising us, dashing us about, to knock the folly out of us and to knock the wisdom in." Those who fail "are either not men and women of God," or have "mistaken their vocation" and ought to "seek employment in some other calling." If the success principle holds in business, politics, and war, "we accept it in spiritual things." Booth's review of how failure had occurred analyzed the mission's numerical losses and gains. Since the 1876 conference, nine stations with 610 members had closed. He named the stations, but did not note that four of the nine were in East London, or that the six new stations were all outside London. Many of the new stations had originated in response to invitations from patrons who asked for evangelists to preach in halls they provided.

Nine evangelists had left the mission, he reported at the 1877 conference; some were unsuitable. Others had gotten "ministerial notions" when they met Baptist or Primitive Methodist preachers or had become "respectable" or doctrinally confused. But Booth felt such departures were bound to occur if the mission stayed true to its purpose; it would happen to Methodists "if Mr. Wesley's standard of rule and labour were restored." One of the nine who had left became a Methodist local preacher; one returned to his previous position because he did not feel he was "adapted for the work." A mission veteran became the "'private evangelist' of a rich gentleman." This brief epitaph shows Booth's disdain for what he termed "deserters." He had asked one applicant: "If your way had been open into the Primitive Methodist ministry you would have gone, would you not?" The applicant said "Yes"; Booth said "No!" As for additions, the mission was growing "our own stuff." Booth hoped that the mission soon would be able to take only those whom it had converted or trained. He expected his own children to enter the mission; "no small token of our confidence in the future and of our willingness to lay aside earthly ambitions and position in order to promote its extension and success. . . . May God accept all nine for this service!" Catherine Booth had borne the last of *eight* children a decade earlier, surely long enough for a busy father to memorize their number.

As his statements at the 1877 conference show, Booth's mind was also on property. He favored rented halls. Ownership meant fundraising bazaars, concerts, entertainments, and "a heap of other worldliness and foolery" such as he had engaged in to pay for the People's Mission Hall in 1870. People said they must have a new chapel to really "get on," but when they got one, they became "deader than ever, besides having a debt to grapple with." To suit him, a building had to meet three standards: it must hold a crowd, stand in a busy location and not a back street, and be attractive. Theaters and music halls met these conditions. They were large, accessible, and cheap to rent.

After discussing all these matters, Booth came to his principal criticism: conferences had been "controversial," taking time to discuss "comparatively trivial matters." They left "essential principles and practices to be mangled about and decided by majorities." At the Christmas meeting with mission leaders, Booth said, he had spelled out his plan. He recalled the mission's origins, when each man managed a station "according to our wishes" and asked for direction. Now he would make conference into a council of war, called by a commander-in-chief to "receive information and counsel." War councils would "receive reinforcements and restation our army," but, mostly, they would "cry together to the living God for the rebaptism of the Holy Ghost." He also abolished the conference committee which advised him as general superintendent. Experienced preachers who once had been its members now led stations outside London and could not assemble quickly.

He exposed a startling fact: the mission had not converted London's heathen or turned the city into a training camp; raw preacher-recruits were led by East End stations. Troubled preachers, Booth had found, did not want to go to a committee. Besides, since no station superintendent was hampered with a committee, why should he be plagued with one? In fact, station superintendents did answer to lay officials concerning finances and statistics. Booth then proclaimed his autocracy: "Confidence in God and in me are absolutely indispensable!" No plan could be adopted without his consent. This was not a new authoritarianism, he pointed out, but a clearer statement of the terms of his rule which came in reaction to perceived flaws in the mission.

Booth presented twelve preachers to be accepted on trial, only one a woman, and permitted challenges by delegates, even though these had proven injurious to individuals in the past. He placed three women in charge of London stations and sent men to the other twenty-four districts. By 1878, he would accept preachers and make appointments without conference's approval; "no committee can have the knowledge of the capacity of the brethren and the wants of the stations I possess." He promised, "If two men are equally eligible to fill the same station I should naturally prefer to send the man who was preferred by the place." This ended the stationing committee's right to appoint evangelists to stations.

Conference then took up the circular of business, but Booth decided there was no time to discuss issues. He simply gave his own views. He liked Sunday schools "in the abstract," but teaching children to read was not the mission's purpose. Only three Sunday schools remained, and he wanted no more. Bible classes had proved divisive unless they were conducted by "right men, and it seems we can't find the right men for them." Booth's new system stripped laymen of their right to participate. As for clashes over temperance, Booth advised that, until there was unanimity, all missioners would be abstainers. On the question of dress, had not the Earl of Shaftesbury quoted a prison chaplain who asserted that the cause of the increase of female prisoners was "drink, trashy literature, and flashy dress?" Evangelists' wives must set the standard in modesty. Booth, like the British Army, would distinguish between "efficients and non-efficients" to recognize "our most devoted and reliable people." This system ended the preachers' plans for promotion.[1]

Elijah Cadman, a converted chimney sweep, led one of the Salvation Army's first assaults when he declared "War on Whitby" and titled himself "Captain" in 1877. Courtesy of the Salvation Army National Archives and Research Center.

In the place of the business Booth had quickly disposed of, he lectured on "Hallelujah Bands" and "Good Singing." While such topics were important to the mission program, Booth used them to draw attention to his autocratic design. He claimed that he had created the hallelujah bands when he was an itinerant evangelist at Walsall in 1863. Bands were groups of lay persons who had been conspicuous sinners—drunkards, prostitutes, and prizefighters—but who now went from place to place holding music hall–type revivals. A leader acting much like a music hall impresario led a lively program by interspersing five-minute testimonies by "celebrities" with ardent prayers and enthusiastic singing. Bands drew people who would not attend church or chapel to a service in a rented hall. They succeeded for awhile, but died, according to Booth, due to a lack of organization, discipline, and management. His mission would efficiently manage the new charismatic spirit which would simulate the best work of the bands.

Conference delegates then told of their hallelujah band encounters, a clue to their reaction to Booth's new structure. William Corbridge agreed that the bands' loose design had caused their failure. He had refused a Methodist rope because it was too tight, but the band rope was too loose: "Now, in the Mission we have both law and liberty." He must have been speaking of the mission as it was, not the tighter system Booth was creating, for he resigned a decade later over differences with Booth. Corbridge wanted "all our people [to] be praying and preaching men and women." Bramwell Booth agreed, "Let us make all our people parsons!" Elijah Cadman's experience with the bands led him to argue that it was the "system to evangelize the world." He had taken a band to Northampton and printed bills which read, "War on Northampton!" He soon would print similar bills for his "War on Whitby," as Booth's "salvation army" took shape in late 1877. The lesson for the Christian Mission was that even the best movements die when there is no discipline. To Booth, effective discipline meant no voting, no free discussion, and virtually blind acceptance of one man as God's chosen voice. As St. John Ervine put it, Booth resolved "to have no priests in his stations; he was equally resolved that he himself should be the High Priest."[2]

Booth's "Good Singing" lecture did not directly bolster his move for more control, but it did provide an opportunity to speak authoritatively. He said that, in almost every case, hearty singing is hampered by musical instruments. He did not use instruments in services till 1880. He was unhappy with the mission's songs, but, in perusing three thousand hymnals, he had found nothing better. He had tired of pretty hymns which did not convert lost souls—no more "bright and beautiful streets and stars and streams of Paradise." He wanted themes of "blood that cleanses, the spirit that empowers, . . . victories and triumphs that await" the soul, put to good tunes whether secular or sacred. "I rather enjoy robbing the devil of tunes," he said. A real tune's distinct melody becomes an obsession. When he introduced the "Lion of Judah" in his 1865–66 Cornwall revival, the tune caught the people even if the sermon failed to do so. Keeping time with their hands gives people confidence and prevents "drag or drawl." Solo singing, in fashion since Sankey came to England in 1873, is boring when "done as a performance." But Sankey enunciated words; "he preached in song."[3]

When Elijah Cadman arrived at his new station at Whitby in September 1877, inspired by the conference, he tacked up placards around town which read "Captain Cadman from London, Evangelist of the Christian Mission," and attracted crowds of fishermen and jet workers to Sunday Services. Cadman had merged the hallelujah band idea with Booth's references to God's army. In six weeks, he reported that seventy-five had professed salvation. When Booth arrived in November, Cadman billed him as "General of the Hallelujah army." Booth would review a march through the streets and then give an open-air address at the Market Place. This was not the first use of the title; missioners had used it as a shortened form of general superintendent. But Cadman's usage reflected the growing notion of that the mission was an army.[4]

By 1878, use of military jargon had increased. Booth held a January war council at Whitechapel with over fifty men and women, including experienced "generals" and newcomers. Bramwell called for brotherly sympathy among our "generals," and new "captains" taught the delegates new songs.

Railton differentiated jingoism from militant Christianity at a time of possible war with Russia. He was appalled at what "blood and charred flesh" would produce as Britain rushed from "honourable and useful paths of peace." Missioners should fight only for God, whatever "Godless governments of our own or any other country do." In Lancashire mill riots, Englishmen had killed fourteen in broad daylight when they fired on their own townsmen. Must we see peaceful people become "murderous mobs" that destroy property and life? Rioting against God could be halted by devotion to God. He was confident:

> We have a shield can quell their rage
>   And drive the alien armies back;
> Portrayed, it bears a bleeding Lamb,
>   We dare believe in Jesu's name.
> Come and join the army, the army of the Lord,
>   Jesus is our Captain, we rally at His word,
> Fierce will be the conflict with powers of sin;
>   But with such a Captain, we are sure to win.

Railton appealed to readers to commit themselves to aggressive Christianity, to "attack high and low alike with the sword of the Spirit" until disorder is turned into salvation.[5]

The mission marched to the provinces in early 1878. Men and women eagerly wandered the streets of strange towns in search of meeting places. Need for money did not inhibit evangelists who operated stations on money raised from the sale of the magazine, from Christian friends, and from offerings at nightly meetings. Sheffield heard Sister Goddard and Rodney "Gypsy" Smith, later a famous independent evangelist, at Temperance Hall on Sundays and at the infidels' Hall of Science on weeknights.[6] Most remarkable, women led three of the four new openings.

Booth was busy. In April, he visited four Yorkshire towns. His Bradford schedule was typical: arriving at 9:40 P.M. Saturday, he was met by evangelist James Dowdle and his people; he attended a 7 A.M. love feast on Sunday, after which a dozen remained to pray from 8 to 10:30, when 130 took the sacrament. Eight hundred attended the afternoon service at Pullan's Hall and about 1,800 the night service. He counted 18 converts and £7 10s. 6d. in the offering. He spent Monday looking at buildings.

Nine stations opened in May. At Felling-upon-Tyne, sisters from Whitechapel unfurled the mission flag in a building owned by a man who remembered Booth as "the man who dealt faithfully with his soul years ago." This was friendly country, unlike London. The mission magazine asked, "Are we going too fast?" and "How about the old stations?" The writer saw problems: stations begun among "wretched populations" had never risen to "a great growth outwardly." Was he thinking of alien East London, where stations had diminished? Booth had sent evangelists from these older stations to the North, part of the reason for East London's statistical decline. Although in May four evangelists had resigned to attempt mission work with "the aid of such of our people as could be induced to assist them," the mission, which had begun in 1878 with thirty-five evangelists, in just five months had sixty.[7]

The last Christian Mission conference, held at Whitechapel in August 1878, signaled the last stage of the military system's development. The conference began with delegates praising God for having added seventeen stations since the 1877 conference, mostly in the North. Only one was in London. By now this was a normal growth pattern. Of the 47 (in 1877) evangelists, 17 were women. The increase in female evangelists—from 11 to 38 percent of all evangelists—was most important change since the 1877 conference, when only 3 women had been in charge of stations. Yet, of the 54 lay delegates, only 6 were women. This was the last time delegates would meet and vote. Booth now would dominate. He personally invited 33 evangelists, largely from small districts, of whom 11 were women. Altogether, 139 attended.

Conferees held "Pentecost" prayer sessions in the East End Spitalfield's Wesleyan Chapel. "War Memories" recounted growth and opposition at new stations. At Bolton and Sheffield, churches had charged them with "proselyting." In Sheffield's Irish area, seven policemen at times were needed to protect their processions. But the evangelist, Mrs. Goddard, was willing to go "across the Atlantic or anywhere." Booth responded, "Ah, I was wondering who we should get for America when we are ready for it." Elijah Cadman had taught his marching columns to sweep all before them into the hall. When a police inspector ordered processions to cease, Cadman appealed to the Lord of the Manor, who sent word to protect Cadman. A Roman Catholic doctor told Cadman that he liked mission people because they all signed the pledge. At Felling, "Hallelujah Lasses" began the mission, during which Primitive Methodists, "almost as bad as the publicans," accused Rachel Agar and her sister of "sheep stealing." Whether stolen from churches or from pubs, in four months they had 450 souls and willing workers.

When Kate Watts left for Wales, she did not realize where Booth had sent her. On arrival, she found Merthyr was "the worst of all the filthy places I had ever seen." Its poverty was awful, its wickedness shocking. With no hall of their own, she and her assistant attended the Wesleyan Chapel the first Sunday and heard a rather dead sermon. Then they held an open-air service but were not allowed to sing in the street. A crowd of fifteen hundred followed their silent procession to the Drill Hall, where their converts included an infidel and a drunkard who soon preached for them. They took names of over five hundred converts besides those they could not make out. Watts found that many of the people were Welsh-speaking, a wonder to an English woman. Already she had been asked to open stations in Aberdare, Tredegar, and Swansea. After these "War Memories," an immense procession filled Brick Lane to march to Whitechapel for tea, at nine pence a ticket, and the annual meeting. Led by musical instruments, the processioners sang, "If the cross we gladly bear, then the crown we shall wear."

The "General's" address focused on organizational reform. Conference, Booth argued, was not for "debating and legislation," but to gather those who "are in perfect harmony with us in purpose and design." If anyone doubted that harmony with the mission meant harmony with Booth, he set them straight. "People who are not with me in purpose and plan must not complain if they do not have my confidence. If they keep secrets from me, they may be sure I get to know it; little birds come to me in the midnight hour with such secrets, and they will be found out." He then gave the mission's history to justify his new power: "We are sent to war," not "to minister to a congregation." The past year he had learned that conceit is "a curse to individuals and societies." He had joined Wesleyan Methodism because it was the liveliest sect. Methodism became "part of my very blood. I have had much to unlearn, and it is very difficult to unlearn being a Methodist." He asked delegates to reject the Methodist system and trust him. He had learned that he had been mistaken to use committees, councils, and conferences, and in his choice of some evangelists who had found fault with the mission and had "set up for themselves." He disputed men who, if they left a concern, would set up shop and offer goods a farthing a pound cheaper, and would tell people that they need not give up smoke or drink or flowers or feathers. It was "dishonourable, un-Christian, and unmanly." Slander upset him more than opposition.

Already some said he had failed in London. He conceded failure, but "'if anybody would like to try their hand with London, come along.' There is a great difference between London people and country people." This was his frankest admission that the mission had left the East End for easier pickings in the provinces. London would be a training ground for work elsewhere. Booth pitied Whitechapel's "Mother Station," where evangelist Brother Dimberline's sect of Tobacconists attacked Booth's "grinding despotism." And a Limehouse evangelist had suffered a marital breakdown. Even so, Poplar had doubled, Hammersmith was better, and Plaistow was as good as in 1877. Yet London was no longer the mission's focus.

Country stations provided better news. Apart from the first two stations organized outside East London—Hastings and Croydon—Booth knew of no country station that had declined. Although some evangelists sought to be respectable, most were doing well. Membership consisted of working people who had been forced to migrate from places like North Ormsby, where half the houses stood empty due to the scourge of the age, unemployment. As a result, forty mission members had moved to towns where they founded new stations. As for leadership, unlike the British Crimean Army, "lions led by asses," Booth saw that his lions were making lions. Problems included evangelists whose methods differed from his and who left the mission when they could not alter it; a need for kinship among evangelists; and superficial work. He needed people who would give up flowers, pipes, and drink, and "not be ashamed to tell everybody what has happened to them." He decreed elimination of debt by assuming all present debt, except for debt of which he had no knowledge. Under the new system, he would permit no new debt. Evangelists who could not raise money would go without it. Every bill would have to be paid before salary could be paid, and, as for salary, "Why more than food, clothes, and a bed to lie on, if he is burning for souls?" As for his own support, Booth, like the queen, was provided for privately. A few gentlemen, some of whom he had fallen out with, sustained him. While Booth joked about his poverty, biographer St. John Ervine found that Booth's income was greater than that of most nonconformist clergymen.

The increased prominence of female preachers became apparent when four reported on their work. Mrs. Burrell found that her greatest foes at Rotherham were infidels and Roman Catholics who physically attacked her adherents. Cadman urged more military jargon and system: "God bless all the captains of the salvation army" [this, before Booth had adopted the name]. He wanted to wear a uniform so that all would know he meant "war to the teeth and salvation for the world." The Booth family became more prominent. Daughter Catherine sang "Only Thee My Soul's Redeemer." In music-hall style, the audience joined in the chorus. Bramwell described the mission as "a machine going about in bits." Then William offered his blueprint for a Christian imperium, "an army of crusaders for the salvation of souls" like those raised "for the recovery of a sepulchre."

But a new system required change in the mission's 1873 Deed Poll. Under a new deed, William Booth personally would control all property and funds (a plan that governed the Salvation Army until a 1931 Act of Parliament altered its government slightly). The new deed placed all decision-making in William's hands and in the hands of successors he would designate. Missioners understood that his heirs likely would be members of his family, his imperial cohorts. Senior evangelists became the army's aristocracy. Proximity to the throne equaled power. Evangelist Tom Blandy and Life Member J. E. Billups moved to annul the 1873 deed. When William offered a new deed, Job Clare and James Dowdle moved its unanimous approval. The magazine hoped that the "unanimous and hearty concurrence" would halt the influence of "slanderers who, taking advantage of the fact that the supreme governing power of the Mission rests in the hands of the General Superintendent, have pretended that he would apply the property of the Mission to his own personal purposes." Booth's solicitor noted that "power over property and funds possessed by the present or any future Superintendent was solely and legally confined by this Deed, to the employment of it for the purposes and advantage of the Mission, and that only."[8]

Some later pondered questions touching the new deed. Was change necessary? Arthur Watts, who in 1878 had been a young evangelist, argued in 1929—near the end of the Booth family's autocracy—that mission growth had come as the result of evangelists' hard work before the 1878 change. Two stimulants to growth, employment of women and the decision to expand to the provinces, occurred before William presented the deed. Had not Catherine Booth already said, "We have turned the corner, we have gone out to the Provinces"? Bramwell agreed: "We are opening our new Stations and making more rapid headway than John Wesley's people." Was there a need to overturn the "representative principle" in favor of one-family rule? Sentimentally attached to a democratic conference, Watts saw no reason to wed military jargon and autocracy to achieve success. Why should Booth stifle free speech? While we cannot diagnose the private workings of committees, it is difficult to believe that others had obstructed William Booth's will. Limiting circles of consultation to a few close advisors was either an act of genius or William's greatest mistake. Men and women of talent outside the circle saw that in a family-run concern. their rise would be limited; defections became numerous. Moreover, the new system caused Booth to become more suspicious of defectors.

Watts disputed Booth's claim that there was no opposition to the change; it was not a unanimous vote. Watts voted against the plan and said that John Allen would have done so, had his health been better. Watts also claimed that "a number of the older men did not vote for the resolution, but they did not actively protest." One of these, Corbridge, told Watts after Corbridge left the Salvation Army in 1888, "I remember you understood the business at that conference." Watts held that the representative principle died because only the Booths, Railton, and the solicitor "had the faintest idea what was going to be introduced." Although he felt Booth's use of power had been beneficent, future problems would arise due to the fact that members and preachers no longer had governance rights.[9] Booth concluded the 1878 conference with this summary: "There have been more than enough conferences, and congresses, and committees, and deliberations. It is time to act. There is not a moment to be lost. No conference with flesh and blood! There cannot be any question about what we have to do."[10]

While autocracy might produce efficient management and short-term growth, the Salvation Army would soon be out of step with a democratizing Anglo-American political culture, already apparent in the growth of trade unions, the proffering of suffrage to most workingmen, and growth of workingmen's political parties. This was no time to set up an autocratic state if one was looking to the future. Booth misread the reasons for his mission's success. He was convinced that it was his authoritarian rule, and not women's ministry and the shift to the provinces, that brought it about. Furthermore, military rule attracted him, his missioners, and his era, and coincided with his authoritarian inclinations.

There is a striking link between Victorian England's use of military metaphors and the naming of the Salvation Army. By 1879, the mission informally had adopted "salvation army" as its title; but the military's new popularity after the Crimean War and Indian Mutiny of the 1850s stimulated formal acceptance. Excitement had surrounded the formation of a Volunteer Army of home guards in 1870. So Booth was not affronting popular norms in adopting a military title; rather he was catching the public eye by co-opting jargon that was then popular. Also, a military motif suited a mission that was evolving an imperial command structure, a London bureaucracy, and, within a year, an international scope.

Booth was influenced by historic examples of the righteous soldier: patriarchs shielded by Yahweh, charismatic warrior-judges, soldier-kings, and militant prophets. Paul of Tarsus urged followers of the Nazarene to take on God's armor to fight Satanic principalities. Crusaders and Jesuits perpetuated this idea of embattled heroes resisting the infidel. Puritan John Winthrop, who founded a Massachusetts "city on a hill" in 1630, wrote on the eve of the English Civil War: "Thus stands the case between God and us: we are entered into a covenant with Him for this work; we have taken out a commission."

But by 1879, it was General Booth and his salvationists who had captured the military figure. The source of their intrigue with the military lay at the surface of Victorian society. Booth was certain that mild religion, practiced by "settled congregations" of both established and nonconformist churches, could not succeed with the masses. Funded by respectable Victorians who, in the 1870s, were enamored of Britain's army, he would "invade" the slums. The Salvation Army, better than other sects, translated Britain's military spirit into the metaphor of "muscular Christianity." Herbert Asquith's poem, "The Volunteer," depicts a clerk who "ever 'twixt the books and his bright eyes the gleaming eagles of the legions came, and horsemen, charging under phantom skies, went thundering past beneath the oriflamme." Booth did not so much invent a novelty as embrace a popular idea. The mission's aggressiveness increased in 1878–79, when it was failing to achieve its primary goal of saving the cities' "heathen."[11]

In 1865, Anglican curate Sabine Baring-Gould in Horbury, Yorkshire, wrote "Onward Christian Soldiers, Marching as to War," as a children's processional. Booth's army would add other hymns to the church's militant hymnody, but no hymn would be more recognizably salvationist than Father Baring-Gould's children's anthem. Charles Kingsley, also an Anglican, invented the phrase "muscular Christianity." His 1853 novel, *Hypatia,* dealt with the conflict between Christianity and heathenism in fifth-century Alexandria.[12]

Historian Olive Anderson sees the 1870s as a decade of "unprecedented adulatory attitudes towards Britain's professional soldiers"; an "imitation of military organization, discipline and paraphernalia, [and] of military sentiments and rhetoric in general."[13] A most important contributor to national enthusiasm for the military was the formation of a citizen army, the "Volunteers," in 1859. Booth's speeches indicate that he was influenced by rising support for the military and the volunteers in the decades preceding the informal rechristening of his mission the "salvation army."

In March 1878, Major General Garnet Wolesley, British army general-in-chief, claimed that the volunteers had "popularized the army." With six hundred thousand trained men scattered around Britain, the military engulfed the public. Wolesley's problem with the volunteers was the same as Booth's with his recruits: how to turn the "ignorant rustic labourer, the urban idler, and the waifs and strays" into disciplined soldiers. But, Wolesley argued, these goals could be accomplished through a national training school, where, using the Prussian model, he would "manufacture" disciplined soldiers in three years and then return them to civilian life for nine years of service. Religious sects, educators, and General Booth adopted this training model. Booth in 1880 opened Salvation Army training homes for men and women cadets, where he manufactured officers from the working class in just three months.

For both armies, public esteem was slow in coming. Hugh Cunningham says that volunteers laughed at themselves as a means of self-protection, suspecting that their "role was non-existent and their organization a sham." After all, for men whose daily work was totally civilian, playing soldier was a bit absurd. As public amusements, the volunteers furnished a model for the salvationists who mimicked volunteer brass bands and uniforms. Volunteers embodied Victorian values of patriotism and self-help. So did Booth's army, which recruited members of the working-class as soldiers and members of the political and manufacturing elite as benefactors of its numerous enterprises for religious and social redemption. The volunteers' imperial spirit would, as the *Volunteer Service Gazette* put it, render them "memorable through all future English history." By the late 1880s, Booth's army had earned similar affection for its earnest, religious patriotism.

Self-conscious volunteers and salvationists made an inviting target for roughs. Was the lower element's abuse due to the fact that both armies depicted established order? An 1878 *Times* editorial stated that to be a volunteer was to take "the opposite side to all disturbers of society from the highest to the lowest." Salvationists, who believed that brewers hired their attackers as Satan's soldiers, felt compelled to seek the support of right-minded Victorians in their crusade. Salvationists and volunteers stood for respectability, however comical, and roughs resented the conversion of their former workmates and pub comrades to at least an appearance of social assent. Kipling's "Tommy Atkins," recruited from London's illiterate cockney workers, typified the mix of respect and loathing soldiers learned to expect: "O it's 'Tommy this, an' Tommy that, an' Tommy, go away'; But it's 'Thank you, Mister Atkins,' when the band begins to play."[14]

There were practical reasons, beyond patriotism or religious experience, why the working class joined these armies. Workingmen had more leisure time than before to pursue recreational, religious, or patriotic diversions. The volunteers and salvationists provided drill as a pastime and offered respectability through a moderate amount of class mixing. Ridicule by former associates could be endured, as long as one made progress toward a better life for one's family.

Each army provided a cause in an era of causes; they attracted Victorian diligence while not neglecting a love of play. But were they effective in their distinct spheres? Gwyn Harries-Jenkins found that the British military was impressive on parade but was not an effective fighting force. Distinctive uniform, ceremonial inspections, and parades pleased the eye, and regulations were effective. But, as a fighting machine, the British Army was, in L. S. Avery's phrase, "largely a sham."[15]

In 1886, the Salvation Army arrived at a similar stage. Its revivalist weapons had failed among the East End "heathen" whom it still dreamed of saving. Even in the provinces, its corps reached a certain stage of growth and stagnated. While the British Army blamed a stingy cabinet for its failures, salvationists blamed "respectable Christians" for not offering support. As a result, both armies turned in new directions. From 1880 to 1885, each set up a territorial command system at home and overseas. When the Salvation Army failed in the tough arena of East London, it found success among populations of the Midlands and North, evangelized earlier by other nonconformists. The British Army expanded the Victorian empire by fighting "little wars" with ill-armed natives in Africa and Asia. By the late 1880s, the Salvation Army had turned to a social service program to redeem its failure in its birthplace, the urban slum. In partially surrendering its revival mission, the Salvation Army survived and grew beyond anything that Booth had envisioned for his East End home mission in 1865.

Evangelical fascination with militancy was due partly to the British Army's acceptance of nonconformists. After 1863, "Other Protestants" could declare their religious affiliation on army registers. These evangelicals had seen the 1857 Indian mutiny as a pagan attack on their "most Christian nation." They heralded General Henry Havelock as an exemplar of Christian soldiers. In the 1860s, evangelicals, including Booth's mission, opened chapels near army bases. Nonconformists joined the volunteers and became convinced that military discipline contributed to a more disciplined society and therefore insured against urban chaos and irreligion.

Love of militarism inspired the age. Volunteers provided a model for the Boys' Brigade (1883), founded by Glasgow volunteer officer William Alexander Smith "to protect the young from moral contamination." Soon there was a Church Lads' Brigade (1890), a Boys' Life Brigade (1899), and Boy Scouts (1908). All used army ranks and organization. Military regimen and Victorian religion were fused. The antisaloon Blue Ribbon Army came to England from America and, in 1874, the militant Women's Christian Temperance Union.[16] The "Purity Crusade" and foreign missions organizations also adopted military nomenclature.

Booth heralded the mission's new name, "a salvation army," in the *Christian Mission Magazine* in September 1878. This war would bring peace to the hearts of "the vilest and roughest people." At the 1878 war congress (formerly conference) musical service, some missioners danced to music by fiddlers, concertinists, and clarion sounders. Those less constrained tossed arms about and rolled on the floor. Four days of nearly ceaseless services ended with a night of prayer, "the most wonderful meeting" ever held in the mission. As they prayed, one collier labored with his fists on the floor and in the air, just as he was accustomed to struggle with rock in his daily toil. Men and women fell on the ground and laid there as if dead, "overwhelmed with the power from on high." Young evangelists acted like boys at play, "locked in one another's arms, and rolling each other over on the floor." They took the sacrament with water; the unintoxicating wine had not been prepared. But no one noticed outward circumstances as souls fed on God. A love feast followed, then they conducted business until one o'clock.

In the month following the congress, the number of stations increased from fifty to sixty, evangelists from 88 to 102. Booth said, "We have never moved so rapidly before." The title *field officer* replaced *evangelist,* and the term *corps* replaced *station.* Corps would be self-supporting, and reports were still to be at London by the twelfth of each month for inclusion in the magazine. In January 1879, Booth changed the title of the official organ, the *Christian Mission Magazine,* to the *Salvationist.* He described the work of salvation people as "getting saved and keeping saved, and then getting somebody else saved, and then getting saved ourselves more and more, until full salvation on earth makes the heaven within, perfected by the full salvation without, on the other side of the river." This orthodox old-fashioned salvation, not "Universalism, Unitarianism, or Nothingarianism, or any other form of infidelity," was found in prophets and apostles, Luther, Wesley, and Whitefield. It had a hell and a way for "drunkards, blasphemers, gamblers, thieves, harlots, money getters, pleasure seekers" to avoid going there. It was salvation for here and now, with assurance of God's presence in the believer's life.

In February, Booth used the title *general* for the first time, in a by-line for his first article in the *Salvationist*. He showed how his system would work. Scripture called believers not just to teach, but to "compel all nations." To bring a rebellious world to God required military tactics uncommon in a church. If five thousand people joined this crusade, they would succeed by working as one army under one plan. When a multitude marches under one standard, it achieves strength from combination. The strong help the weak, and fresh troops constantly join in. Booth justified his absolutism by arguing that success comes from one plan, executed under one head. Did a committee "emancipate the Israelites," or command or govern them afterward? He judged one bad general to be preferable to two good ones. While he needed subordinate leaders, one directing will must be followed if five thousand soldiers were to be unified. And soldiers must be trained; God does not despise anyone's gift or sex. Booth would assign the right person to the right job. Obedience would be crucial. Could a regiment succeed that resolved to storm a redoubt after they had taken a majority vote? Of course not, Booth argued. Hence the defiant must be "degraded, punished, expelled." Likewise, a disciplined army must be kept busy. "Nothing demoralizes salvation soldiers more than inactivity."[17]

In January 1879, W. J. Pearson wrote the Salvation Army's first war song to the tune, "Ring the Bell, Watchman":

> Come join our Army, to battle we go,
> Jesus will help us to conquer the foe;
> Defending the right and opposing the wrong,
> The Salvation Army is marching along.[18]

For all this masculine trumpeting, it was women who brought growth, as a 1879 *Northern Express* article showed. When Catherine Booth spoke in Newcastle on "Hallelujah Lasses and Aggressive Christianity," explaining army principles, Gateshead Mayor J. W. Robinson, a man the Booths had known as a member of William's congregation there, chaired the meeting. He announced that after the Hallelujah Lasses had arrived in Gateshead in December 1878, the chief constable had reported a decline in arrests for drunkenness. That month, eighty-three males and twenty-eight females were convicted, but by March 1879, only fifty-three males and six females were convicted. Assaults also decreased. The Mayor had attended army services to attest that those who frequently came before him were at the meetings. The writer of the *Express* report found the success of these mission women even more remarkable in that they were uneducated and without influence, introduction, or friends. A *Salvationist* report pointed to the army's fascination with collecting ethnics. At least twelve Negroes and "a Chinaman" had attended the Limehouse corps. The publication wanted one of each nationality, even poor Turks, to join. A Jarrow synagogue was the site of weeknight meetings.[19] By the mid-1880s, the army had corps for Germans, Italians, and Swedes in London and New York. Booth wanted his empire to encompass all nations.

A May 1879 Tyne war council heralded army advances in the North since August. At Newcastle, Sisters Louisa Agar and Lizzie Jackson preached to twelve hundred on weeknights, of whom only six were women, which again proved that female preachers attracted male audiences. At Gateshead, three corps were in full swing, all led by lasses. Catherine Booth presented the army's "colours" to nine newly formed corps, a function Queen Victoria handled in the British imperial system. When Catherine no longer could present the flag after cancer struck her in the late 1880s, her daughters filled this role. The army had its own imperial family. By now field officers had ranks: Captains Fawcett, Cadman, and Ballington Booth took part in the council. To the *Northern Express,* Salvationists were strange folk, whom "[neither] Whigs, Tories, nor Radicals could make out, and which beat Church and State, Bishops and Bradlaugh," the atheist member of Parliament. The public called the missioners various names— "Bleeding Lambs," "Jesus," "Salvationists," "Ranters," and "Shakers"—but the editor noted that all obeyed Booth's orders.

SALVATION ARMY!

TWO HALLELUJA FEMALES

FROM ENGLAND,

will speak and sing on behalf of GOD and PRECIOUS SOULS,

Commencing

SUNDAY, OCTOBER 5TH, 1879,

IN THE

Salvation Factory,

Formerly used as a Furniture Factory,

OXFORD ST., between 5th and 6th Streets.

Service to commence in the morning at 11 o'clock, afternoon three and evening at seven.

Other Cristian friends will take part in the meetings.

RICH AND POOR, COME IN CROWDS.

EXCELSIOR PRINTING HOUSE, 1646 Germantown Av n'e

Poster: "Two Halleluja Females." Courtesy of the Salvation Army National Archives and Research Center.

Catherine defended the military approach in her answer to the question, "Could you not march without a flag?" (She had designed the emblem.) The flag was useful in leading processions; it represented militancy. Emblematically, its crimson stood for the redeeming blood of Christ; its blue for purity; and its motto, "Blood and Fire," for the blood of Christ and the fire of the Holy Ghost. She declared, lack of proof notwithstanding, that the army was the only hope the church had to win the heathen. The church had lost the spirit of Pentecost. She pointed to a new start, a new Christian kingdom. The flag symbolized spiritual victory, not attained by "learning, fine buildings, wealth, respectability, numbers." After just over a year of fighting, since the two Agar sisters had come from Whitechapel to the Tyne, there were twenty-two corps, forty-seven officers, and nearly three thousand members.[20]

But at London's war council in June, other reports of success did not equal those from the Tyne. Booth had slighted London due to growth elsewhere. He admitted that there were evil reports about the strength of the oldest corps. He scolded the Hammersmith (London) Corps, where he found open-air work done constantly at the same location, not among the dwellings of those hardened against the gospel. By now his officers had learned that there was easier terrain than the Irish back courts of urban slums. Surrounded by popery, publicanism, and infidelity, Hammersmith had accomplished little. At Millwall, where the mission for a decade had occupied a cowshed in a back street, the corps had moved into a "Salvation Factory" with Captain Louise Agar and Lieutenant Jackson in command. Whitechapel had attacked Mile-end Waste, where missioners were received with curses and a savage attack on Jeremiah Lamplough, which he bore admirably. Again women proved useful when those who hooted the men listened in silence to female pleading.[21] Yet there is no evidence that the new militancy had had any positive impact on East London. After a year under its new name, provincial growth barely managed to obscure the continuing abysmal failure of Booth's mission at the heart of what, in 1865, he had seen as his destiny.

William had spent the year on the run. A schism in Rotherham took him and Catherine to the scene. The army lost heavily from internal splits. At Bradford, he once again found that the mission did not attract the poor. At Whitehaven, he found that "efforts to graft other opinions and usages upon our people" had caused schism. At Roach, a Cardiff suburb, he opened a hall which, he felt, should have been four times larger. At Maesteg, the army had been injured by "untoward circumstances," but churches had received as many as a hundred new members as a result of the army's work. He stopped at Ebbw Vale to help the captain find a building, then walked over the mountain to Tredegar for a night meeting at Temperance Hall. He returned to Ebbw Vale and negotiated a ninety-nine-year lease at nominal rent on an Iron Works Company's land. A builder offered to erect a hall for eight hundred people for about six hundred pounds, but buildings, he recalled, cost time and anxiety as well as money. Only when it was necessary would he permit the purchase of a hall. On Sunday at Ebbw Vale, Booth inspected a pavilion with an attached public-house, which he bought. He no doubt saw this as a bargain, not at odds with his opposition to purchasing buildings. There were five hundred at the 7 A.M. prayer meeting and about ninety for a 9 A.M. Sunday school to teach reading. The eleven o'clock service, with about 1,000 present, was preceded by an open-air meeting and procession; at 2:30 P.M., there was another open-air and indoor service, with testimonies and addresses. An evening march brought a crowd of two thousand, by newspaper count. The *South Wales Daily News* reported that "the town appears to have undergone a complete change" under Captain Kate Shepherd. Booth spent the next week visiting Merthyr, Aberdare, Porth, Ystrad, and Cardiff, and then passed a weekend at Stroud before beginning another week of corps-hopping. By the time he returned to London after two weeks, he had preached twenty-two times indoors and nine times outdoors, had traveled over seven hundred miles, had spent thirty-two hours in trains doing business—all to feel "better in health than when I started."[22]

Reporters' accounts of salvationists were sagacious. A reporter from the *Secular Review,* called by the *Salvationist* an "infidel publication," visited Whitechapel's Salvation Hall to study the "downright, most unfashionable earnest" salvationists. The service began with a hymn to the tune "Ye Banks and Braes of Bonnie Doon," with no instrumental accompaniment. Nor was any needed; on the chorus, sung over and over, the gathering clapped time to the singing. Preacher Peter Kern had loose grammar but spoke in an untheatrical manner that "Oxford and Cambridge theologians might profitably strive to emulate." Kern's pure Antinomian creed insisted on a need to throw everything on Jesus, a reformation doctrine of hell's fires and heaven's pearly gates that had lost none of its force. Salvationist worship, like the early church, did without white-robed choir and "gaudy bedizened priests." The *Sheffield Independent,* recalling Thackeray's hatred of dingy tabernacles where "'men howled about hell fire in bad grammar,'" felt that the satirist had forgotten the "dregs of society" into whose "steel-plated hearts salvation must be shouted." Captain Fawcett's forces sang in Ira Sankey fashion, but with more energy.[23]

A war council at Booth's native Nottingham in November was the fall highlight. Catherine gave flags to groups from Leicester, Basford, and Bradford. William offered his mission history, which, as it always did, began with the myth, "a man alone in the East of London." Success had come in the last two years. Now the army had 122 stations, over two hundred officers, and four thousand speakers who spoke to two million in the streets every week. Catherine spoke of how like Jesus the army was: respectable people had thought, "He'll come to the temple, to the doctors of divinity; He'll come in pomp and majesty and dignity, and in His dignity we shall be dignified," but it was not so. He came to a manger, fled to Egypt, went about healing common folk who heard him gladly; then the "respectabilities crucified Him and said, 'Now surely we've got rid of this vulgar Jesus!'" Now He comes to "not the select few, but the masses of men." When some denounced the army's tactics, Catherine asked, "Are you doing the work?" If not, "for Christ's sake, let us alone, for we are." After early morning love feasts, three processions led by cornet and flags met at Sneinton Market. Eight thousand heard testimonies where infidel lecturers normally held sway. Sunday ended with a night of prayer. Penitents threw away pipes, feathers, and ornaments.[24]

After the council, Booth toured surrounding corps. Basford, formerly a village, was now a populous working-class suburb. At Bulwell, he arranged for opening a corps. At Arnold, the "little Gospel Trumpet" was in charge; and at Leicester, Booth worried about the "Rest and be thankful spirit" that destroys movements. The earth was full of movements that "became proper and temperate"; would this happen to his army? He believed that God would gather a multitude from England to shake the nations of the earth. If God thinned the army's ranks, it would be all right; an army can afford to be smaller if it is one in purpose, prepared for "losses, and crosses, and agonies, and deaths." A trade depression had sent people into the streets, where "you can attack and harass them all day long." With less money for pleasure, their hearts would open to salvation. Booth found enough new opportunities to consume a thousand officers. His vision of a Christian imperium began to encompass a global sphere. Ireland, France, and other nations would follow the army's Glasgow opening.[25] At the end of 1879, Booth described "A Good Soldier of Jesus Christ" as one who dislodged Satan. Satan was everywhere, in superstitious savage nations and in professedly religious ones. A good soldier may have a trade, but salvation warfare is his business. He studies men's hearts, Satan's devices, and sinners' hiding places, and knows how to shower sinners with red-hot truth. He is a fighter, not just orthodox in creed; neither is he a deserter nor a schismatic.[26]

Booth printed a Methodist discipline as *Orders and Regulations* in 1880. He adopted ranks, brass bands, and volunteer-style uniforms. This system in turn was copied by several Church of England missions ("bogus armies," he called them) which merged into a Church Army in 1882. At that time, a bishops' committee aspired to entice Booth to bring his army into the church as its evangelistic wing in the slums.[27] He declined the honor.

As Booth adopted a military plan, he also formed an imperial order around his family and leadership. He then moved to bring America, Europe, even India and Africa, under his flag. Gradually his mind moved from older principles of individualistic revivalism to a dream of a disciplined society. Although he did not publish a social scheme until 1890, by 1880 his army already was broadening its scope from soul-saving in London's East End to a worldwide imperium aimed at altering society through evangelism. Booth would marry revivalism to imperialism, to create a new social order which he saw in millennialist terms, as the coming kingdom of God, a new Jerusalem. By now he was certain that an army under his own control, a Christian imperium, would conquer all. He had no doubt that he was the man and that the Salvation Army was the mode by which God would produce a millennial dream.

There are those who deny that the Salvation Army is a genuine reflection of 1880s Anglo-American culture. They accept only its caricature and reject its ideological and organizational development.[28] Such a view ignores comments by contemporaries outside army ranks, social thinkers such as Josephine Butler, Henry George, Rider Haggard, Cecil Rhodes, W. T. Stead, Beatrice Webb, Arnold White, Francis Willard, and Theodore Roosevelt who applauded Booth's desire to create a disciplined social order. That his new order would include military discipline did not frighten Victorians. That military discipline would be cloaked in religious revivalism frightened only a few.

PART III.

Christian Imperium to

Social Reform: The 1880s

After Booth named his Christian Mission "a salvation army" in 1878, the organization experienced phenomenal growth, due to four factors: the mission had accepted women into ministry equal with men; it had adopted a popular military title and jargon; it had moved beyond East London; and it remained free of the established church, thereby avoiding an exclusively English identity that might hamper realization of its international ambitions. But by 1886, the Salvation Army's growth had come to a halt in England, much as the Christian Mission's growth had ceased in East London by 1874. The army's failure to reach the "heathen masses," as Booth had set out to do in 1865, had become apparent to critics. The organization grew outside cities but failed to hold converts at its oldest stations. Failure in London pained Booth; he now denied it. He feared the day when his army might be merely another sect perpetuating itself. Revival, not sedentary ecclesiasticism, was his ambition. He was a disciple of Caughey, Finney, and Palmer. As a result of the army's failure to grow, and in response to international concern for the wretched conditions in cities, between 1883 and 1890 socially-minded salvationists slowly turned the Booths' attention toward social reform.

The Salvation Army's first social services, in 1883–84, were totally congruent with the Christian Mission's soul-saving charity work in the 1870s. And they were no different from the charities of other urban missions. The army sponsored rescue homes for fallen women, brigades to save drunkards and prisoners, and slum sisters (district visitors) to care for London's poor women and children. Booth had rejected these efforts in 1874, along with Sunday schools, as work which dissipated evangelists' energies and wasted limited funds. Recommencement of this work in the 1880s was not his doing, but the result of efforts by women who pushed him to attack the squalor of East London, as described in the secular press. Publication in 1883 of Andrew Mearns's *Bitter Cry of Outcast London* intensified pressure from army women. Always open to the "outside" world, Booth reluctantly permitted his army to join the outcry against woeful conditions in the East End, which was, after all, his "home." At first, Booth's solution to the poverty problem was the mission's evangelism. When that proved inadequate by 1888, he joined the reform battle aided by salvationist commissioner Frank Smith and W. T. Stead, crusading editor of the *Pall Mall Gazette*. Together, in summer 1890, the three gathered material for *In Darkest England and the Way Out*.

6.

A Christian Imperium's

Growth and Stagnation

The early 1880s were a period of remarkable growth for the Salvation Army. William Booth instituted a military regime in 1878–79, with orders flowing from general to chief of staff (the Booths' son Bramwell) and thence to territorial, divisional, and corps commanders. William no longer consulted with clergy or laity; now he called councils, issued orders, and inspired advances. During the 1880s, the army, without acknowledging that it was doing so, fled its extradenominational origins to become a sect, although Booth still followed methods laid out by James Caughey, Charles G. Finney, and Phoebe Palmer. If the military style was more picturesque—with cornet, banners, and tambourine—the message was still that of 1840s revivalism. By marrying revivalism to ecclesiastical polity, Booth assuaged his earlier fear that his mission, like other sects, would settle down. He had revised his preference for uninhibited lay activity by the new regimentation. In fact, he was copying the stultifying ecclesiology he had so resented in his youth and in 1861 as a clerical renegade. Despite his own desire for independence from stifling authority, he meant for his army to follow his command.

Booth's clergy were not "Reverends," a title he had rejected for mission evangelists in the 1870s. But they were "ordained" (until the 1980s, the army opted to "commission") as "officers" who exercised priestly functions matching those of other clergy. The *War Cry,* founded in 1879, carried the army's written message, and its soldiers sang songs of its own making, printed in its own hymnal, led by brass bands which played only army tunes.[1] For a decade, the army's growth was as striking as that of any post-apostolic missionary movement; it manufactured and sent out officers in an age of Christian imperialism. A systematizer, Booth had no patience with chaotic ventures, either when he served Reformers in the 1850s, or when he worked with hallelujah bands in the 1860s. He

"The Salvation Army"—drawn by W. P. Snyder, 1880s, New York. Courtesy of North Wind Picture Archives.

wanted well-organized revival efforts with notable results. So, in 1878, he had merged ideas of itinerant evangelism, lay enterprise, Methodist polity, and love for the military to produce a new sect with a sectarian polity, dogma, and discipline. That its form was disguised, so as to avoid the appearance of being a sect, was partly a result of Booth's hatred of sectarianism. His aim in the 1880s was to return to first-century Christianity as he saw it, to turn men and women into soul winners and slum saviors. By 1880, his army had spread across the United Kingdom and had made inroads in the United States, Europe, and the British colonies. It succeeded in Protestant pockets but failed in Catholic areas.[2] Growth was the preeminent feature of the army in the early 1880s.

By 1885, however, Booth was adopting new goals and tactics which drastically altered the army. He had founded an urban mission to preach salvation from sin in East London slums in 1865. By 1874, he had given up the normal mission program of mixing salvation with soup as being both beyond his financial resources and counterproductive in that social service programs attracted a following of "soupers." In fact, by 1876, he was aware of his inability to deal with the slum clientele he felt led by God to save. Increasingly the mission turned to the "respectable" working class that Wesley, Finney, Caughey, Palmer, and now Moody had found to be receptive to revival efforts. Among this population, the army experienced significant growth in the early 1880s. But as the decade progressed, the soul-saving methods of Booth's formative years no longer were working as they once had, even with the working class.

By 1885–87, the army stagnated, just as the Christian Mission had in East London by 1877. Booth found that growth could be perpetuated only by moving to new areas. Old corps, not only in East London, were struggling. Unfortunately, a decrease in the number of officer-candidates and in income meant that movement to new areas also slowed. In this pivotal decade, Booth sensed that he was living in an increasingly secular society that had little interest in soul salvation. In this climate, he would turn toward social salvation. By 1890, he would offer a grand scheme to abate England's unemployment, poverty, and urban vice. Thus it was the army's failure to grow as a revivalist sect, first among the "heathen" and then among the working classes in the provinces, that turned it in the direction of social service. The army soon became a religious sect with a social service ministry.

While a cause for the army's failure to gain members lay in the 1880s' pluralistic-secular society, its structure speeded the decline. In an era of rising democracy, Booth led an anachronistic autocracy. Members had either to conform or leave. Booth sent out directives from the secret councils of his family and a few chosen leaders. In its charismatic, formative state in the early 1880s, the army's discipline and unitary command gave it the ability to maneuver, but in its settled state by 1886, many officers resisted discipline. As the army lost personnel and money, a new approach was in order. The Booths, as usual, proved adaptable. Although they had founded a revivalist mission in 1865, by the mid-1880s they were ready to launch a crusade for social salvation, although they expected personal conversions to continue as a major element in the redemption of society.

The army experienced phenomenal growth from 1878 to 1886. In August 1877, there were 36 stations and 31 evangelists, 9 of whom were women. By June 1878, there were 50 stations and 88 preachers; about half were women. This expansion proved Watts's prediction concerning the growth potential of a democratic mission before the organization had become a "salvation army." By Christmas 1878, due to the amazing increase in staff (principally women), there were 127 evangelists and 81 stations. Growth continued until 1886, when, in the United Kingdom alone, there were 1,006 corps (formerly stations) run by 2,260 officers (formerly evangelists). The Booths saw this surge as a sign of providential favor, but with growth came problems—where to get enough funds to maintain the level attained; and how to recruit the necessary officers to fuel future growth.

In 1880, the army spread overseas, beginning in the U.S., where in 1872 a Christian Mission layman had started a mission in Cleveland, Ohio. This work had ceased before the Shirley family migrated from Coventry to Philadelphia to begin an unofficial corps in 1879. Booth then sent his commissioner, George Scott Railton, to America to make the Shirley's work official. With seven hallelujah lasses, Railton arrived in New York in March 1880. In 1881, Booth sent his eldest daughter Catherine to France to start work as the *Marechale*. Soon India and Australia were outposts of the London-based army. By 1886, there were 743 corps and 1,932 officers overseas, not far behind the numbers in the mother country.[3]

Certainly a general and chief of staff could provide strong leadership for an international movement. They moved officers around the globe on command. A 1884 schism in America resulted in the dispatch of a new commander, Frank Smith, and over fifty English officers to save the work. But the social class from which the army recruited could not produce enough officers who were fit to manage its operations at great distances from the London headquarters. Although the Booths set up training schools in London for men and women under their second daughter Emma and second son Ballington, the cadets' illiteracy caused their brief three-month stay to be used as much for basic education as for administrative and evangelistic training, to say nothing of theology and pastoral care. Demand for workers in the field caused Booth to commission cadets early, so that teenagers with less than three months' training commanded corps.

When the army sent lieutenants to command corps, they spent as much time raising their living as preaching the gospel. *War Cry* sales yielded more funds than did offerings from impoverished audiences at

Six of the seven "Hallelujah Lasses" who helped "Commissioner" George Scott Railton commence "official" Salvation Army operations in New York in 1880. Courtesy of the Salvation Army National Archives and Research Center.

nightly meetings. Headquarters received ten percent of all income, and other money had to be set aside for overseas expansion through "Self Denial." The U.S. commander wrote in 1885 that "no officer can reckon on remaining in any station above a few months at the outside, and not one can be sure of remaining a week" before being moved. No salary was guaranteed, and poor *War Cry* sales might mean little food. Rent had to be paid before an officer drew a specified "allowance." Headquarters officers were not under similar pressure to raise their own salaries,[4] and some field officers resented the privileges of the staff.

The autocratic system's efficiency rested on generating enthusiasm among the troops. Rallies led by the Booths and other leaders kept spirits high, at least temporarily. By the 1880s, Herbert and Eva, the Booths' third son and third daughter, joined their siblings in lifting the morale of English forces. Soon they toured Australasia, the U.S., Canada, and Europe to heighten zeal for the war. Beyond this internal spirit-raising, the army could count on opposition in the streets to rally its soldiers. The era of growth was also that of greatest persecution. In 1882, roughs assaulted 669 soldiers. By the end of 1884, 600 salvationists had gone to jail, mainly for obstructing streets while parading or holding open-air services. Between 1881 and 1885, 250,000 knelt at army penitents' benches, but, as Foreign Secretary A. M. Nicol noted, its failure as a sect was that it did not turn converts into members. Maybe an autocratic system is incapable of providing a nurturing atmosphere. In the 1880s, the army claimed a million converts, but its membership did not equal a tenth of that number.[5]

More embarrassing, had the facts been generally known, was the army's failure in London. While it grew in provincial towns, by 1882 it again was waning in London. Work in provinces so outpaced city growth that salvationists told strangers, "You must not judge the Salvation Army by what you see in London. Go to Bristol, or Hull, or the Rhondda Valley, and you will find what it is capable of accomplishing." The army increased its property holdings in London when William bought Clapton Congress Hall, formerly the London Orphan Asylum, and, sensationally, the notorious Eagle Tavern and Grecian Theater, both in East London. But Booth's new headquarters at 101 Queen Victoria Street was in the City (financial district), and the showcase Regent Hall Corps was near Oxford Circus. Booth was escaping the organization's East End origins.

An indication of Booth's London failure came in 1882, when he appointed twenty-eight-year-old Frank Smith, with only a year's experience, to command the army's London division and to consolidate the corps.[6] Consolidation at London freed money and personnel for work in more fertile fields. When Booth sent Smith to the U.S. to repair a schism there in 1884, A. M. Nicol succeeded him in London. Nicol expanded the division geographically, but growth occurred only at London's periphery, where Baptists, Methodists, and independents had gone, according to the 1888 *British Weekly* survey of London churches. Surveyors found that the army's 1887 London attendance encompassed only .7 percent of the populace. By comparison, 1881 figures had shown that the army attracted 11 percent in Scarborough, 7.4 in Hull, 6.8 in Barnsley, 5.3 in Bristol, 4.2 in Barrow, and 3.3 in Portsmouth.[7] Not only was the army finding less success in East London, but London as a whole also had largely rejected it. In poor areas of Bethnal Green and Whitechapel, surveyors could scarcely find a salvationist. While Booth reached a lower social class than other nonconformists, his main hall at Clapton was set "among artisans and clerks."[8]

After two decades in London, Booth found that the few soldiers he had won from the masses were moving, like the Methodists before them, into working-class neighborhoods. And his officers were finding that, by working in provincial Britain, they could raise their meager allowance to support their families. While the army still claimed to be the most formidable mission in attracting the lower classes, its success came in fields occupied by working-class sects. Booth tried to discredit the 1887 *British Weekly* survey by noting that the army had a larger weeknight attendance in London than the Church of England. The argument was true but unimpressive, since the church had few weeknight services, while the army met every night.

War Cry articles detailed the army's East End problems. In 1887, all but one of the twelve East End corps were in serious debt, a problem that district officer Staff Captain Atherton said he had solved by 1889. During this time, he reported, there had been an increase of 308 soldiers. But in April 1889, a new district officer gave a membership count at each of fifteen corps in northeast London, remarkable since the army almost never released such figures. Average corps membership was 71.6. Ponder's End was the smallest, with 20 soldiers; King's Cross the largest, with "about 200." Only Withamstow, 75; Wood Green, 72; Haggerstown, 71; and Blackfriars were over 70. Hackney claimed 120 "adherents," a word which included all who attended services. Limehouse and Edmonton gave no figures. The total number of soldiers was about one thousand, the same as that of four stations (Whitechapel, Limehouse, Poplar, and Shoreditch) in 1874, fifteen years earlier.[9]

Decreases in *War Cry* sales, an important part of a corps' income, are another measure of East End decline. The first ten Christian Mission stations, six of which were in East London, showed massive declines in sales. In October 1880, Whitechapel had sold 1,728 *War Crys* weekly; but by March 1886, it made only 325 such sales. The *War Cry* used the word "hardness" to describe work required in East London. The paper applied the word to Whitechapel in the wake of Andrew Mearns's *Bitter Cry of Outcast London,* which exposed the hard life of the district in fall 1883. Again, it used the term at the time of the Whitechapel "Jack the

Ripper" murders in summer and fall 1888. As the army focused on the provinces, it frequently reminded itself of how little it had done for London. Given the greater time it had worked there, it was less successful than had been the Christian Mission, with its more democratic structure. That disparity cast doubt upon Booth's assertion that success rested on authoritarian rule. Whatever the system's strengths, it did not nurture a regular membership in urban slums. And if the East End was not amenable to militant revival methods, then a new approach would have to be formulated. The Booths soon would turn to social salvation as a means to the end of individual salvation, which they had clung to as the only hope of mankind.

Salvation Army membership also declined all over Britain by 1887, especially in areas where it had worked for a decade. Part of the decline was due to its autocratic system and part to an inability of its officers and soldiers to sustain the level of energy growth required. As the army grew less aggressive, opposition to its work decreased. By 1890, there were few arrests for obstructing streets. In the four years before General Booth's death in 1912, there were only seven imprisonments, compared with six hundred in 1884.

Booth stopped publishing membership statistics in the 1870s, at the time of the mission's first decline in London, and he again halted publication around 1887. But he did admit a decline in the number of British corps. In 1888 there were 1,412 corps; 1,395 in 1889; 1,375 in 1890; and 1,211 by 1894. *War Cry* sales fell from 350,000 a week in 1883 to under 290,000 in 1890. During this period of decline, Booth's interest in social salvation grew.

Outside Britain, growth continued by adding territory until 1929, the year the high council deposed Bramwell Booth, who had succeeded his father as general in 1912. That year there were 25,427 officers internationally. The 1994 *Salvation Army Year Book* reported 24,366 officers worldwide, of whom 16,455 were active (the rest being retired), a serious drop from 1929.[10] Changes begun in the 1880s still affect the army as it deals with its failure as an urban revivalist mission, an identity it is still loathe to forsake.

Strain on Salvation Army personnel and income caused leaders to ponder new approaches by 1886. Training officers and raising funds from a constituency that had no say in the army's program depended on a wellspring of *esprit d'corps* which the organization found difficult to sustain over time. There was a serious decline in officer recruits in Britain. By the late 1880s, the army's new social institutions further strained Booth's ability to provide officers for evangelistic programs. In its charismatic stage the army had grown at unprecedented rates, but by 1886 it grew only by plowing new fields overseas. When officers and funds no longer could be spared for overseas expansion, the army as a whole declined.

In the 1880s, the army's internal cohesion depended on the Booths. Catherine, Bramwell, and their boarder George Scott Railton had encouraged William to turn the mission into a military-style Salvation Army in 1878. Older leaders gave way to new talent, literally as it emerged from Catherine's nursery. On-the-job training was the best experience for future leaders, and the Booth children led singing, preached, and learned the rudiments of administration while still early adolescents. Catherine did not trust secular education, so, like her mother, she taught the children herself. To some, the Booths were the Salvation Army; and, to some Booths, the army existed as a family fiefdom. Seven of the eight children graduated to leadership and produced a family dynasty possibly unrivaled in church history.

The Booths were a typical Victorian family. While some social historians stress the father's strict rule, middle-class Victorian homes were largely a mother's domain; due to the father's absence, she supervised a domestic staff, children, and the domestic economy. Mrs. Booth, despite other duties, insisted on guiding her children's lives. With William and Catherine, family government was mainly democratic, but obedience was the principle they applied in childrearing—obedience laced with affection. In spite of her many absences on preaching missions, Catherine was an overpowering mother. While other Victorian sons rebelled early and often, hers walked a narrow path of obedience into their middle years. Only after her death in 1890 did rebellion break out. Her granddaughter surmised that, had she lived, Catherine would "have been able to dispel the misunderstandings which after her death caused her lonely William such grief."[11] Whatever the family's later problems, official army historian Arch R. Wiggins wrote that its early years were "indisputably and understandably largely a Booth affair." All except the retarded Marian held high positions with a distinctive personal rank;[12] until the family disintegrated around 1900, it served the army well.

MRS. BALLINGTON BOOTH.   MR. BALLINGTON BOOTH.

MR. BRAMWELL BOOTH.   "GENERAL" BOOTH.   MISS EVA BOOTH.
CHIEF OF THE STAFF.

THE   SALVATION   ARMY   DISSENSIONS   IN   NEW   YORK.

The "Booth Dynasty"—a Christian Imperium—Dissensions in New York in the 1890s. Courtesy of North Wind Picture Archives.

Second son Ballington (1857–1940) joined his parents' work in 1879, when he took charge of the new Manchester Temple. In 1880, he became the Men's Training Home principal. He fell in love with the daughter of a Church of England rector, Maud Charlesworth, who married him against her father's wishes in 1886. The army attracted "women of gentility," who craved more exciting work than tract distribution and district visiting, according to Ervine. In 1885, William promoted Ballington to marshal, a rank he alone held, and gave him command in Australia. In 1887, when Frank Smith's health broke, Ballington and Maud went as joint commanders to America, where they named the Booths' first grandson William—a name they altered to Charles Brandon Booth when they left the army in 1896 to found the Volunteers of America.[13]

Eldest daughter Catherine (1858–1955) became *La Marechale* when she opened the army in France and Switzerland in 1881–82. In February

1887, she married her chief-of-staff, Arthur Sydney Booth-Clibborn, who had altered his name five days earlier by deed poll. Due to personal slights and anger at the army's central command system, the Booth-Clibborns resigned in 1902 and joined Dr. Alexander Dowie of Chicago. Kate later wrote, "To the Masses I was sent as a child, and my greatest and deepest spiritual blessings and lessons have come in following my calling."[14]

When Emma Moss Booth-Tucker (1860–1903) died in a train wreck in Deans Lake, Missouri, she was serving with her husband as joint commander in the U.S., following Ballington's defection. From 1880 to 1888, she had taken charge of the Women's Training Home, where she taught recruits rudimentary English, army tactics, and discipline. In 1888, she had married Frederick St. George de Latour Tucker who, like Clibborn, appended Booth to his name. Emma had gone with her husband to India as joint commander in 1888, adopting Indian garb and taking an Indian name, Raheeman.[15]

Herbert Howard Booth, (1862–1926), like his sister Catherine, left the army in 1902 to become an independent evangelist. In 1880–84, he had campaigned in England, assisted Kate in France, formed Auxiliary Leagues of army friends, and succeeded Ballington as Men's Training Home principal. In 1889, he commanded Britain. In September 1890, he married Cornelie Schoch, daughter of an army pioneer in Holland, and then, at his own request, took command in Canada because of problems with Bramwell.[16] The Booths' sixth child, Marian Billups (1864–1937), was the only one not to become an army leader. Described variously as an invalid or retarded, her malady was traced to severe convulsions soon after birth or to an accident from which she "developed serious physical weakness."[17]

Eveline Cory (1865–1950) changed her name to Evangeline at Francis Willard's suggestion. Eva played a major role in deposing her brother Bramwell as general in 1929 and retired as the fourth general in 1939. In spite of her youth, her duties during the dynamic 1880s included assisting Emma at the Training Home with oversight of cadets at a slum home in 1884. During six months of 1886–87, she was captain at Marylebone Corps, where John Bright attended meetings and admired her forceful command. In 1889, she commanded the London division. She led the army in Canada (1896–1904) and the U.S. (1904–33).[18]

Lucy Milward (1867–1953), the last of the eight children, went to India with the Booth-Tuckers in 1888 and remained in charge there in 1891. In 1892, the family announced her engagement to Colonel Lampard, who immediately thereafter wrote to tell the general that he was unfit to be the husband of such a fine lady. A court marshal found the reason for Lampard's cold feet; he was deranged. Ervine says that Lampard was "stigmatized as a sort of lunatic so that the face of the Booth family might be saved." He left for America, "where his eccentricities, if he had any, would not be noticed, and there became an evangelist." Lucy soon met Emanuel Daniel Hellberg, an officer from Sweden, whom she married. She led the army in Scandinavia and became her father's companion during his final illness. She stood with Bramwell in the 1929 deposition.[19]

T. H. Huxley assailed the army's "corybantic Christianity" and lampooned its family rule. But nepotism was common among Victorians. Only in the 1920s, when Britain's model imperial family was no longer respected, was the overwhelming influence of one family on a mature organization seen as unfair. In the 1880s, the Booths' combined influence as they perambulated the globe was a factor in Salvation Army growth. Although William angered some army leaders when he appointed his juveniles to command at tender ages, there was no denying their capacities. Besides bearing their parents' name, the children's musical talent, organizing skill, and dramatic sense of what would catch the public eye allowed the young Booths to foster an imperial dynasty.

By the late 1880s, the army's pattern of growth, stagnation, and adaptation had reached the Ballington Booths' command in the U.S., the army's first overseas colony. Commissioner (the rank implied diplomatic powers) Railton, who had come to New York in March 1880, remained till 1882, when he reluctantly returned to England. The army's first efforts in the U.S. were unimpressive. The brand of revivalism brought to England by Caughey, Palmer, and Finney no longer was common in America. While evangelicals aided the army's attempt to re-ignite that style, the urban milieu, as its population became increasingly heterogeneous, had become noticeably hostile to revivalism. Although nostalgically applauded by those who hoped for a revival of Protestant values, the army's effort in New York collapsed, necessitating a "re-opening" there in 1882; of the ten corps established by Railton in 1880, only five remained when he left in 1882.[20]

Railton's successor was Thomas E. Moore, a man of affairs who had lived in the U.S. Born in 1840 in Worcestershire, he first experienced conviction of sin at age fourteen through fear of death, common in religious adolescents. At age twenty, an open-air preacher convinced him of his sin and he joined a church, but he soon became a backslider. He spent eight years in America, to which he later returned for three years to make a fortune, leaving his family in London. His fortune-seeking was interrupted by an experience of holiness, and he spent six months preaching in towns before returning to London, where he managed a West End firm. An account of the Salvation Army in *The Christian* caught his eye, and he joined in 1879. After two years, he became London's commander, a sign of the army's desperate need for officers with leadership skills. His American command greatly improved upon Railton's two-year effort, opening 120 corps, mostly in towns where Methodism was strong. By 1884, his 230 officers sold twenty thousand copies of the *War Cry* weekly. In 1884, Moore extended his American command into Canada.[21]

Moore, who did not have the long-term connection to Booth that Railton enjoyed, became increasingly independent. He became a citizen in order to fulfill Booth's wish that all army property be kept under Booth's personal control. As an English citizen, Booth could not own property under U.S. state laws, so Moore registered army property in his own name as Booth's surrogate. Legal action against army holdings, therefore, was directed at Moore personally. To avoid legal harassment, as early as 1882 Moore tried to get Booth to incorporate the army in America, to no avail. Finally, in October 1884, Moore incorporated the "Salvation Army of America" after he met with officers at his headquarters in Brooklyn. They voted 121 to 4 to incorporate, in light of pending litigation in New Brunswick, New Jersey; and Newburgh, New York, where local members resisted removal of capital funds from their towns to Moore's account. After Booth rejected Moore's appeal to incorporate, Moore made himself general of his Salvation Army and took the *War Cry* copyright and army insignia with him into a new corporation. Booth did not see the need to incorporate the army, until after the 1896 schism led by his son Ballington. To protect army patents, copyrights, and property, the Booth-Tuckers incorporated the army under New York law in April 1899. Today Salvation Army leaders in America constitute a corporation in Alexandria, Virginia, with a board of trustees.

Thomas E. Moore, the Army's Divisional Commander in London, became its second commander in the United States. He led a schism in 1884, the first break-away from the Booths' imperial control. Courtesy of the Salvation Army National Archives and Research Center.

In 1884, Booth at once sent over a new commissioner, Major Frank Smith, and America was now blessed with two Salvation Armies, one American and one international. Smith, an excellent organizer-publicist, soon had the larger force. Booth sent along over fifty English officers to recoup, so far as was possible, the ruinous losses inflicted by the "traitorous" Moore. Smith sensed American antipathy to English rule and mounted a campaign to win over the enormous "coloured" population, with only temporary results. With his personal charm and bounding energy, Smith's two and a half years took the army from seventeen corps and an indeterminate number of officers in 1884, when loyalists and rebels were not easily sorted out; to three hundred corps and 656 officers when, in April 1887, he asked to be relieved due to broken health. Again the army's system had succeeded under a charismatic leader. But in America, as in England, salvationists found no real success with their revivalistic message in urban slums.[22]

A great anxiety to Booth was his organization's tendency toward schism, which betrayed a fundamental defect in his centralized government. Moore's departure epitomized local commanders' desire for a more federal system which would allow them freedom for maneuver. Booth earlier had noted the tendency of Christian Mission evangelists to split off from his mission and set up shop on their own. Self-rule was on the rise. Local problems forced governments to allow colonial regimes more liberty. Booth's lack of sympathy with federalism made him unsympathetic to salvationists' desires to participate in decision making. His autocracy kept him at odds with his American constituents, who chafed under English domination. Although he was delighted with this "Mighty England over the ocean" in 1886, when he first went to America, he found that the Americans "vote on everything . . . except in The Salvation Army." To Booth, it was unthinkable that leaders should share decision-making powers with followers.

Railton sensed Booth's concern over the 1884 Moore schism, which led later to demands by other territorial leaders for shared rule and to other democratic rebellions against and within Booth's London headquarters. Railton hailed Booth as a man "set forth by God to be a leader of His people," and said that he would "follow him as he followed Christ, even to death." But commissioners in distant lands of Booth's imperium wanted to be consulted on where their organization was going. For all of his sensitivity to his era, Booth failed to read the signs of the time, visible in the 1880s in increased worker restiveness, trade union organization, and reforms that gave male suffrage to nearly all workers and initiated compulsory education and literacy.

In the U.S., increased desire for self-rule was compounded by national maturity. As Britain's equal, America would not accept subjugation by a London-based general, whether chosen by God or not. An English army in America would have to take on the character of American culture. Thinking of 75 degrees Fahrenheit as hot, the English found the U.S. climate terribly uncomfortable. And the political atmosphere was just as challenging for the English nervous system. With democracy mounting on both sides of the Atlantic, a changed attitude toward the right of working-class people to advise concerning their own destinies was in order. Salvation Army commanders in America, even Booths, understood that Yankees would assert their rights.

Less provincial Americans like Major Suzie F. Swift,[23] editor of the army's *All the World* missionary magazine in the 1880s, were appalled by such chauvinistic American practices as the use of American flags in army halls and marches, and the use of the eagle in place of the crown atop the army's international banner. But nationalist idiom became a prerequisite for the army's continued existence in America. Booth grasped the desire of others to be unique, but he would not permit self-rule. This fixity even led to tension between him and the reliable Railton while the latter was commissioner in America. Booth feared that his friend had become a captive of his new homeland—one reason for his recall. Others proved totally unreliable, as two of the next three U.S. commissioners, Moore and Ballington Booth, led schisms; and there is evidence that the third, Frank Smith, may have considered doing so.

Smith's 1887 departure from America caused another relapse in the American army, though not due to any known perfidy on Smith's part. His successors, the Ballington Booths, assured Americans that Smith's exodus was not another Boothian plot to curtail their liberty. By December 1887, Ballington reported stability, with 265 corps and 550 officers, a decrease from Smith's statistics. But eight years later, he and Maud complained of William's and Bramwell's restrictive leadership and left the army to found the Volunteers of America. Before leaving England to take over his command in 1887, Ballington had told a Liverpool audience, "I am growing daily into the views and feelings of our General." Feelings acquired in London were not retained in the U.S. Although, in many ways, Ballington's 1896 split was the great schism led by a member of the imperial family, the reason once again was the general's aversion to accepting federal rather than centralized government. Still, in 1896 recovery seems to have been rapid. The army in America by that time was more mature, with around two thousand officers.

After Smith's departure, Booth treated the U.S. forces with benign neglect. The London *War Cry* reported American news less often than events from other territories. Booth made only one visit to the U.S. in the 1880s, while he frequently toured the continent. During his 1886 visit, he was taken by a country where "everyone does as he likes" and "people learn to take care of themselves." He met many British converts; the army in America was to a large extent an Anglo-Saxon affair. Booth expected soldiers to find a corps after emigrating abroad. Booth's enjoyment of his first trip to America was raised by a meeting with captured Chiricahua Indian chief Mangus on a train in Indiana. Booth wanted the

Salvation Army Charioteers taking the gospel to English Villages in the 1880s. Courtesy of the Salvation Army National Archives and Research Center.

government to hand over Indian affairs to the Salvation Army. The *Chicago Tribune* compared him to evangelists Dwight L. Moody and Sam Jones. Booth met his old mentor James Caughey in New Jersey and attended Dr. Palmer's Tuesday Meeting in New York, renewing his ties with his revivalist heritage. Still, efforts to discredit the army in the U.S. as "altogether English" troubled him. Why could Americans not see the inefficiency of a system that was built on shared decision making rather than on divine rule by one? Booth, an autocrat with an imperial regime, could not comprehend the American mentality. He also had increasing trouble with demands from the rising working classes of his homeland.

In 1887, Field Secretary Brindley Boon, in a remarkably candid mood, asked, "Are we settling down?" Boon knew from statistics that the army was not growing and that it had moved from core cities into working-class suburbs occupied by Methodists, independents, and Baptists. "We go to a town of 20 or 30,000 people, take a Barracks [hall] at some street corner, get a Corps of 100 or 200 Soldiers, then we consider our work done." The urban slum was no longer the army's native habitat; there, as we have seen, a roster of 100 to 200 was not the average membership. Boon envisioned Bolton, a city of 106,000 inhabitants, filled with salvationists. But the army had only one barracks with two officers. Boon noted that many villages of under 4,000 population had as large a hall as Bolton. Buildings had become ends in themselves, just as Booth had predicted they might. Boon mused, "If we are not the people whom God has sent to subdue the earth, if we are only one more sect, one more collection of churches, then our days are numbered, and we shall become like others." He concluded that the army's best chance for growth was its open-air work, its most aggressive ministry. But he found bandsmen "tootle tooting" in the streets, with little sense of purpose. His solution: make at least half an hour of witnessing a rule for open-air work. Of course, this idea that the army could increase spirit by setting down rules was just another sign of its decadence and settling down.

Booth had published *Field Officer's Orders and Regulations* in 1881, but by 1887 leaders feverishly tried to halt stagnation by making a matter of duty activities that in earlier days had been done cheerfully. A week after Boon wrote of his frustration, he found that the army's 148,000 conversions in 1886 were in no way reflected in membership. To halt the "leakage between the penitent-form and the Soldiers' Roll," he proposed that each of the 430 converts who knelt at London penitent-forms in one week make just one convert per week. In fourteen weeks, the entire population of London would be saved. He wondered why, after twenty-two years of Salvation Army work, "so little has yet been accomplished?" Revivalism's critics often pointed to a lack of interest in nurturing converts. The army's solution was to order the staff council to develop a new report form to insure better follow-up of "personnel."[24]

Stratification into ranks grew rigid. The army's military rank structure separated the clergy from the laity and the field from headquarters staff. Minute 44 of October 3, 1888 made staff officers more distinguishable from those "of lower rank" by ordering subordinates not to wear shoulder straps. The chief of staff would not countenance junior officers addressing ensigns and adjutants as staff-captains and staff-captains as majors. Disregard for rank "must be discontinued." A new Statistical Department collected a monthly "up and down form" in 1889 to chart the progress of corps. The general told Bristol Circus Corps' sergeants to obey their superior officers. Had not Wesley said, "Your business is not to mend the rules but to keep them." It apparently did not occur to him that he was speaking not in the late eighteenth century but in the late nineteenth, when a newly literate trade-unionist working class had come of age and was eager to participate in making its own rules.[25] Soon the staff produced a *Field Officer's Book* to examine knowledge of regulations and to find those who strove to be efficient. Getting ahead in the army was the aim. By November 1888, headquarters also had created an exam system for staff officers and thus established a virtual civil service system. Railton proposed an exam to require soldiers on command to "speak outdoors or in"; to sell the *War Cry* in the streets and in pubs; and to "go to any part of the world." Next came regulations for corps secretaries and treasurers, as well as pages of "Band Rules."[26]

Increasingly, the army's numbers (not analyzed by historians) reflected the findings of the 1886 *British Weekly* survey that counted those who went to services in various London churches. The survey uncovered the army's weakness in the slums and found that it had moved into areas already cultivated by other nonconformists, a point that Booth would not concede. Spending a Sunday at London's Regent Hall Corps in 1888, he tried to answer the accusation that "the number of your soldiers does not very much increase" by noting that the Regent Hall had produced three hundred officers in its six years of existence. But Regent Hall was a West End middle-class showcase, hardly representative of the army as a whole. When he addressed a twenty-third anniversary celebration in July, he pointed to improved discipline and uniforms as the year's achievement; but he did not make his usual comparison with 1887's statistics.[27]

Booth's unpublished statistics are most significant. In the 1890 May meeting (voluntary societies published annual reports in May) at Exeter Hall, Booth listed the number of officers and corps abroad, but not the British totals, which had declined by fifty corps since May 1889. At his sixtieth birthday celebration in 1889, Booth had said that his "new, mighty, aggressive, and successful agency" was making the world bow at Jesus's feet. But he did not back up his bravado with the numbers he once had loved to quote. He claimed to have turned drones into workers by giving soldiers the "liberty to fight the devil, the world, sin, and selfishness." But those who fought *him* would have to leave his army. Autocracy, he held, was God-invented government, as seen in Eden, the family, and heaven. We are "hallelujah Jews." His ordeal had been coping with traitors.[28] Perhaps we should not make too much of Booth's autocratic talk, but it suggested that he was out of touch with the populist mood.

Charges of failure dogged Booth in 1889. In January, the *Times* quoted Anglican clergyman Llewellan Davies's charge that the army was "a unique failure" in London's Marylebone district. The *Times* asked a probing question: "Did The Salvation Army aim principally at reaching those whom every Christian agency had failed to reach—the outcast of society, the uncared for, the lowest and the worst?" The question had until now escaped notice. Was the army a mission to the heathen, or just another working-class sect? Booth answered that the army never had aimed only at saving drunkards, harlots, and slum dwellers, but had meant "to go to those of the working classes who were without Christ." Its scope, he said, ran from "Rotten Row" to "Royalty."

This admission that the army had become a working-class sect opened the way for its re-formation into two wings by late 1890—a religious wing and a social wing. The religious wing would deal with a working-class membership that the army was cultivating in suburbs and small towns; the social wing would serve the masses whom Booth still meant to save. As Booth's social program took shape in the 1880s, he claimed that he was discovering how to deal with the "ignorant and vicious and naked people, whom a generous government and a wealthy nation left to thieve under the shadow of the Church and the throne." But in spite of his claim that the army could fill Printing House Square with its converts for the church and the *Times* to see, it was not filling its East End halls with converts. This was now apparent. So the *Times* asked, was it true that converts were backslidden church members? If Booth's army did not reach the heathen, was it at least reaching those who once had been in the church? Booth admitted that converts were mainly former church members; after all, 80 percent of one prison populace had been Sunday school attendees.[29] This group included nonconformist defectors who had joined the Salvation Army.

In 1886, Railton warned against "extravagant expectations," pointing out that, before 1877, the mission had had few successes. But Booth more than anyone had raised expectations. He projected twentieth-century growth, when, by his estimate, the army would outstrip all other religious sects. When he sent 760 English officers overseas in 1886, he

English Lady-Preacher of the Salvation Army in a Swiss Tavern in the 1880s.
Picture by the Swedish artist G. Cederstrom. Courtesy of North Wind Picture
Archives.

claimed that this was a greater number than had been sent out that year
by "all the rest of the Protestant world put together?" The annual report
of May 1890 stifled these claims; only 163 had gone abroad that year.[30]
Was the decline due to unfair expectations or to some defect in the army?
Why was the army not turning converts into soldiers? Why did it have
no viable corps in the slums?

The army's focus no longer was London. Booth moved the training
of cadets away from London. The new training program, aimed at the
country, moved cadets through three two-month stages: first, training in
country depots; next, command of a village corps; and, finally, finishing
in London. By 1886, the army had five thousand soldiers in six hundred
villages where it had begun in 1885. The hope was to extend work to
eighteen thousand villages where evangelicals hoped to save country
folk from Anglo-Catholic missions. Booth planned to turn five thousand
soldiers into officers and local officers: (1) "readies" would become officers immediately upon passing a simple test; others would be (2) "can-

didates" and form the "reserves" to continue training in corps until they became (3) "cadets" in training. Booth the Methodist would put all salvationists "on the plan." But, in 1888, Booth began moving "training depots" back to London,[31] as his emphasis became less how to prepare preachers than how to expose cadets to new social operations in the metropolis.

In 1887, Boon made an amazing statement: Booth had stopped all openings for six months. Demand for officers overseas and at home had outstripped the training homes' ability to produce them. Problems of the army's survival plagued Booth. He assured others that his system was self-sustaining. If the general died, he said, "there would still be The Army to reckon with; still Mrs. Booth and the seven [eight?] sons and daughters," then commissioners, majors, other officers, and tens of thousands of soldiers and little soldiers. Here we see Booth's hierarchy, from his family down to little soldiers. Indeed, little soldiers were getting a great deal of notice, as concern for the army's future grew. To supply needed officers, converted children first would become soldiers and then, at a rate of one per corps per year for ten years, would constitute ten thousand Salvation Army clergymen and clergywomen. On the rolls in 1888 were 15,149 junior soldiers. A children's paper, the *Young Soldier,* edited by a female staff, had a larger youth circulation than any religious paper other than the American *Sunday School Times.*[32] But, as the number of British officers declined, Booth worried about the future.

By 1888, overseas expansion made the Salvation Army the world's fastest growing Christian sect in an age of missions. Beginning in 1879 with the U.S., the army had invaded thirty-four countries by 1890. Greatest growth came in 1885–86, when it sent hundreds of officers to Europe, America, Australasia, Asia, and Africa. According to A. M. Nicol, the army's foreign secretary, Booth wanted to found an empire of "states throughout the world, conforming to the laws and customs of the country in which they are formed, paying homage, obedience, and tithe to a central power." In this federated autocracy, territories would take direction from the general and chief of staff in London, who would see to their support.[33] Ideally it was a federation, but in colonial territories, its autocratic international command diluted even limited autonomy.

By 1889, the army in Europe had corps in France, Switzerland, Italy, Holland, Belgium, and Germany. Only in Denmark, Sweden, and Nor-

Robert Harris's (1849–1919) Salvation Army Parade, Toronto, circa 1880, shows exhuberant Salvationists and sympathetic evangelicals at a time when the army was opening hundreds of corps, particularly in Anglo-American countries. Courtesy of Confederation Centre Art Gallery and Museum, Prince Edward Island. Robert Harris Collection.

way did it flourish. Booth, tending to overstate, claimed that the army's growth in Scandinavia was the most remarkable of "any religious movement on the face of the earth." The army had entered Catholic Argentina, the sole South American venture in the 1880s, with poor results. Booth claimed that salvationists were not Protestants, were "not sent into the world to convert Catholics from their errors," but the *War Cry* contradicted his claim when it announced Catholic conversions. Nicol found that, in France, the army had "a pretense of a hold" in only one or two towns, and recruits were mainly the children of Protestants. Major James Vint was "starved out" of Rome. The army aided disaster victims in Italy, but Nicol, writing as an ex-officer, noted that its charity "always [had] a handle to it."[34]

In 1882, India became the army's first non-Western territory and a major test of its ability to adapt. As Booth pointed out, three problems faced Europeans in India: (1) how to close the gap between European and native; (2) how to get Indians converted; (3) how to make the Indian work self-sustaining. He asserted that two great Salvation Army principles were "self-sustenation and self-propagation." He could have added that, in East London, neither had been attained. Officers adopted Indian names, a yellow and red robe, and sandals. In this, the army followed Francis Xavier's 1542–45 humble life among fishermen of southeastern India. Xavier had assumed a Tamil name and worn Tamil garb. Still, Nicol's 1910 assessment of the army's experience in India was harsh: it had succeeded in catching only "converts of other missions." Converts were unreliable, corps work fluctuated, and "the officers, un-Christian in their spirit and conduct, [make] too frequent use of the collecting-box." Nicol doubted that the army had been as successful as normal British or American missions, whose missionaries did not "eat and dress as do the heathen." His charge that the army was a "sheep-stealer" echoed the claims of others. Some prayed that the army would not come to India, but one Methodist missionary named Gladwin joined the army's pioneers as a captain, and his wife became a lieutenant.[35]

Harry Williams, Booth-Tucker's biographer, says that the army recruited few soldiers from Hindu, Parsi, and Muslim homes. Indian recruits came from Christian families. Ervine earlier had said the same. *Harvest Field,* a missionary journal, reported Tucker's financial appeals as based on "inflated statistics and impermanent results." Older missions' negative reactions no doubt were partly due to the army's disregard for the zones of influence into which the missions had carved India before the army arrived. Without a zone of their own, salvationists trespassed on territory claimed by others. Irish Presbyterians in Gujarat said that the army was the "greatest religious swindle of the 19th century." Salvationists were "barefooted, peripatetic theologians in buff." American Methodist Missionary Bishop J. Wascom Pickett censured the army's rejection of baptism, which Indians saw as a rite of passage into Christianity from heathenism. He found that salvationists were not cooperative and, as far as evangelization was concerned, a negative force. The *Times* told "orderly communities" that, despite defects, unencumbered salvationists recalled a distant past when the older sects too had conducted themselves with vivacity "though with more self-respect." Even *Harvest Fields* praised salvationists' "tireless enthusiasm and abounding hopefulness" in their "readiness for any new exploit anywhere; the impatience with plans to which the people have grown accustomed and perhaps indifferent." And Pickett noted that new missionaries achieved miracles which older missionaries had termed impossible.[36] The army goaded older missions, but its method, theology, and tactlessness placed it outside their good graces.

Frederick Tucker (1853–1929) took the name Fakir Singh when he returned to India with the Salvation Army in 1882. He had been converted in the 1875 London campaign of evangelists Moody and Sankey and received his Indian Civil Service appointment in 1876. In the Indian Civil Service, he had risen to the rank of assistant commissioner. In 1881, he took leave to go to London to investigate the army after he read of it in a Christian journal. Once Tucker became a Salvation Army officer, Booth almost immediately assigned him to form a party to invade India. With Captain Henry Bullard, Lieutenant Arthur Norman, Mary Thompson, and Sister Jennings, the Tuckers left from Liverpool. In September 1882, all but Sister Jennings, who had fallen ill en route and returned to England with Mrs. Tucker, landed at Bombay. During the first year, after notable legal battles, the group gained the right to preach in the streets. The government was afraid that religious strife might break out. The party extended the army's work from Bombay to Calcutta, Madras, Poona, Lahore, and Colombo, opened training homes for men and women; and issued a weekly *War Cry* in English and a monthly in Marathi and Gujerati. By 1889, there were 263 officers, 103 of whom were Indian or Singhalese nationals, and 57 corps.

Tucker's rigid rules for native living by Europeans led to protests which Booth investigated on his first trip there in 1886. Booth's compromise meant that officers ceased begging for rice or living in huts. Tucker's wife died of cholera in February 1887. In April 1888, he married Emma Booth and changed his name to Booth-Tucker. By 1889, of 192 western officers the army had sent to India since 1886, 4 had died, 9 had gone home as invalids, 10 had paid their own passage home but stayed in the army, 1 had resigned, 2 had been dismissed, and 5 had joined other missions. The remaining 161 presumably served their missionary terms acceptably.

The Booth-Tuckers returned to England in 1891, due to Emma's health. When Emma's death ended Booth-Tucker's 1896–1904 term as U.S. commander, he became foreign secretary in London in 1904–7 and then returned to India to set up settlements for criminal tribes. He had plotted these farm colonies in cooperation with the government during his first term in India. By 1925, there were thirty-five thousand farm settlers in the army's Indian settlements. In 1898, he organized U.S. farm colonies to move the urban poor to farms. Tucker's career ended in 1929, in a debate with Bramwell Booth about army government.[37]

In the New World, the army had more success than in Catholic Europe or Hindu India. Lay soldiers from England spread the army to the U.S., Canada, and Australasia. By 1889, there were 380 corps and 926 officers in the U.S. In April (Easter was a time for enrollments), they claimed 9,500 soldiers, 2,500 more than in March but still a tiny membership averaging only 25 soldiers per corps. *War Cry* circulation had reached 103,500. In Canada, there were 350 corps and 1,000 officers. By 1890, Canadians had sent more officers to India than they had received from England. In May 1887, Commissioner Coombs told the London *War Cry* that he could find jobs for servant girls and farm laborers on government land out west.[38] But even Canada claimed just 12,000 soldiers, a mere 34.3 per corps. *War Cry* sales there were 95,000 per week. In Australasia (five Australian colonies, New Zealand, and Tazmania) there were 314 corps. Of the 900 officers, 850 were of Australian origin. Membership was over 14,000, 44.6 per corps, and *War Cry* sales were 95,000 copies. All in all, the number of members per corps was small, particularly as the army claimed to be making 150,000 converts per year.

While the numbers of corps, officers, and *War Cry* sales in these three areas equaled those in Britain by 1890, Britain's pattern of growth and stagnation was replicated overseas. The army's small membership meant that its support came largely from *War Cry* sales in shops and taverns and from other external donations. Field officers bore the burden personally when revenues did not pay their rent and small allowance. Still, growth in the number of corps and officers (most were under thirty years of age in 1890) was striking. But growth came at high personal cost. Many new corps quickly closed or maintained a precarious existence. For this reason, by 1886 the army published the number of corps and officers but withheld the number of soldiers and the amount of their donations. It failed to make itself into a self-supporting sect. Nicol said of the army in the U.S.: "It has no numerical following worth naming," but rather is "an organised charity"; its recruits did not come from "the world outside the Church."[39] Because, by 1890, its worldwide membership was small, the army had begun to look elsewhere for prestige. In fact, by 1890, it already was known largely as a social service agency.

Outsiders who knew it for its social programs did not realize it was a church as well.

In 1886, Booth faced a dilemma: whether to democratize his methods in order to hold working-class converts or find work which would not require a membership to supply income. He adopted social service as the army's means of renewal. What moved him in this direction? The first motivator was the army's failure to nurture its members. If it had had a membership which sustained it financially, the Salvation Army would have developed into a sect, just as other Methodists had done. Instead, autocracy kept laypersons from finding fulfillment within its ranks, and so it drove toward social service after 1887. Perpetuating itself was its paramount worry. Now turning converts into members was no longer essential to its existence as an organization.

Between 1884 and 1887, Booth gradually formed a rationale for the army as a worldwide Christian imperium. In 1885, he asked, "Are all to become [Salvation Army] officers?" He described his imperial aim: "My business is to get the world saved; if this involves the standing still of the looms and the shutting up of the factories and the staying of the sailing of the ships, let them all stand still. When we have got everybody converted they can go on again." He was convinced that, when God's people woke up to the import of Christian warfare and engaged in it sincerely, the millennium would not be far off. As a postmillennialist, he was convinced that his army could so alter the world as to introduce a Christian era prior to the second advent of Christ. When Booth presented his global creed of salvationist optimism, the idea that Christ's earthly reign could be brought about by human effort, a nineteenth-century evangelical conviction, was taking on international scope due to Anglo-American imperialism.

Moore's 1884 schism focused Booth's imperial aim. He saw the army as one body with one head, one law. While territorial leaders could adapt methods to native cultures, all property must belong to one Salvation Army; it could not be severed from that organization. Union was God's will and prevailed in heaven. Corps in towns united under one captain; it was equally wise for corps worldwide to comprise one army under one general. "Unity is strength"; strong corps assisted weak ones, as strong nations aided the weak, but this only occurred when they were parts of one whole. Soon, forces of infidelity and godliness would face each other in the final war to possess the earth. Then "will the value of union be realised."[40]

In discussing possible war between England and Russia in May 1885, Booth mixed pre- and postmillennial ideas. In gloomy moods, he argued that righteousness would not rule until "the Prince of Peace at the head of some great Salvation Army has overcome the devil," outlawed wholesale murder, and ushered in the millennium. His mood turned harshly premillennial in August 1887, due to frustration with Christianity's—and, quite likely, his own army's—numerical failures. Since 1785, three million had become Christian, but over twenty million babies had been born. "Tell me not that we are on the eve of the millennium, that things are not so bad as they seem." But more often he was optimistic and postmillennialist. He saw his army as a catalyst of Christ's Second Coming: "I don't say there are no other Israels, but I do believe that Jesus has come again now in the flesh of The Salvation Army."[41] Did he intend this notion to be taken literally, or was it his way of stimulating hope in his troops?

In 1890, Booth told his Birmingham soldiers that some people wished that there were only one denomination. "So do I," he said, "and I wish it was all The Salvation Army!" If he were a prophet, he might tell them "that the little stone cut out of the mountain without hands that is to go on increasing till it fills the whole earth, which we read of in Daniel, might be The Salvation Army." But "I am not a prophet." What separated him from cultists was his humor; he often made claims for his army in jest. Was he correct when he said the army was the fastest growing missionary society, the greatest tract society, and the largest temperance society in the world? He was building a benevolent empire, a Christian imperium. Even Jews, whom Railton was recruiting (in 1887 he collected the names of Jewish salvationists for an advance on Jerusalem), were not beyond Booth's dream.[42]

Booth saw that federal principles were in vogue and tried to make his empire appear to conform to them. While he insisted that there had to be one international center with one general, he held that the nation where the headquarters was located did not have supremacy over other nations. Just as the U.S. was a number of small federated states, "we seek a Federation of all the States of the world." The fact that all prior efforts to form a worldwide Christian federation had failed was no reason why he should not make an attempt. Referring to Moore's 1884 schism, Booth argued that when someone rebels in the name of liberty, in order to become the head himself, union becomes more difficult. Yet, in spite of Moore's schism, Booth claimed that Americans would see that his army was not English "but that it is a Kingdom, world-wide in its scope." He also saw that it would be tyranny and folly to impose Western ideas on Eastern peoples. He accepted the China Inland Mission goal of developing indigenous leadership overseas.

Booth adopted from William Carey, who went to India in 1793, a view of missions as self-sustaining and self-propagating. Carey held that "the chief responsibility for winning a people to the faith must be borne by indigenous Christians." Booth was proud of the Indian, American, Canadian, and Australian officers he recruited. Another mentor, James Hudson Taylor, founder in 1865 of the China Inland Mission, provided missionaries with no money. They had to rely on faith for their income. Booth used this mode in Western countries, where he asked officers to raise their support in towns to which he sent them through *War Cry* sales and donations by nightly congregations. When Booth sent 203 officers to India in 1886, he told them to raise their support locally, as soldiers had in Britain and America. But when Anglo-American-Australasian officers resisted use of Tucker's begging bowl, contributions from the West supported the Indian army. In 1885, Booth defined what he meant by self-support: "a large proportion of the money" must be supplied by the army's members.[43] When Booth failed to grasp the link between self-support and self-rule, he forfeited the support of his dwindling number of soldiers, and his ambitions for a worldwide empire of revivalists foundered.

Even soldiers in the West failed to support corps' expenses. After a corps had been in a town for a decade, its officers still sought income from *War Cry* sales in shops and taverns. Booth did not see his soldiers' giving as linked to a desire to have a say in spending the income. He also would forfeit officers and soldiers who would not sacrifice for a concern owned by the Booth family and not by them. A federalist structure without shared authority was not true federalism. As for self-rule, Booth would not have it.

He did not grasp federalism. At a 1886 meeting of officers in London, he declared that he would allow no controversy in army councils. Voting and committees were wasteful. Bramwell met with London's Grecian Corps soldiers and gave "money, prosperity, politics" as reasons for the half-heartedness of soldiers after conversion. But these were the hopes of a rising working class that no longer was submissive to rule by others. When membership fell, headquarters complained that officers were making unauthorized removals of names from soldiers' rolls. The 1884–86 depression caused offerings to drop at a time when the need for officers and funds increased. Booth still excluded soldiers from decision making, an exclusion he had begun in 1878. He employed the device of stringent regulations and inaugurated a "Self-Denial Week," during which soldiers and friends were to put aside money from some pleasure for the cause. Booth wrote in 1887, "Divine Rule is the true Home Rule." "I am a Unionist, I am for uniting everybody under the King."[44] In the army, Booth was king.

Inconsistency of rule, as much as rules themselves, angered the rank and file. Critics saw as a tragedy, in the army's socially stratified system, the fact that field officers existed on subsistence income while staff officers' salaries were guaranteed. A rule existed requiring a captain to be engaged to another officer for twelve months; this Booth justified fairly as being no more rigid than the discipline imposed by other sects. Yet, early in 1887, he permitted two colonels to marry non-officers.

Increasingly, ex-officers, now growing in number, voiced their frustrations in public. Defections in 1886 by Colonel Day, the Southern Division commander, and Commissioner Corbridge, Booth's friend from Christian Mission days, pointed to dissension in the staff concerning Booth's arbitrary rule. Day later recanted his complaints; but Corbridge, whose charges had to do with financial reports sent him by army accountants, threatened to sue and contact the press. He had been the official fund-raiser. Day, Corbridge, and others held meetings to denounce the army. From 1886 to 1889, former staff officers brought court cases, all won by the army, which spawned negative press reports at a time when the army needed more income. Two of Booth's Aide-de-camps, Major Hodges and Colonel Edmunds, resigned.[45] These officers knew how to litigate and knew how much the army needed a good press. They also saw how little influence they had in an organization controlled by the Booth family. Thousands of lesser officers resigned due either to illness or to despair at their hard lot and the lack of influence they had in a system that profited from their labor.

In May 1889, at Exeter Hall, London, Booth defined a Christian imperium. In "The Future of Missions and the Mission of the Future," he saw Christianity losing a world population race, due to inefficient missionary societies; they must get more results at less expense. To achieve this goal, he would dissolve the entire church into one vast missionary society. He would sort the human race into friends and enemies of Christ, on a declining scale beginning with the royal family, and descending through the House of Lords, newspaper people, and the stock exchange, down to the poorest beggar. Soldiers of Christ then would "charge down upon the enemy" until all had fallen at Christ's feet. A year before he published his social reform manifesto, he was railing against those whom he saw as "paradise mongers" with "humanitarian wishes." He found it hard to reconcile revivalism with the social services he had already begun to develop. Social reform without personal salvation from sin was no solution, he argued. Humanitarians had "stolen the idea of our heaven" and tried to get people into it without Christ. They wanted to civilize people with stone houses and trousers before Christianizing them. What had civilization done for natives of America, Australia, or South Africa? Neither had education solved the human problem, he argued. A person who can read the Bible can also "read Huxley and Darwin, and that whole generation of unbelievers and doubters." Apostles did not teach pagans to read, they converted them; then they educated themselves. And they had Jews to deal with; anyone "would sooner undertake to save a Heathen than a Jew." To yield results equal to expense, the church must send missionaries equal to the work to be done. If the queen needed eighty thousand soldiers to subdue India, the King of Kings could need no fewer.[46]

Booth continued to be, above everything else, a revivalist, a disciple of Caughey, Finney, and Palmer. But in the 1880s, events pressured him to modify his allegiance. By 1887, Frank Smith, W. T. Stead, and others were reeducating him to become a social reformer. Reeducation was not easy. Booth always had been sure that a Christian world would be achieved by revival means he had learned in the 1840s. But the world of the 1880s had frustrated that hope, in all churches and missions, and in his own Salvation Army, which was experiencing stagnation. By 1889, Booth was turning in new directions, but old ways died hard.

7.

Wholesale Salvation:

Darkest England's Social Reform

In 1883, five years after William Booth made his mission into a militant Salvation Army in order to save more souls from hell, he opened a rescue home to save fallen women from an evil environment. What turned this revivalist into one of the world's leading social reformers, and who changed Booth's mind about how mankind's salvation could be achieved? And why did he publish, in 1890, a social scheme which would take the "submerged tenth" from city workshops back to the land? In fact, a symphony of 1880s ideas changed Booth's mind. The message came from Mount Olympus and Mount Sinai, from outsiders and from salvationists. Booth, like Saint Paul, was a debtor to Jew and Gentile, intellectual and barbarian. From 1883 on, he heard salvationists, mainly women and Frank Smith; was prodded by Andrew Mearns's *Bitter Cry of Outcast London* (1883);[1] joined in W. T. Stead's 1885 "Maiden Tribute of Modern Babylon" crusade; and supported London's dock strikers in 1889.

By 1890, Booth's contemporaries mostly lauded his "Darkest England" scheme to end unemployment by moving wasted labor in the cities to the wastelands of colonies. Some, however, flayed him as a religious dictator who hoped to raid national funds to build his Christian imperium, now that his revival methods had failed. But neither view of this revivalist turned social reformer was fair. One historian saw Booth as a practical man who scorned "promising the destitute either the rewards of heaven, or of a socialist utopia after the revolution."[2] He would solve the world's ills by practical means. In the end, his scheme, as one of many 1880s schemes, had limited success. Like Edward Bellamy in *Looking Backward* (1888), Booth pondered how best to delay the revolution of the laboring masses. The most important outcome of his program was that it became the basis of Salvation Army social services.[3]

Booth apologists argue that his conversion from revivalist into social reformer after 1883 was a minor alteration, and that his mind was bent on reform due to his boyhood poverty in Nottingham. After all, his East London mission had opened soup kitchens in 1870, albeit to raise funds. "Darkest England," they claim, was only the result of renewed interest in the physical needs of the poor.[4] Not so. The 1890 scheme differed in kind, and not just in scope, from the temporary handout aid his mission offered, aid he had halted in 1877 when it impeded his revival program. His fixation was on saving souls. Darkest England was a new departure for Booth and for the army. As its evangelistic program stagnated in the 1880s, social salvation replaced evangelism as the army's mission.

When cities became more ethnically mixed, the army had to deal with people less amenable to revivalism. By 1883, it began to turn from a fixed concern for revival to social concern for fallen women, drunkards, and released prisoners. Necessity drove Booth, a practical man, to meet human need and at the same time to save his failing mission. Previously he had won souls through street services and home visitation. But by the mid-1880s, critics saw that the army, unable to "win the masses to the Gospel," was recruiting its soldiers from the working classes whom Methodism had attracted in the eighteenth century. Booth became aware that he needed new solutions to the problem of converting the "heathen."

In 1883, Mearns's *Bitter Cry* exposed London's unsanitary, crime-infested, starving condition. Booth supported Mearns's findings but not his appraisal that poverty was the cause. Society did not create slums, according to Booth. Squalor resulted from rebellion against God, from sinful nature; "the way to help the prodigal son was not to build him a comfortable hut, or to give him an allowance from the parish, or provide for his education, but to get him to see and acknowledge his sin." Nonetheless, Booth was upset that London, the center from which he hoped to save the world, gave such a bad impression—"extreme wealth of a few and the miserable poverty of hundreds of thousands," open harlotry, and only ninety thousand seats in its churches. How could such a city be the center from which he would evangelize the world? After reflection, he remarked that model dwellings were a good thing. Education, art, more work, and better wages were useful. But he still held the revivalist's view that the prodigal with a new home, a new suit, a loaf of

Catherine Mumford Booth (1829–90) died of cancer just as William was launching his great social experiment with the publication of *In Darkest England and the Way Out*. Courtesy of the Salvation Army National Archives and Research Center.

bread, and half a crown weekly from the parish still would not be a new man. Sin was at the root of poverty; only confessing it would produce a cure. Catherine Booth's response to *Bitter Cry* was a plea for money from the "respectable and well-to-do classes," to get London's authorities to help the army save these multitudes.[5]

Meanwhile, salvationist women had found that evangelism was not the first solution to the poverty they met in the slum homes they visited. As attendance declined at mission meetings, they became convinced that social conditions must improve in tandem with soul-salvation. Booth grudgingly embraced social efforts but saw no new source of income to support them and at the same time continue funding evangelism. Booth first experienced pressure from within the organization when he became aware that lay-salvationist Mrs. Cottrill had been taking hapless girls home with her from the Whitechapel corps since 1881. For this pale copy of Josephine Butler's purity crusade, Booth provided a Whitechapel rescue home in May 1884, but his interest waned until he put his daughter-in-law, Mrs. Bramwell (Florence) Booth, in charge.[6] Also in 1883, Marianne Parkyn began to evangelize released prisoners. She placed a "saved thief" decoy outside Wandsworth jail, who brought the released prisoner to the house of Sergeant Ward. Ward's wife provided breakfast

William Booth (1829–1912) was aged 61 when he published *In Darkest England and the Way Out,* a program to end unemployment in England. Courtesy of the Salvation Army National Archives and Research Center.

and prayed with him, then took him to the noon prayer meeting and led him "straight to the Saviour." They gave him wood-chopping work until he found lasting employment. This home closed in 1888, but work with prisoners spread elsewhere.[7]

In 1884, women cadets rented a room in London's notorious Seven Dials district. With only a few educated women, Booth used what Mrs. Butler termed "surplus womanhood" of lower-class origins to swarm the slums. With conversion and cleanliness as goals, Soap and Water Brigades marched into poor homes to help mothers, talk with drunken fathers, and save "the most wretched poor and outcast people that had ever dwelt in the slums of London." That same year, two Oxford students opened Toynbee House in the East End, the first settlement house. Rescue, prison, and slum work all were done by women, under female leadership.[8] This was simple handout charity which did not meet the standards of scientific charity set down by Charles Loch's Charity Organisation Society (COS), which held that only indoor work-relief was uplifting.

In 1885, W. T. Stead, *Pall Mall Gazette* editor, asked Booth to join his crusade to pass the Criminal Law Amendment Bill to raise to sixteen the age at which a girl could agree to act as a prostitute.[9] The House of Commons twice had failed to pass the bill. Stead had an idea which would break teenage prostitution and end "White Slave Trade" scandals. To aid Stead, Booth introduced him to brothel-keeper-turned-salvationist Rebecca Jarrett, who procured thirteen-year-old Eliza Armstrong from her mother for two pounds, had Eliza's virginity certified, and took her to a brothel. Stead appeared at the door to make a supposed seduction and then left. A doctor recertified Eliza's virginity. Next day Bramwell Booth arranged Eliza's passage to France, where the army found her work.

A month later, Mrs. Armstrong sought Eliza through Marylebone Police Court, and Bramwell returned Eliza to her mother. Mrs. Armstrong signed a receipt which said that Eliza was "safe and sound" and had received double wages; she also signed charges against Stead, Jarrett, and Bramwell Booth. Meanwhile, the Tories had succeeded Gladstone. Given the Tories' weak position, Stead hoped that his "Maiden Tribute" articles, which depicted his abduction of thirteen-year-old "Lily" (Eliza Armstrong), would give them backbone. Stead pictured democracy and socialism as united against the excesses of the rich, who had created modern Babylon's "brotheldom."[10]

Booth exulted over the effect of Stead's revelations: multitudes cried out for the bill, he claimed. At a public meeting to support the bill's passage, Catherine for the first time called for woman's suffrage, to give women a voice in choosing the lawmakers who consigned England's helpless daughters to the 329,000 fallen men who prowled London. William Booth proposed to set up Houses of Enquiry to gather fallen women and then move restored girls to overseas rural Homes of Refuge in Canada and the western United States. Catherine Booth asked the government to give four to five thousand London prostitutes under sixteen to the Salvation Army. The Melbourne (Australia) government had paid the army to reclaim them and teach them a living at a per head cost which was less than shooting "a few Zulus or Arabs." Some 150 Salvation Life Guards in red jerseys and white helmets, together with English mothers, marched from East London to deliver a "Mothers of the Nation Petition to the Queen" at the House of Commons. The army's first effort to improve England's laws asked that girls be defended until age eighteen. Salvation Army officers sold the *Pall Mall Gazette* at train stations when bookseller W. H. Smith refused to sell it.[11] After a Mansion House committee announced that Stead's claims were basically true, Commons passed the bill on August 7.

As Parliament passed the bill, clouds gathered. The prospect of government by religious fanatics appalled Member of Parliament George Cavendish-Bentinck, who called "Maiden Tribute" an "enthusiastic spasm of virtue." He asked Commons if Stead could be prosecuted for distributing obscene materials. Stead, Jarrett, and Bramwell Booth, charged with child abduction under an 1861 act that had never been used to punish child abductors, were tried with others at the Old Bailey. Jarrett's muddled story of her arrangement with Mrs. Armstrong reflected poorly on her and Stead. The court sentenced Jarrett to six months and Stead to three months (his motives were pure, the court noted), and Bramwell Booth was acquitted. On the whole, the crusade succeeded. Parliament raised the age of consent to sixteen and suppressed homosexual activity.

The reputations of Stead and Bramwell Booth recovered, and the Salvation Army, having made this step into politics and social reform, was now prepared to advocate more advanced programs for social betterment.

William Booth soon shifted from revivalism to become the leader of a religious sect *cum* social agency. The 1886 *British Weekly* survey's criticism of his failure to reach the masses propelled him to seek a better method. While clerical critics argued that his claim to save the masses was unsupported, Catherine pleaded with wealthy Christians concerned for self-preservation to support the army as "the only organization whose members to any appreciable extent buttonhole the dangerous classes on their own ground" and turn them away from anarchy, socialism, and infidelity.[12] The Booths, in response to critics, needed new ways to save the "vicious" poor. Gradually they invented a distinct form of work which embraced a sectarian creed but also conducted a nonsectarian social service program.

After the 1886 Trafalgar Riots, Booth wrote on "Socialism," which showed how his revivalist's mind slowly changed. Opposed to "Socialism of Infidelity," he proposed "Salvation Socialism." Nothing is "gained by destroying society's foundations in order to rectify its wrongs." Society needs radical mending by God. At Nottingham, he recalled that, as a boy, he had admired Chartist Fergus O'Connor; but he now saw that the Chartist ladder to bliss was a mirage. Realizing that a new message was called for, Booth still offered only spiritual solutions to the chasm between rich and poor.[13]

Still, Booth's "Maiden Tribute" role and his well-publicized rescue homes and slum posts were securing his reputation as a social activist. Stead's *Pall Mall Gazette* recorded that Huxley, M. Renan, Morley, and Frederick Harrison, experts on human efforts, had been outdone by Booth's work with the lowest of the low. Australian Francis W. L. Adams praised the army's "religious socialism" and its attack on middle-class hypocrisy. He praised its "sweet true women" as "the essence of Christianity," the daughters of Mary Magdalene and Monica.[14] By the end of 1886, Salvation Army women were operating rescue homes for 150 girls.

By 1887, salvationists were divided over the role of social services. Booth indicated that rescue work lay outside the army's sphere unless salvationists could make it completely a salvation work. That goal he claimed had been achieved, as over 80 percent of the army's fallen girls had been converted. As a result of the Maiden Tribute crisis, Mrs. Bramwell Booth had expanded rescue homes, conforming to scientific social work in classifying the girls by type. By the end of 1887, she had four London homes and eight in provincial towns. The army was on the threshold of a new era. But in its large corps, it was not reaching the lowest via ordinary evangelistic services. After February 1887, it separated stable working-class corps outside the slums from the slum corps, at which it accommodated the "vilest offender."

More than anyone, Frank Smith got Booth to champion the lot of the poor after 1887. Under Smith's tutelage, Booth adopted ideas from Henry George, Arnold White, H. Rider Haggard, Sidney and Beatrice Webb, and others. Smith had converted to what he called Booth's "religion of enjoyment" in 1879. In 1881, Booth asked him to give up his art furnishing trade and take over the Liverpool I. Corps. After just a year, Booth asked the "Red Major" to consolidate the London corps. In 1884, Smith replaced Major Moore in the U.S., remaining there until 1887. In New York he met Henry George, whose *Progress and Poverty* he had read on his passage over. George's reform theory became Smith's social creed. At an 1886 international congress, Smith described the army as a "great leveling machine." To deal with sin and poverty in slums spawned by the uncaring rich, the army would march up palace steps and turn salvation guns on sinful ease. Smith called the rich the true "dangerous classes" who must be saved in order to eliminate poverty.[15] When Smith returned to London in July 1887, he told a welcoming crowd, "Those

Frank Smith, the first "Social Wing Commissioner," was the compiler of material for *In Darkest England and the Way Out,* and the father of the new departures in Salvation Army social services from 1887 to 1890. Courtesy of the Salvation Army National Archives and Research Center.

that are high up we bring down, and those that are low down we bring up." He wrote in the *War Cry* that one of the greatest leaders of advanced social reform had called the army "the coming revolution." Now, as Booth's private secretary and traveling companion, Smith filled Booth's ears with social reform and used *War Cry* reports to represent his own social views as Booth's. From Glasgow he wrote that foul courts and barefoot women and children "made us feel sick at heart." Some held that there must be these extremes of masses and, above them, classes. But he and Booth had seen prisoners whose vice and poverty had been "promoted by the hard-hearted pitiless avarice of their betters." He and Booth longed to "lift them to a platform of temporal as well as spiritual comfort and happiness."[16]

Some headquarters officers resisted Smith's urging that the army become active in social reform. Colonel Brindley Boon, leader of spiritual work, held that unemployment could only be altered by inner change. Land laws, aristocracy, and religious people did not create the condition of the unemployed.

In September, Smith suffered a breakdown related to his health. This may have been physical or may have been part of a manic-depressive cycle. Booth put him on leave; yet, in October, Smith participated in Trafalgar Square and Hyde Park rallies at which the *War Cry* reported that the unemployed blasphemed religion as a force that kept the people down. During the next six months, Smith joined the Law and Liberty League and extended his other secular contacts.[17]

In February 1888, as three thousand walked London's streets due to high unemployment, Booth opened Food and Shelter Depots. He rented a warehouse in Limehouse and sold adults a meal for a penny; supper and bed for three pence. He agreed with his chief of staff, Bramwell Booth, that the dole impoverished the spirit, so, at morning and evening meetings, he promoted the salvation of those who received assistance. The work supported itself after an initial four hundred pounds to prepare the building. Other voluntary groups followed the same pattern. Though it was a new venture, the operation was like the Food Shops that Booth had given up in 1874 in order to devote more time to evangelism. The *War Cry* ran articles on slum and rescue work just before interest in Whitechapel peaked in October, with exposes of the "Jack the Ripper" murders. The army had a post in the vicinity of Angel Alley next to George's Yard, where several of Jack's murders occurred. With renewed public interest in slums, Booth announced in November that he would extend slum work to other British cities.[18]

The rift between spiritual and social officers widened. The former felt that social work was an auxiliary project. When Catherine Booth commissioned rescue work officers in July 1888 (she had given her last public address at the City Temple in June, just before cancer forced her retirement from public life), she told them not to wish that they had been called to do more spiritual work. They could be as spiritual in sewing on buttons as in dealing with girls about their souls. The *War Cry* called for slum sisters who were godly but did not possess great powers of leadership. Major Cooke, the Slum Division commander, exploded when a spiritual-side divisional commander wrote on a candidate's form, "A nice little lass she has offered herself for the slums, but is really fit for the field." Cooke fumed: "I suppose they think if a girl is good and sympathetic, and loves the people, and is willing to scrub their floors, these qualifications are all that are needed." Beatrice Webb later depicted Salvation Army officers as a Samurai caste characterized by equality between men and women; "home life and married life are combined with a complete dedication of the individual to spiritual service." They were more cultivated than most persons of their social status, she claimed, and better at conversation than an elementary school teacher or trade union official. They exuded "a power of command." She particularly liked social officers: "Officers on the spiritual side have more the characteristics of the artist or public performer—more emotion and less intelligence."[19]

The clergy continued to criticize in 1888. Old Ford's vicar charged that the army had offered to make matchboxes at two pence per gross, undercutting wages at private firms; that male and female members lived in the same barracks; and that the army competed with poor women for laundry work. This criticism came just as fourteen hundred female employees of Bryant and May's match factory in Bow had decided to go on strike. The *Times* printed Bramwell Booth's denial, and the vicar retracted his charges. Bramwell felt that some opposed the army because it did not support legislative remedies for social ills but rather proclaimed the gospel as the quickest, most complete means of lifting the poor. A Marylebone vicar revived the charge that the army was a "unique failure" in evangelizing the heathen. This being true, he argued that Booth was unfit to administer state charity. To prove his point, he asked for names of those in his parish who had been reclaimed by the army. Booth gave him names of six soldiers saved at Marylebone's Great Western Hall. The vicar cited two of these as working men who had been of exceptional character before they joined the army; Booth had not produced names of those who were spiritually derelict. Booth responded that army rescue homes had satisfactorily handled fourteen cases from Marylebone and that his had never been exclusively a slum mission.[20]

Discord came at a bad time. In late 1888, Booth was for the first time asking government aid for his rescue, slum, and shelter work. For his "largest Rescue Society," he requested fifteen thousand pounds to outfit ten homes to rescue one thousand girls annually. He wanted ten Food and Shelter Depots in London and ten outside. The Australian government in Victoria had made several grants of five hundred pounds and offered the use of buildings in Melbourne, but Westminster rejected his appeal; he went ahead with his plan. At a food and shelter meeting, he told the men to give their hearts to God. But the *Times* reported that Booth did nothing on condition that the men do something religious in return. Booth referred to the Earl of Meath's pamphlet, whose ideas on

Suzie Forest Swift claims to have assisted with the writing of *In Darkest England and the Way Out* in 1890 as a Salvation Army officer, but left the army in 1896 to join the Roman Catholic Church's Dominican order. Courtesy of the Sinsinawa Dominican Archives.

poverty he shared. Although he said that he would prefer to return to re-vivalism, his "legitimate work," he opened a third food and shelter depot in Marylebone in February 1889 and a women's shelter in Whitechapel in March.[21]

Spiritual-side advocates got Booth to halt public lectures dealing with social problems. Railton, who defended revivalism as the army's sole mission, was pleased that staff officers now could preach to crowds who preferred to listen to lectures or anything else than to the voice of God. But Booth had become enthralled with his "Wonderful Salvation Army Machine," which changed earthly materials into new shapes of human nature. His twelve British Rescue Homes had saved one thousand girls a year at seven pounds each.[22] Booth knew how to appeal to cost-con-scious Victorians.

Besides pressure from salvationists and public events, the August 1889 London dock strike aroused Booth's social concern. He fed and sheltered striking families and even turned the 272 Whitechapel Road corps into a Food Depot and served meals there on Sundays. Nicol explained this social use of the army's "Mother Corps" by quoting a converted former Holloway Jail convict: "272 has a chance of regaining its old lustre and power." Booth observed, "It was hard work to get at people's souls, and so we went round about and got at their souls through their bodies." The strike by 75,000 workers led to formation of the Darkest England Social Scheme. But Booth the revivalist watched the strikers march with brass band through the city each day and wondered: Could not these thousands of dock workers be convinced to "strike for souls?" His dream for the East End's salvation revived, as roughs no longer jeered the Salvation Army but cheered the "Starvation Army." Strike organizers Ben Tillett and John Burns deemed the army's work the most practical next to that of the Catholics. Worldly Wiseman wrote in the *Daily News* that the army was the only church, chapel, or mission that came "heart and soul into the strike, sympathizing cordially with the strikers." Booth was "manufacturing friends wholesale."[23]

Salvationists debated how to save the poor by weaving social and spiritual work together. A Vassar College graduate, Major Suzie F. Swift, gave numbers to show that thirty field officers and nearly one hundred social officers dealt with East End squalor at twelve slum corps, seven rescue homes, three shelters, and two cheap food depots. She claimed that people lived in slums due to stimulants for which there was only one "moral disinfectant," namely, the Spirit of God. "Long Fellow" said that by aiding strikers, the army had proved that it was for easing the world's social and spiritual miseries, and that East London one day might be as "widely known for its godly population and happy homes as now unfortunately it is for the reverse."[24] The army wanted to retain the public esteem it gained during the dock strike. In January 1890, Booth brought Colonel James Barker from Australia, where he had opened prisoners' homes with government aid. Barker proposed similar schemes in England. Booth now was clearly committed to social services. Colonel Boon concluded that there was no distinction between social and spiritual work; Commissioner Railton took part in meetings at shelters. Before being commissioned, every cadet spent two weeks in the slums; and the *New York World* carried an article on American slum work. By winter 1890, change was in the air.[25]

Prayer meeting at a London
Salvation Army workshop
in the 1890s. Courtesy of
North Wind Picture
Archives.

At this juncture, in March 1890, Bramwell Booth announced that
Commissioner Frank Smith had returned, his health improved and his
former spirit restored. For months, Bramwell had shielded Smith from a
visible role, likely due to his political radicalism; his connections with
trade unionists and with Annie Besant, the atheist; and his fiercely secular speech at a dockers' Hyde Park rally. Bramwell diplomatically explained that Smith's absence had been due to private and family matters
now disposed of. Booth had conferred with aides before deciding that
Smith should lead the social program. Colonel Boon foresaw additional
departures of every kind, now that Smith had "landed." Smith came into
the limelight just as the city workshops he had organized to relieve unemployment got under way.

In April, Booth publicly made it plain that preaching was not enough.
He had tired of saving souls retail and wanted to "go into this business in
the wholesale line"; a coherent scheme was in the works. He would find
work for all who were willing to leave their evil ways. The army would
go to prison gates; it would open a thieves' retreat, an inebriates' home,
and, for those who could afford a better lodging, a hotel. It would set up
a workhouse where a starving wretch could earn a meal, a labor bureau,

and a farm. These were the principal ideas of the scheme, still six months from publication; Booth mentioned them just a month after Frank Smith's official return to the ranks.

Smith told the press that the army would end starvation that was caused by lack of available work. He set up shop on Upper Thames Street, behind the army's headquarters. Sensitive to opponents who thought that social services departed from the army's main concern for soul salvation, he took saved dossers (residents of cheap lodging-houses) around London to "witness," but most of his time was taken with work on the Darkest England scheme. He saw his social reform wing as resulting from communion between "hearts touched by an ardent love of the world's Saviour" and the despondent hordes. The wing aimed at saving body and soul. Present remedies—indiscriminate distribution of charity, and the Poor Laws' stone breaking and oakum picking—did not work. The homeless poor were a burden and a danger caused by poor distribution. Each corps would have a social-wing agent; every salvationist, a coworker. He was readying hallelujah workshops, for which he needed information on manufacturing black lead, brushes, cocoa matting, mat making, basketry, tinware, chair making and caning, woodchopping and tilling apparatuses, and all sorts of tools. He already employed fifty men. His articles in the *Daily Telegraph,* the *Daily Chronicle,* the *Evening News and Post,* and the *Star* asserted that the vagrant poor were willing to work.[26]

Meanwhile, a court ruled that the army's shelters must conform to common lodging-house regulations. The army argued that it should be exempted from such requirements since it served people who would have no shelter apart from its overcrowded warehouses. In *Booth v. Ferritt* (1890), the court found for the army.[27]

W. T. Stead praised the scheme without revealing that he was one of its authors: "General Booth is now standing on the eve of a new and momentous departure" which would solve social problems at home and multiply "the ties which unite the mother country with her colonies." Booth, Smith, and Stead fashioned a social program in three phases. City colonies would gather unemployed men from the streets and enlist them in household salvage brigades to collect waste materials from middle-class homes. In return, the men would receive food and shelter. Next the army would move those it could not employ in salvage brigades,

Making up bundles of firewood at the Salvation Army workshop, Hanbury Street, East London, 1890s. Courtesy of North Wind Picture Archives.

and for whom it could not find employers, to farm colonies in Britain. There they would prepare for a third step, emigration to a colony overseas. Harold Begbie described the scheme as an attempt to systematize charity, to make it "masculine, practical, and scientific." The army had accepted the chief-of-staff, Bramwell Booth's negative attitude toward the dole. As William Booth put it, mere charity demoralizes the recipient.[28]

Although Booth claimed sole authorship, *In Darkest England and the Way Out* was the product of three minds. Smith in particular created it, forwarding ideas and data to Booth, who annotated them with his opinions. Stead boiled down this massive document to produce the text. It was not Booth the revivalist who produced the scheme, nor the outsider Stead, who never sufficiently gained Booth's confidence to be able to adjust the general's ideas along these lines. Booth did not trust Stead, who was closer to Catherine and Bramwell.

Frank Smith, influenced by Henry George's ideas for redistributing wealth, gave the scheme to Booth. Smith found land colony ideas in England, Ireland, and Europe, where he traveled in spring 1888. Smith was the genius behind the army's post-1887 social programs. Stead, in the *Star*, gave Booth full credit as author. He wrote to a friend, "The sole responsibility and the dominating mind was his and his alone"; however, "you will recognize my fine Roman hand in most chapters." He told Cecil Rhodes that he had secured Booth not only "for Social Reform but also for Imperial Unity." Stead's biographer argued that the end of the first chapter was taken almost verbatim from the lead article in the *Pall Mall Gazette* of October 16, 1883, in which Stead had praised Mearns's *The Bitter Cry of Outcast London*. Stead noted that, as late as 1889, Booth had not wished to use the army as an agent of social reform, yet "Smith wanted it to be so employed."[29] There can be no doubt that Smith convinced Booth the revivalist to create a social wing for his Christian imperium.

Booth opposed hurting capitalists while he aided those who did not benefit from capitalism; he did not share Smith's socialism. He did want to repair capitalism's flaws, however. Booth's aim was to change a man when character was the reason for failure. For him, man's nature was grounded in the heart, not the environment. He was not a classical Christian Socialist; he believed that only conversion could rid the heart of sin and change outer maladies, although at times the cause of ruin was beyond one's control.

Under the system by which Booth ran the army, he would run the three colonies; he would be the final arbiter of personnel and program.[30] Graduation from each colony—city to farm to overseas—moved people to progressively healthier conditions, under the supervision of the army's social officers, who would gauge each individual's potential to move ahead in the system. Foremen would demonstrate successful work habits, and beneficiaries would become increasingly self-sufficient. Booth rejected division of the poor into "deserving" and "vicious," adopting instead Thomas Carlyle's maxim that even a London cab horse had a right to feed and a stall. Could any man deserve less?

Smith was already running a city colony program, composed of rescue homes, slum posts, food and shelter depots, and workshops. His newest plan, a salvage brigade, survives as the army's most visible urban program, the only lasting part of the scheme. The unemployed picked up used furniture, clothes, and items that could be sold for scrap. Salvation Army stores sold the salvaged goods to those unable to buy them new. In the process, the army provided jobs and a place to live, while it restored self-respect. Sale of salvageable goods made the city colony self-sufficient.

The farm colony, the most clearly defined part of the plan, mirrored the uplifting work of the city colony. Environment now assisted rather than hindered. Smith and Booth shared a widely-held desire to return the cities' unemployed masses to the soil. This colony would teach intensive small-scale agriculture (farms were three to five acres), produce bricks for homes, make furniture and clothing, and recreate the self-sufficient family farm that then was beginning to pass from existence, as large farms proved more efficient. As colonists bought land, buildings, and equipment from the army, their interest payments would make this venture, like the city colony, self-reliant. Booth foresaw an interdependent relationship between city and farm. Food from the farm would be consumed in the city's food depots, while city products would be consumed on the farm.[31] Like his salvation empire, his social empire would be a federated one, an organic, interdependent whole.

In 1891, Booth bought 800 acres—later increased to 3,200—at Hadleigh, Essex, and sent 215 men from London as the property's first settlers. The aim was to reverse rural migration by sending people back to the land— that is, "back again to 'the Garden!'" The army owned a light railway, a wharf on the Thames, and barges to take farm produce to London and bring back supplies. Income from stores, a bakery, dormitories, and a hospital supported the colony. There were halls for meetings, reading, and dining. Salvationist foremen lived in demonstration homes with gardens. Social critic Walter Besant found that, due to poor health and ignorance of farming, men taken from the gutter took three weeks to become productive. This led to a deficit of £4,000 per year. Besant rationalized the debt by claiming that the army took men who had consumed £40 worth of food, clothes, and shelter a year instead of producing £60 worth of goods, causing a net loss to the community of £100. This amount, multiplied by 260 men, equaled £26,000 that the army saved the nation by finding men work. Since Hadleigh lost £4,000 a year, this left a £22,000 net gain. Booth's promise of self-sufficiency thus was salvaged. Area farmers employed the men once they were healthy. Some remained as part of the staff. The army paid wages according to personal need but kept part of the pay to buy clothing for the time when residents would leave the colony. About 55 percent were permanently restored.[32] Hadleigh never fit Booth's plan for a workers' agricultural university to prepare colonists for emigration to overseas colonies, but, in its early years, it moved urban workers to the land as farm workers. In 1905, Balfour's Tories commissioned Rider Haggard, novelist and back-to-the-land advocate, to study the army's farm colonies in England and America and to advise the government whether to support such experiments. Haggard proposed support for the army's work, but a new Liberal government was not inclined to follow the advice. Haggard had discovered that the colonies lacked sufficient capital and able settlers to succeed without government help.[33]

The overseas colony, the third element of the plan, expressed an imperial idea that Booth shared with W. T. Stead and Cecil Rhodes, who at one time was inclined to provide capital to help Booth colonize within the empire. Colonial governments would donate land divided into family plots. The army would find emigrants, provide transit, and supervise them. Booth's machine would take thieves, harlots, paupers, and drunkards, on condition that they would accept discipline, and pour them onto virgin soil to create "pieces of Britain" in the richest parts of the earth. When Booth could not convince government or private philanthropy to back the idea, he began an emigration program without a colony at the other end. Emigrants were not the "submerged tenth" he first intended to assist, but rather were working families who needed someone to supply cheap conveyance. By 1938, the army's emigration bureau had settled nearly 250,000 Englishmen overseas, primarily in Canada where the government assisted in finding employment for the newcomers.[34]

Frank Smith caused what army historian Robert Sandall called Booth's "change of mind." While labor unrest helped, and while the army needed new methods to stem its membership decline, it took a forceful individual to redirect Booth's thinking. Smith captained the salvationists who urged the army to become a social movement. Historian K. S. Inglis suspects that Smith's subsequent resignation caused writers sympathetic to Booth to neglect the former's role. Harold C. Steele noted that, from the beginning, Smith believed that the army could be effective in large-scale relief. Contemporaries conceded his role. A *Times* correspondent rightly observed that "the ideas of the substantial parts of the scheme . . . had their origin in the mind of Mr. Frank Smith" and "were accepted most reluctantly by Mr. Booth." Smith hid his role, but his friend Keir Hardie, founder of Britain's Independent Labour Party, unveiled Smith's behind-the-scenes part: "It is doing no injustice to the other prominent men of the Salvation Army to state that the social side of the army's work is largely due to Mr. Smith's initiative and activity; and when at length it came to be a recognized feature of Salvation Army work he was put in command."[35]

Hugh Price Hughes, social reform editor of *Methodist Times,* worried that Booth was not "fully aware how far Commissioner Smith has gone, in his name, in certain recent very important correspondence with the London Trades Council [which] consented to supply the General with certain information upon condition that the labour bureau of the Salvation Army acts up to the creed of the 'New Unionism,' and boycotts blacklegs." Did Booth know that Smith, a Salvation Army "turn-about," espoused Henry George's one-tax theory? Is it surprising that George had "said he thought the scheme was the most remarkable thing he had seen since leaving the States?"[36]

Numerous ideas formed the basis of *Darkest England;* none was original with its authors. They studied Owenite E. T. Craig's 1831 communal farm experiment at Ralahine, Ireland; Count Rumford's military tactic for solving Bavaria's beggary problem in 1789–90; and the Earl of Meath's ideas on imperial migration. Out of these ideas they produced the city-farm-overseas colony format. They took ideas from Anglo-American back-to-the-farm advocates Henry George, Arnold White, H. Rider Haggard, and Herbert Mill, and from Rees's *From Poverty to Plenty.* Booth shared Stead's concern that Britain's surplus populace was emigrating to the U.S. at a time when tracts in her own empire, in Canada, Australasia, and southern Africa, remained unsettled. But this part of the plan to develop overseas colonies did not succeed.[37]

Despite Booth's hope of being accepted by the establishment, reaction to *Darkest England* was not altogether friendly. Thomas Huxley joined Anglican clerics who rejected Booth as an agent of state philanthropy. Huxley was vexed by Booth's autocracy and "corybantic Christianity." As the Church of England did not bring Booth under its wing in 1882, so the 1906 Liberal government rejected Haggard's report, which

recommended giving Booth government funds. Thus the established order did not absorb the Salvation Army. Instead, its social program, like
its revival mission, would be carried out with private donations, along
the lines of a voluntary agency outside the control of church or state.
Anglo-American private philanthropy and Charity Organisation Societies
also disavowed Booth's conversion to scientific social work.[38]

As a package, Darkest England failed. The overseas colony never
found support, despite Stead's exuberance. By 1906, farm colonies no
longer functioned as intended. Only those social services which Frank
Smith organized as the city colony remained: rescue homes and crèches
(day care centers), a missing persons' inquiry bureau, drunkards' brigades
and an inebriates' home, prisoners' brigades and homes, slum posts, and
food and shelter depots, to which Smith added workshops and a household salvage brigade to employ men until they found permanent jobs.
Darkest England's reception, while at first hopeful, did not gain the support of organized philanthropy, whether sponsored by church or state.
More important to the army was the division created between its spiritual
and its social wings—two wings that never completely meshed. Salvationists who had accepted Booth's call to revivalism saw social work as a
distraction, much as Booth himself had despised handout welfare in 1874.

Although Catherine Booth had embraced social remedies by the time
she died on October 4, 1890, she told Henry George that her position
would not allow her to advocate his views publicly. In the same vein
she wrote to Stead, "Praise up humanitarianism as much as you like, but
don't confuse it with Christianity, nor suppose that it will ultimately lead
its followers to Christ."[39] Her Wesleyan creed rested on the doctrine of
human depravity. Soup and soap were, at best, ancillary to soul saving.
Had she lived longer, she might have shared others' concerns about the
gap between the army's spiritual and its social work.

Speaking for spiritual-wing officers who were angered by the army's
new direction, Railton voiced the most ardent critique of what he saw as
the diversionary nature of social programs. As Booth's first lieutenant in
the 1870s, he had championed equal status and pay for women, led in
forsaking sacraments, and forged the mission's doctrine of holiness. But
when commercial aspects of the Darkest England scheme—a deposit
bank and insurance company—came to light, he protested. Bernard
Watson says that Railton had the misfortune to feel that he was the cus-

todian of Catherine Booth's strict evangelical tradition. In July 1894, when public approval had brought the army prominence, Railton stood barefoot and in sackcloth in Queen's Hall, London, to attack the insurance plan. When he refused to recant, Booth assigned him to a series of minor posts until he died in 1913. As leader in France in 1901, he was a renowned foe of social work; France, he argued, could not be saved by "soup nor coffee." Had not the general said, "You don't cleanse a man by washing his shirt."[40]

Meanwhile, Smith's mind drifted from soul salvation, even as he continued to lead evangelistic meetings with saved dossers. His mind was on "sociology." Using the Lord's Prayer as his text, he argued that the clever took advantage of the simple by force or duplicity, leaving their hapless brethren to starve. Christians would be shocked to hear that God predestined some to be shut out of his kingdom, yet many judged it fair for some to be "predestined to live in filthy surroundings, homeless, breadless, idle." Consent to one's lot was a "*sine qua non* of indwelling grace." Surely, daily bread included essential clothing, shelter, a job, and things that supply life's needs and comforts. Keir Hardie later noted that Smith had learned "that however godlike the work of saving the wreckage of our social system would be, it would be more godlike to put an end to the causes which produced it."[41] To be free to grapple with poverty's root causes through political activity, Smith resigned from the Salvation Army.

The *Times* headlined Smith's exit in December 1890 and echoed his belief that the army's social scheme should be kept distinct from its religious work. Smith opposed commingling different kinds of work or the funds raised to support them. Booth defended moving account books from Smith's office to the accounting bureau in order to release Smith for planning duties. The *War Cry* noted that Smith had not been as free as he wished, but it did not term him treasonous. Booth had suffered "a great disappointment." Smith spoke of no unfriendliness and assured Booth, "I do not contemplate anything on the lines of opposition"; he agreed with Booth on the desired end but differed with him on methods.

Others who left sued the army. The *Times* noted that Smith was one of a few men outside Booth's family who had held high position in the army. The paper predicted that Smith's successor would be a Booth, but instead the general appointed Colonel Elijah Cadman, an old-line Christian Missioner to head the social program. Later, in 1901–3, and again in 1905, Smith resigned his London County Council seat and returned to the army. He served on the London County Council for eighteen years and ran a dozen strenuous campaigns for Parliament before being elected a member from Nuneaton in 1929 at age seventy-five. During this last campaign, he wrote a defense of Bramwell Booth, as the latter was being deposed as general in 1929. Frank Smith's enduring legacy is that he turned the mind of William Booth the revivalist to social reform.[42]

The Booth-Smith dispute rests on the public record. But it points to a tension between spiritual and social work in the Salvation Army. Smith, heart and soul, endorsed social reform. Booth supported him, culled useful ideas from him, and encouraged his scheme. But, by 1890, the gulf between the army's two wings—one spiritual, one social—was widened by Booth's autocratic style of government. As general, Booth was unclear on the army's mission. He desired revivalism's day to return; he told Bramwell that social reformers "have no sympathy with The Salvation Army nor with salvation from worldliness and sin." Doubt loosened the army's grip on its mission, generating a confusion that endures today. Many wanted to renew the spiritual crusade and emphasize membership growth. Others realized that the army's genius, the basis of its financial support and public approval, was in its social services to an urban population it never had succeeded in reaching with the gospel.[43]

Epilogue

Today's Salvation Army cannot be understood apart from the impact of mid-nineteenth-century culture on its founders, William and Catherine Booth. Its initial creed, that of American revivalism, persists in the army's theology, its training of officers, and in its goal to convert sinners and enroll laypersons. But the army, as it now stands, is also the result of failure to win the masses of city slums to the gospel. William Booth failed as a revivalist in London's East End, and twentieth-century salvationists also fail in large, heterogeneous cities, in winning the masses to their brand of Wesleyan Christianity. But failure did not persuade Booth to relinquish his desire to establish a godly kingdom among people disinclined to embrace it.

As the army grew into a Christian imperium, it found a second solution to the problem of urban poverty—social services, which Booth called "wholesale salvation." As early as 1881, salvationist women had worked with "fallen" women; by 1883, drunkards and prisoners had been added. The army's program was not the scientific social work which Charity Organisation Societies claimed to practice, but handout relief, which the Christian Mission had done up to 1874, when Booth rejected such programs as a detour from his evangelistic mission.

Several influences pushed the Booths toward social reform in the 1880s. One was the decline of their urban mission. From within, mostly women salvationists urged them to respond to newly publicized slum conditions, and, in 1887, reform champion Frank Smith returned from America to add his voice to calls for social programs. From outside, Andrew Mearns's *Bitter Cry of Outcast London* (1883), the "Maiden Tribute" articles (1885), and the London Dock Strike (1889) pushed the Booths to inaugurate social services among fallen women and dock strikers. These forces, along with the army's failure to win East London's "heathen" to the gospel, spurred the Booths' interest in social programs. The Darkest

William Booth (1829–1912) with "Gyp." Courtesy of the Salvation Army National Archives and Research Center.

England scheme of 1890, "authored" by Booth but based on ideas fed to him by Frank Smith, sealed the commitment to social services. The Salvation Army now had become an international Christian imperium with two wings—one for revival and one for social service.

One other element dominated the army until 1929—the despotic rule of the Booths. Up to 1929, when a high council of commissioners deposed General Bramwell Booth, the army was a highly centralized, imperial family concern. After 1929, it assumed a federal bureaucratic structure at last. Although formal power is still vested in the general, the present incumbent, Paul A. Rader, shares it with territorial commanders.

To a large degree, the army's program is determined by its funding sources. In the 1860s, Booth began his urban mission with financial aid from nondenominational evangelical societies. As the army turned to social services in the mid-1880s, it appealed to a secular, nonevangelical public for its funds. The Darkest England scheme began by soliciting £100,000, and Booth sought government aid for the first time (1889). With public contributions, the army built homes for unwed mothers, hospitals, children's homes, summer camps, and rehabilitation centers. These social centers, mainly in cities where the army had failed to evangelize the poor, absorbed an ever higher share of its funds and personnel. By the 1920s, most of the army's income in the U.S. came from federated community funds. As the army sought ways to increase its income, it tempered its aggressive Christianity in both verbiage and action.

By the 1920s, annual reports seldom referred to the number of "conversions," but rather emphasized "character building," a phrase the army's secular donors found palatable. Although its revivalist program—including occasional street services, an evangelical creed, and salvation and holiness meetings—remains, it has become ritualized. That is, spiritual programs became irrelevant to the organization's financial survival; converting sinners was not essential to its survival. Those who give money to the army do not expect, and many do not desire, that the poor might be converted to Wesleyan Christianity. They only want the poor to be improved in character.

Tensions that existed within the army by 1888, between its revivalist wing, which worked to build the kingdom of God, and its social wing, which gave material succor to the poor to improve the kingdom of man, exist to the present. The Salvation Army trains its officers primarily as evangelists but then assigns them to serve under two administrative wings which compete for status within the movement. Within its ranks, the army argues over whether or not the two wings are congruous and whether or not social reform fits with its original nineteenth-century revival aim. In some cities, social programs absorb as much as 90 percent of its budget. Still, the army has not considered excising either the social service or the religious program to achieve a singular ministry. Tension between the wings has been contained, with only occasional expressions of frustration. The army has been able to maintain a revival legacy at least ritualistically, although it has altered its lexicon to conform to the expectations of those who provide community funds—e.g., "conversion" becomes "character building." In most places, social programs predominate. But the Salvation Army never has succeeded where William Booth failed; it never has won the heathen masses of the cities to its Wesleyan gospel.

APPENDIX A

Doctrines

Methodist New Connexion Doctrines (1838)

(1) We believe that there is one God, who is infinitely perfect, the Creator, Preserver, and Governor of all things.

(2) We believe that the Scriptures of the Old and New Testament are given by Divine Inspiration and form a complete rule of faith and practice.

(3) We believe that three persons exist in the Godhead: the Father, the Son, and the Holy Ghost, undivided in essence, and co-equal in power and glory.

(4) We believe that in the person of Jesus Christ the Divine and human natures are united, so that he is truly and properly God, and truly and properly man.

(5) We believe that man was created in righteousness and true holiness, but that by his disobedience, Adam lost the purity and happiness of his nature; and, in consequence, all his posterity are involved in depravity and guilt.

(6) We believe that Jesus Christ has become the propitiation for the sins of the whole world, that he rose from the dead, and that he ever liveth to make intercession for us.

(7) We believe that repentance toward God, and faith in our Lord Jesus Christ, are necessary to salvation.

(8) We believe that justification is by grace, through faith, and that he that believeth hath the witness in himself: and that it is our privilege to be fully sanctified in the name of the Lord Jesus Christ, and by the spirit of our God.

(9) We believe that man's salvation is of God, and that his damnation is of himself. We believe, also, that in the Gospel plan of redemption, men are treated as rational, accountable creatures; that "it is God that worketh in us to will and to do of his own good pleasure;" and that we are to "work out our own salvation, with fear and trembling."

(10) We believe that it is possible for man to fall finally from grace.

(11) We believe the soul to be immortal, and that after death it immediately enters upon a state of happiness or misery.

(12) We believe in the resurrection of the body—in the general judgment at the

last day—in the eternal happiness of the righteous—and in the endless punishment of the wicked.

Evangelical Alliance Doctrines (1846)

(1) The Divine inspiration, authority and sufficiency of Holy Scriptures.

(2) The right and duty of private judgment in the interpretation of Holy Scriptures.

(3) The Unity of the Godhead, and the Trinity of Persons therein.

(4) The utter depravity of human nature in consequence of the fall.

(5) The incarnation of the Son of God, his work of atonement for sinners of mankind, and His mediatorial intercession and reign.

(6) The justification of the sinner by faith alone.

(7) The work of the Holy Spirit in the conversion and sanctification of the sinner.

(8) The immortality of the soul, the resurrection of the body, the judgment of the world by our Lord Jesus Christ, with the eternal blessedness of the righteous, and the eternal punishment of the wicked.

(9) The divine institution of the Christian ministry, and the obligation and perpetuity of the ordinances of baptism and the Lord's Supper.

Christian Mission Doctrines (1870)

(1) We believe that the Scriptures of the Old and New Testaments were given by inspiration of God, and are the only rule of Christian faith and practice.

(2) We believe that there is only one living and true God; the Father, the Son and the Holy Ghost—three persons in one God—equal in power and glory; and the only proper object of religious worship.

(3) We believe that in the person of Jesus Christ the Divine and human natures are united, so that He is truly and properly God, and truly and properly man.

(4) We believe that all mankind, in consequence of the disobedience of Adam, are sinners, destitute of holiness, and justly exposed to the penalty of the Divine Law.

(5) We believe that the Lord Jesus Christ has, by His suffering and death, made an atonement for the whole world, so that whosoever will be saved.

(6) We believe that repentance toward God, faith in our Lord Jesus Christ, and regeneration by the Holy Spirit are necessary to Salvation.

(7) We believe in the immortality of the soul—in the resurrection of the body—in the general judgment at the end of the world—in the eternal happiness of the righteous—and in the endless punishment of the wicked.

Sources for Doctrines

Methodist New Connexion: *The General Rules of the Methodists of the New Connexion,* 1838. (See 1834 brief list.)

Evangelical Alliance: J. W. Massey, *The Evangelical Alliance: Its Origin and Development* (London: John Snow, 1847), 303; John W. Ewing, *Godly Fellowship: A Centenary Tribute to the Life and Work of the World's Evangelical Alliance, 1846–1946* (London: Marshall, Morgan, Scott, 1946), 17–18, 129; *Conference on Christian Union: Narrative of the Proceedings of the Meeting in Liverpool* (London: James Nesbit, 1845), 33; J. B. A. Kessler, *A Study of the Evangelical Alliance in Great Britain* (Goes, Netherlands: Oosterbaan and Le Cointre N.V., 1968), 68.

Christian Mission: *Minutes,* 1st Conference of the Christian Mission, People's Mission Hall, London, June 15–18, 1870; Robert Sandall, *The History of the Salvation Army* (London: Thomas Nelson and Sons, 1947), 1: 262–63. Norman H. Murdoch, "Evangelical Sources of Salvation Army Doctrine," *Evangelical Quarterly* 59 (July 1987): 235–44. I am grateful to Dr. John Coutts, Major Dr. John Rhemick, and Major Jenty Fairbank for aid with this doctrinal issue.

APPENDIX B

Christian Mission Organization, 1870–78

The Christian Mission's polity from 1870 to 1878 was methodism's conference plan from its founding by John Wesley. In structure and discipline, Booth's Christian Mission was Wesleyan.

Christian Mission Conference System

Annual Conference: met the 2nd Monday in June, the Rev. Wm. Booth, president. Members: full-time evangelists and two lay persons from each circuit. Officers were elected and votes taken on resolutions.

Circuit Quarterly Conference: two or more stations (meeting places). A circuit superintendent appointed by annual conference reported to the general superintendent. Members discussed all questions before they voted on them. To hold office, a person had to accept the doctrines, "lead a godly life," and abstain from alcohol and tobacco, except when ill.

Society Conference: the members of the mission at one station.

Christian Mission Hierarchy

Mission Member: believed in Christ for salvation and behaved well as evidence of faith, attended a believers' meeting, contributed at least a penny a week "when convenient," but was not disqualified by a "minor questions of doctrine" unless it hindered "usefulness." A member should "abstain from all intoxicating drinks," except when ill; and from smoking and "other evil offensive habits"; and would not sell intoxicants or frequent a public house "except on business"; or sell "obscene books or pictures, fortune telling books, or ballads"; or exhibit theater, concert, or ball bills, or read literature like the *London Journal* or *Family Herald*. Members would avoid "foolish fashions" in dress as well as "falsehood, slander, backbiting, habitual frivolous or foolish jesting, drunkenness, divisive or quarrelsome conduct."

Class Leader: the lowest level of leadership was an exemplary lay person elected or appointed to meet a class of members weekly and lead them in sharing their religious experiences.

Stewards: were elected annually to take care of the hall, ushering, finances, the poor fund, and distribution of notices for services.

Exhorters: lay speakers who assisted the itinerant preacher in conducting services, particularly open air and cottage meetings.

Local Preachers: the level on the plan above exhorters, these were lay persons who preached as they had opportunity.

Evangelists (Itinerant Preachers): the highest ministerial office, it was still unordained but paid. Conference appointed them to stations.

APPENDIX C

Christian Mission Membership,

1871–77

London Districts	1871	1873	1874	1875	1876	1877
Whitechapel	253	300	372	230	221	221
Poplar	129	272	199	90	88	32
Shoreditch	325	329	283	323	60	—
Limehouse	111		183	101	71	75
Bethnal Green	—	—	—	—	69	80
Stratford	—	—	—	19	25	20
Millwall	—	—	—	—	27	15
Canning Town	—	—	—	30	52	60
Plaistow	—	—	—	12	44	34
Croydon	85	100	109	89	45	38
Hammersmith	—	—	—	170	233	142
Soho	—	—	—	36	50	50
Barking	—	—	—	41	75	82
Cubbittown	—	—	—	—	16	—
Hackney	—	—	—	—	110	55
Stoke Newington	—	—	—	—	19	21
Tottenham	—	—	—	—	18	—
North Woolwich	—	—	—	—	30	—
Bromley	—	—	—	—	18	—
Country Districts	1871	1873	1874	1875	1876	1877
Hastings	95	—	149	125	116	62
Portsmouth	—	30	290	271	70	103
Wellingborough	—	31	50	92	87	90
Kettering	—	—	60	50	46	—
Chatham	—	—	55	101	105	129
Tunbridge Wells	50	—	—	—	—	—
Cardiff	—	—	—	50	140	174

Stockton	—	—	—	81	320	240
Middlesboro						
(Odd Fellows)				70	250	196
#2 Princes	—	—	—	—	—	158
#3 North Ormsby	—	—	—	—	—	120
Rye	—	—	—	—	12	—
Ninfield	—	—	—	—	38	36
East Hartlepool	—	—	—	—	—	100
Leeds	—	—	—	—	—	80
Bradford	—	—	—	—	—	40
Leicester	—	—	—	—	—	100
Saint Leonards	—	—	—	—	—	23
Totals Per Year	1871	1873	1874	1875	1876	1877
London Districts	493	1,001	1,146	1,1411	1,192	925
Country Districts	95	61	604	840	1,068	1,651
Entire Mission	588	1,062	1,750	1,981	2,376	2,576

Source: Christian Mission, Annual Conferences, *Minutes,* 1871–77. No conference was held in 1872.

Notes

Preface

1. Cushing Strout, *The New Heavens and the New Earth* (New York, 1974), xiv.
2. Howard R. Murphy, "Review: Arch R. Wiggins, The History of the Salvation Army," vol. iv in *Victorian Studies* 8 (Dec. 1964): 185.
3. Ibid., 186.
4. The myth that the army succeeded in the London slums has persisted throughout the 20th century. See Maj. Michael Pressland, "Whither the City?" in *The Officer* 29 (Aug.–Sept. 1978): 348–51, 399–401, and letters to the editor which followed this extended article.
5. Norman H. Murdoch, "The Salvation Army's U.S. Arrival," *Organization of American Historians Newsletter* 15 (May 1987): 12-13.
6. George Scott Railton, *General Booth* (London, 1912), 17.
7. W. T. Stead, *General Booth* (London, 1891), 38–39.
8. Rom. 1:14.

Part I

1. Humphrey Wallis, *The Happy Warrior: The Life Story of Commissioner Elijah Cadman* (London, 1928).
2. Booth to John Savage, 30 Oct. 1849, quoted in Harold Begbie, *The Life of General William Booth,* 2 vols. (New York, 1920), 1:108.

1. The Salvation Army's Roots in American Revivalism

1. "In Satan's Stronghold," *New York Herald,* rptd. in *War Cry,* 17 Apr. 1880, 1.
2. David D. Hall, "The Victorian Connection," in *Victorian America,* ed. Daniel Walker (Philadelphia, 1976), 81–94, called the evangelical movement in Brit-

ain and America "the basis of a transatlantic network or 'connection' across which flowed ideas of immense significance." Richard Carwardine, *Transatlantic Revivalism: Popular Evangelicalism in Britain and America, 1790–1865* (London, 1978), xiii–xv; and John Kent, *Holding the Fort: Studies in Victorian Revivalism* (London, 1978), saw in revivalism the major influence that both shaped American society and, through American revivalists, altered the direction of British evangelicalism. Arthur R. Mountfield, *The Quaker Methodists* (Ngion, England, 1924). Arthur R. Mountfield, "The Coming of Lorenzo Dow," in Charles A. Johnson, ed., *The Frontier Camp Meeting* (Dallas, Texas, 1955), 25–32.

3. Charles C. Goss, *Statistical History of the First Century of Methodism* (New York, 1866), 110ff. Gerald B. Kauvar and Gerald C. Sorensen, eds., *The Victorian Mind: An Anthology* (New York, 1969), 91, wrote, "Evangelicalism determined the tone of much controversy over social problems."

4. Wreford J. Devoto, comp., *The Rev. James Caughey, The Man Who Influenced William Booth to the Ministry* (n.p.: n.d.), 1–2. *Christian Advocate,* 29 June 1837, Jan. 1846, and 5 March 1890. Joseph Hillman, *The History of Methodism in Troy, New York* (Troy, N.Y., 1888), 75. James Caughey, *Earnest Christianity Illustrated* (London, 1857), 7. Benjamin Gregory, *Sidelights on the Conflicts of Methodism, 1827–1852* (London, 1898), 368–69. Joseph Dyson, "James Caughey," in Newspaper Cuttings, Sheffield City Library, Sheffield, England. Daniel Wise, ed., *Methodism in Earnest* (Boston, 1850), v–vi.

5. On Booth's experience in the South Docks area, see Norman H. Murdoch, "From Militancy to Social Mission: The Salvation Army and Street Disturbances in Liverpool, 1879–1887," Chapter 7 in *Popular Politics , Riot and Labour: Essays in Liverpool History, 1790-1940,* John Belchem, ed., (Liverpool, England: 1992), 160–172.

6. Devoto, *Rev. James Caughey,* 3–5. James Caughey, *Letters on Various Subjects,* 3 vols. (London, 1844–47), 1:2, 1:6–9, 1:82, 1:92–100, 1:115, 1:146–50, 1:159, 1:186, 1:203, 1:229–39, 2:67.

7. E. R. Wickham, *Church and People in an Industrial City* (London, 1957), 79–106, 20–22, 46–84. E. P. Thompson, *The Making of the English Working Class* (New York, 1966), 427–30, 917–23. Robert F. Wearmouth, *Methodism and the Working-class Movements of England, 1800–1850* (London, 1937), 133.

8. Caughey, *Letters,* 1:211. James Caughey, *Report of a Farewell Sermon Delivered in the Methodist New Connexion Chapel, Parliament St., Nottingham*

(1847), 2. Caughey, *Earnest Christianity,* 154. James Caughey, *Revival Miscellanies* (London, n.d.), 408–9. Begbie, *Life of Booth,* 1:69, 1:9–14, 1:175. St. John Ervine, *God's Soldier: General William Booth* (New York, 1935), 1:37. George S. Railton, *Twenty-One Years Salvation Army* (London, 1886), 7–8. Stead, *General Booth,* 26–29, confused Caughey's 1846 Nottingham revival with Booth's 1844 conversion, a mistake repeated by others.

9. The terms *penitent form, knee drill,* and *fishing* in the pews for converts all continue in Salvation Army parlance. Neither John Wesley nor William Bramwell employed the "call to the communion rail." The practice became common in British Methodism in the late 1820s, to put pressure on the undecided to become penitent; it was referred to as "the American custom." Caughey, *Letters,* 1:175–76, 2:222, 2:59, 2:99, 2:233–38, 4:78–81, 4:264–66, 4:107–8, 5:5, 5:134. James Caughey, *Voice from America* (Manchester, England, 1847), 5–22, 37. Begbie, *Life of Booth,* 1:83–84, 1:163. Caughey salted his Nottingham sermons with militant jargon: "But this is not the first victory that has been won more by the valour of officers and troops, than by the wisdom and foresight and good generalship of the Commander-in-Chief!!" James Caughey, *The Triumph of Truth and Continental Letters and Sketches from Journal, Letters, and Sermons* (Philadelphia, 1857), 46–47.

10. *Whig Morning Chronicle,* 16 Apr. 1846, p. 15. Caughey, *Earnest Christianity,* 290–94, 364–70. Caughey, *Letters,* 2:121–24, 2:196–97; 3:155–56, 3:183–84, 3:240; 4:133–35. C. W. Andrews, *William Bramwell, Revivalist* (London, ca. 1910), 17, 47, 71, indicates that Bramwell, who "lived a very strict life" and "ruled the church with a severe discipline," worked at "getting up a revival" long before Caughey came to England.

11. Gregory, *Sidelights,* 72–74, 357, 400–403, 496. *Protest in Favor of the Rev. James Caughey* (Sheffield, England, n.d.), 2, 10. Caughey, *Brief Memoir,* 2, 23, 30, 53–60, 64. Caughey, *Review of the Whole Case* (n.d.), 3–17. Caughey, *Letters,* 3:236–45. *A Faithful Verbatim Report of the 'Fly Sheets'* (London, 1849), 65–66, 72. *Sheffield Daily Telegraph,* 1 June 1927. Joseph Dyson, "United Methodist Free Churches: History of the Movement in Sheffield," Newspaper Clippings, Sheffield City Library. Ervine, *God's Soldier,* 1:47–48.

12. Catherine Booth to her mother, Feb. 1858, Booth Papers, British Library. See Catherine Bramwell-Booth, *Catherine Booth: The Story of Her Loves* (London, 1970), 176.

13. See *Revivalist,* 1860–67, on Caughey's meetings. For all Caughey's 11 sanctification sermons, see Ralph W. Allen and Daniel Wise, eds., *Helps to a Life of Holiness and Usefulness, or, Revival Miscellanies* (Boston, 1851).

14. Col. Edmund C. Hoffman, "James Caughey and William Booth," *Officer Review* (Jan. 1944): 32–37. Hoffman indicates that Booth did not receive a kind reception at Caughey's home. Caughey had retired in 1886, married a "very disagreeable person," and acquired a home in New Brunswick, N.J., where he was pastor emeritus of Pitman M. E. Church until his death. He was buried in Elmwood Cemetery. The Salvation Army cares for his grave. See Begbie, *Life of Booth,* 1:13.

15. See the superb treatment of Caughey in Carwardine, *Transatlantic Revivalism.*

16. Ervine, *God's Soldier,* 1:364–65. George S. Railton, *Twenty-One Years,* 21. George S. Railton, *General Booth,* 21, 17.

17. Frederick deL. Booth-Tucker, *The Life of Catherine Booth,* 3rd ed., 2 vols., (London, 1924), 2:69–70. Bramwell-Booth, *Catherine Booth: The Story,* 111.

18. Sydney E. Ahlstrom, *A Religious History of the American People* (Garden City, N.Y., 1975), 1:557–58, listed Charles Finney's "new measures" as: protracted meetings; the anxious bench; public witness by women; use of publicity; a team approach to evangelism; "emphasis on the human production of conversions"; and emphasis on entire sanctification. All were featured in the Booths' ministry.

19. Charles G. Finney, *Memoirs of Rev. Charles G. Finney* (New York, 1976), 76–77, 89–90.

20. See reports on Charles Finney's London mission in *Christian Witness* (1849): 513–15; *Christian Witness* (1850): 545–46; *Christian Witness* (1851): 1–5; *Christian Witness* (1853): 209–11, 255–63. David E. Ford, *Alarm in Zion* (London, 1848), 41–44. *British Banner,* 1 Sept. 1852. Ervine, *God's Soldier,* 1:63–9. Carwardine, *Transatlantic Revivalism,* 145–54. In 1851, the Booths may have heard Charles Finney at Campbell's Tabernacle, at about the time William gave up his pawnbroker's trade for preaching.

21. Charles Finney, *Memoirs,* 400. G. Redford to C. Finney, 2 Dec. 1850, Finney Collection, Oberlin College, Oberlin, Ohio. Bramwell-Booth, *Catherine Booth: The Story,* 235, noted that in 1868 Catherine Booth declined a tabernacle, offered by businessmen, that was larger than Spurgeon's Metropolitan Tabernacle in London.

22. Emory S. Bucke, ed., *The History of American Methodism* (New York, 1964), 2:196–99. Timothy Smith, *Revivalism and Social Reform in Mid-Nineteenth-Century America* (New York, 1957), 180–88. Clifford S. Griffin, "The Abolitionists and the Benevolent Societies, 1831–1861," *Journal of Negro History* 44 (1959): 195–216.

23. Booth-Tucker, *Life of Catherine Booth,* 1:145f. Booth wrote in his diary that Spurgeon's "simple, earnest, and faithful sermon" pleased him.

24. *Revivalist* (1862): 68–70. Timothy Smith, *Revivalism and Social Reform,* 94, 8, 143, reports that American revivalism was "lay centered, tolerant of minor sectarian differences, ethically vital and democratically Arminian."

25. For an excellent discussion of evangelicals and abolition, see Lawrence J. Friedman, *Gregarious Saints: Self and Community in American Abolitionism, 1830–1870* (Cambridge, England, 1982).

26. *Wesleyan Times,* 6 Aug. 1860. Phoebe Palmer, *Four Years in the Old World* (New York, 1886). Carwardine, *Transatlantic Revivalism,* 176–79. Kent, *Holding the Fort,* 313–40. Frederick Coutts, "As Others See Us," *Officer* 37: (June–July 1986): 253–255, 309–311, disputes Kent's claims concerning Phoebe Palmer's theological influence on the Booths.

27. Catherine's preaching provided the basic Booth family income until 1881. William wrote to their eldest son Bramwell in 1872, "Mama must earn some money by preaching." Bramwell-Booth, *Catherine Booth: The Story,* 181, 197, 227, 253, 356. See Norman H. Murdoch, "Female Ministry in the Thought and Work of Catherine Booth," *Church History* 53 (Sept. 1984): 363–78; and Olive Anderson, "Women Preachers in Mid-Victorian Britain," *Historical Journal* 12 (1969): 467–84. Arthur Augustus Rees, "Reasons for Not Co-operating in the Alleged Sunderland Revivals" (Sunderland, England, 1859), is not available.

28. Timothy Smith, *Revivalism and Social Reform,* 107. *Christian Advocate,* 2 and 23 Mar. 1856, and 19 July 1860. Robert Sandall, *The History of the Salvation Army,* 3 vols. (London, 1947–55), 1:22. Palmer, *Four Years in the Old World,* 105. *Revivalist,* 1859, 125. William Carter, *The Power of God* (London, 1863), 78. Booth's 1870s Food for the Million shops and his 1888 world missions vision epitomize a postmillennialist tendency to view the world as perfectible; preaching the gospel would bring an era of peace *prior* to Christ's *parousia.* Timothy Smith, *Revivalism and Social Reform,* 103, 111–12, traced Finney's perfectionism to his study of John Wesley's *Plain Account of Christian Perfection* and a 1836 biography of James Brainerd Taylor. Carwardine, *Transatlantic Revivalism,* 192–97, finds that revivals in Britain coincided with activities of American evangelists, rather than the economic cycle. Peter Brierly, *Mission to London: Phase 2: Who Went Forward* (London, 1985), indicates that Luis Palau's 16,000 converts in 1984, like those of Caughey, Finney, and Palmer, were young and church-connected.

2. The Booths as Wesleyan Revivalists

1. Ervine, *God's Soldier*, 1:11.

2. Ibid., 1:28f., 1:117, 1:255, 1:361. Begbie, *Life of Booth*, 1:15–34. Bramwell-Booth, *Catherine Booth: The Story*, 129, 153f., 163, 191.

3. Bramwell-Booth, *Catherine Booth: The Story*, 17–18, 26–28. W. T. Stead, *Mrs. Booth of the Salvation Army* (London, 1909), 22–31. Booth-Tucker, *Life of Catherine Booth*. Ervine, *God's Soldier*, 1:11–27.

4. Erik H. Erikson, *Young Man Luther* (New York, 1958), 97, 43, 47, 54, 67, 123, examines Martin Luther's "somber and harsh childhood" which precipitated "a severe identity crisis." He depicts a father who is reminiscent of Samuel Booth—"a father to whom he could not get close and from whom he could not get away—faced with such a father, how was he going to submit without being emasculated, or rebel without emasculating the father?" (67)

5. George S. Railton, *General Booth*, 9, states that Booth's conversion occurred "in one of the smaller meetings." Begbie, *Life of Booth*, 1:35–37, 1:44–45, 1:53, cites a street conversion. Ervine, *God's Soldier*, 1:33–35, notes that Booth could not recall the "precise moment." Also see George S. Railton, *Twenty-One Years*, 7; and Frederick Coutts, *Bread for My Neighbour* (London, 1978), 27.

6. Booth-Tucker, *Life of Catherine Booth*, 1:36–38. Bramwell-Booth, *Catherine Booth: The Story*, 33–38. Stead, *Mrs. Booth of the Salvation Army*, 36, 39, dates her conversion to a "great crisis of soul" at age 15.

7. Ervine, *God's Soldier*, 1:37. Begbie, *Life of Booth*, 1:9–10. Erikson, *Young Man Luther*, 101. George S. Railton, *Twenty-One Years*, 7–8. William James, *Varieties of Religious Experience*, (London: Longmans, 1902), 200, observes that Booth considered "that the first vital step in saving outcasts consists in making them feel that some decent human being cares enough for them to take an interest in the question whether they are to rise or sink."

8. George S. Railton, *General Booth*, 20–56, records Booth's four crises as: the death of Sansom and his loss of employment with Eames; an 1852 failure to progress toward formal ministry and rejection by his pastor who suspected him of Reform leanings; the 1861 Methodist New Connexion Conference which denied him evangelistic work; and an 1865 crisis when he saw London's masses "evidently without God or hope in the world."

9. George S. Railton, *Twenty-One Years*, 10. Begbie, *Life of Booth*, 1:83, 1:104–6. Ervine, *God's Soldier*, 1:42–47, 1:191–93. The Wesleyans later expelled

Dunn as a reformer, at the same time that Caughey was "banished from Nottingham."

10. Ervine, God's Soldier, 1:44–45.

11. Begbie, *Life of Booth,* 1:86–90, 1:99–108, observes that Booth's "call" was not dramatic. William was lonely in London (1849–52), with only a sister in the city, whose atheist husband treated William shabbily.

12. Ervine, *God's Soldier,* 1:47–54. Stead, *General Booth,* 37–8.

13. Begbie, *Life of Booth,* 1:104–7, 1:111–15, 1:123; and Bramwell-Booth, *Catherine Booth: The Story,* 60–61, describe Rabbits's deal with Booth and the meeting at Rabbits's house.

14. The Booth Papers at the British Library consist mainly of letters between William and Catherine during the period when he was an itinerant preacher.

15. George S. Railton, *General Booth,* 31. Stead, *General Booth,* 39–40. Begbie, *Life of Booth,* 1:145. Bramwell-Booth, *Catherine Booth: The Story,* 74. Ervine, *God's Soldier,* 1:61–69, quotes from the Calvinist George Payne, *Divine Sovereignty* (n.p.,1836), which Booth had been urged to read: "If there had been an obligation upon God to save men, there would doubtless have been a decree to save all men. But if God were under no obligation to save men, but might have left all to perish, there is no principle on which it can be maintained that a decree to save a part of the race only violates goodness." This is an interesting indication of how Calvinism was being turned into Universalism in the 1830s.

16. The term "circuit" refers to Methodist societies meeting in several towns under one superintendent. Booth held similar services for each congregation and directed the work of ministers in charge of individual societies and/or of local lay preachers whose training and performance were his concern.

17. Correspondence of William and Catherine Booth, 1852–March 1853, Booth Papers, British Library, MS 64799. Ervine, *God's Soldier,* 1:69–95, 1:106–9, 1:135–94. Frederick Coutts, *Bread for My Neighbour,* 15. Begbie, *Life of Booth,* 1:146–202, 1:207–9. Bramwell-Booth, *Catherine Booth: The Story,* 75–127. Stead, *Mrs. Booth* 42. George S. Railton, *General Booth,* 32–40. Booth-Tucker, *Life of Catherine Booth,* 1:74, gives Nov. 1852–Feb. 1854 as the period of William's Spalding pastorate.

18. At Dr. Cooke's home, three or four students prepared for the Methodist ministry. Cooke was president of the Methodist New Connexion Conference in 1843, 1859, and 1869. He received a D.D. degree at Shurtliff Col-

lege, near Alton, Ill., in 1861. See Samuel Hulme, *Memoir of Rev. Cooke, D.D.* (n.p., n.d.)

19. Booth Papers, British Library, MS 64799. Booth-Tucker, *Life of Catherine Booth,* 1:111. Bramwell-Booth, *Catherine Booth: The Story,* 145. See also Begbie, *Life of Booth,* 1:203–5, 1:210, 1:216, 1:224; Ervine, *God's Soldier,* 1:130, and 1:110–14; Stead, *Mrs. Booth,* 70; and Catherine Bramwell-Booth, *Bramwell Booth* (London, 1933), 7f.

20. On emotion and revival, several sources merit mention. Catherine Booth to William Booth, 20 Mar. 1853, Booth Papers, British Library, MS 64800. Begbie, *Life of Booth,* 1:162–66. Ervine, *God's Soldier,* 1:78–79. William Booth to Catherine Booth, 1 Feb. 1855, Booth Papers, British Library, MS 64802. Begbie, *Life of Booth,* 1:224–25. George S. Railton, *General Booth,* ch. 6. Begbie, *Life of Booth,* 1:149, 1:178–80, 1:195, 1:204. Bramwell-Booth, *Catherine Booth: The Story,* 101–5. Booth-Tucker, *Life of Catherine Booth,* 1:152.

21. On temperance, consult the following. William Booth to Catherine Booth, 17 Nov. 1852; and Catherine Booth to William Booth, 27 Dec. 1852; both in Booth Papers, British Library, MS 64799. Begbie, *Life of Booth,* 1:149, 1:154–55. Ervine, *God's Soldier,* 1:71–2. Bramwell-Booth, *Catherine Booth: The Story,* 79, 82, 86–87. William Booth wrote to Catherine Booth, 28 Mar. 1855, Booth Papers, British Library, MS 64802: "I believe that the beer agreed with me wonderfully—I am as different as possible; I believe that bitter ale or porter would be very beneficial in this respect—but, do not fear, I will stick to the pledge." Also see Begbie, *Life of Booth,* 1:232–33; and Ervine, *God's Soldier,* 1:120–21. Brian Harrison, *Drink and the Victorians* (Pittsburgh, Pa., 1971).

22. On illness and medicine, several works are informative here. Booth Papers, British Library, MSS 64799–64806. Begbie, *Life of Booth,* 1:10, 1:189–92, 1:198, 1:274. Bramwell-Booth, *Catherine Booth: The Story,* 98, 152, 188f., 221, 252, 257–63, 296. Ervine, *God's Soldier,* 1:200–207, 1:227–28, 1:267, and the appendix "Hints on Health and the Water Treatment." William Booth, *Letters to Salvationists on Religion for Every Day* (London, n.d.). Each morning William washed his chest with cold water, then rubbed it vigorously before eating two raw eggs in his tea. This meal he repeated in the evening with milk and oatmeal for a queasy stomach. Edward H. Madden and James E. Hamilton, in *The Life of Asa Mahan* (Metuchen, N.J., 1982), note connections among advocates of health reform, Grahamism, homeopathic medicine, temperance, women's rights, holiness, abolitionism, educational reform, and vegetarianism.

23. The following sources are relevant on family life and holy living. The Booths' letters in the Booth Papers, British Library, MSS 64799–64806. Begbie, *Life of Booth,* 1:156–61, 1:172, 1:178, 1:195, 1:200. Bramwell-Booth, *Catherine Booth: The Story,* 87–89, 105–6. Timothy L. Smith, *Revivalism and Social Reform,* introduced the idea that Wesleyans fostered the reform notion in America.

24. Stead, *Mrs. Booth,* 29. Booth-Tucker, *Life of Catherine Booth,* 1:27–33. Bramwell-Booth, *Catherine Booth: The Story,* 26–27. Ervine, *God's Soldier,* 1:29–30, 1:129. Ford C. Ottman, *Herbert Booth* (New York, 1928), 59f. On music, see Ervine, *God's Soldier,* 1:93, 1:101. William was already thinking of wedding secular tunes to religious words, as Wesley, Whitefield, and others already had done.

25. Begbie, *Life of Booth,* 1:61, 1:121, 1:260–67, 1:188–89, 1:217.

26. Catherine Booth, *Female Ministry: Woman's Right to Preach the Gospel,* abridged ed. (New York, 1975), 22; the 1859 unexpurgated original has not been found. Bramwell-Booth, *Catherine Booth: The Story,* 49–52, 79, 88–89, 138–43, 176, 291. Stead, *Mrs. Booth,* 92f., 214–16. Booth-Tucker, *Life of Catherine Booth,* 1:117–23. Begbie, *Life of Booth,* 1:150–55. Ervine, *God's Soldier,* 1:71. Constance M. Coltman, qtd. in A. Maude Royden, *The Church and Women* (London, 1924), 110, says that one factor in the success of the English Primitive Methodists in 1823 was its 13 women preachers. See Murdoch, "Female Ministry," 363–78; Fred D. Layman, "Male Headship in Paul's Thought," *Wesleyan Theological Journal* 15 (Spring 1980): 46–67; Donald W. Dayton, in *Discovering an Evangelical Heritage* (New York, 1976), 88–95; and Anderson, "Women Preachers," 467–84.

27. Stead, *Mrs. Booth,* 29. Booth-Tucker, *Life of Catherine Booth,* 1:27–33. Bramwell-Booth, *Catherine Booth: The Story,* 26–27. Ervine, *God's Soldier,* 1:29–30, 1:129. Begbie, *Life of Booth,* 1:121, 1:61, 1:260–61, 1:188–89, 1:217. Ervine estimated William's pay at £100 per year plus travel expenses, £30 to £40 more than other young men in similar circumstances in the 1850s. See William Booth to Catherine Booth, 1 June 1855, Booth Papers, British Library, MS 64802.

28. William to Catherine, 1 June 1855, and William to the Mumfords, n.d., both in Booth Papers, British Library, MS 64802. Begbie, *Life of Booth,* 1:243, 1:262, 1:267, 1:286–92. Sandall, *History of the Army,* 1:10–11. George S. Railton, *Twenty-One Years,* 13. Bramwell-Booth, *Catherine Booth: The Story,* 165, 180–86.

29. George S. Railton, *Twenty-One Years,* 13–15. Bramwell-Booth, *Catherine Booth: The Story,* 204, 176, 213–33. Begbie, *Life of Booth,* 1:292–95. Booth-

Tucker, *Life of Catherine Booth,* 2:39–57, quotes the *Wesleyan Times,* 1862. Carwardine, *Transatlantic Revivalism,* 183–84. Stead, *General Booth,* 56, quotes *Minutes of the Methodist Conference, 1862,* 15:326, par. 4, on the Booths' exclusion from Methodist pulpits. *Christian Advocate,* 9 Oct. 1862. *Minutes of Several Conversations between the Methodist Ministers . . . at their . . . annual conference in 1862* (London), 326–27. Ervine, *God's Soldier,* 1:235–60, provides a full, balanced treatment of Booth's resignation. Bramwell-Booth, *Catherine Booth: The Story,* 206–11. Stead, *Mrs. Booth* 161. Conference accepted Booth's resignation "formally and ungraciously" at Dudley in 1862, closing the door to the New Connexion. For Catherine's feelings, see Catherine Booth to her mother, 24 June 1861, quoted in Bramwell-Booth, *Catherine Booth: The Story,* 209.

30. Bramwell-Booth, *Catherine Booth: The Story,* 221, 291, indicates that Caughey's converts had built the Walsall Chapel. George S. Railton, *Twenty-One Years,* 16. Ervine, *God's Soldier,* 1:264–68. Stead, *Mrs. Booth,* 58–60, 214–16. Begbie, *Life of Booth,* 1:295–96. The Hallelujah Band movement continued in the Black Country until its leaders disagreed. Because of the "squalor of industrial life," Ervine found Booth's sensationalism necessary to lure workers away from the "allurements of the public house," in which they found "gaiety and warmth." George S. Railton, *Twenty-One Years,* 17, writes that Booth believed the band died out due to a lack of "acknowledged authority" or "distinctive teaching beyond that of conversion." But Booth remained convinced that such a movement, if properly directed, could be a "powerful force" among the "vast continent of rampant wickedness that I saw around me everywhere."

31. Bramwell-Booth, *Catherine Booth: The Story,* 221–28. Begbie, *Life of Booth,* 1:292–312. Booth-Tucker, *Life of Catherine Booth,* 1:273–80. Ervine, *God's Soldier,* 1:263–80. Bramwell-Booth, *Bramwell Booth,* 27–30.

32. Bramwell Booth, *Echoes and Memories* (London, 1925), 32.

Part II

3. An East London Home Mission, 1865–70

1. Ervine, *God's Soldier,* 1:381, 1:283. William Booth, *Heathen England and What to Do for It* (London, 1877). George S. Railton, *General Booth,* 56. Begbie, *Life of Booth,* 1:355. Booth-Tucker, *Life of Catherine Booth,* 1:279–80, 1:291. Bramwell-Booth, *Catherine Booth: The Story,* 266–80.

2. Ervine, *God's Soldier,* 1:277. Sandall, *History of the Army,* 1:26. Booth-Tucker, *Life of Catherine Booth,* 1:280–81. Begbie, *Life of Booth,* 1:309.

3. Sandall, *History of the Army,* 1:27. By the term "Irregular Agencies," the *Christian Year Book* meant extradenominational voluntary agencies.

4. Sandall, *History of the Army,* 1:24–26. Herbert A. Wisbey, Jr., "A Salvation Army Prelude: The Christian Mission in Cleveland, Ohio," *Ohio Historical Quarterly* 64 (Jan. 1955), 77–81.

5. J. B. A. Kessler, *A Study of the Evangelical Alliance in Great Britain* (Goes, Netherlands, 1968), 17, says that the idea for an Evangelical Alliance came from Dr. Paton of New York to Rev. John Angell James in May 1842. See *Conference on Christian Union* (London, 1845), 9; and John W. Ewing, *Goodly Fellowship* (London, 1946), 13.

6. Carwardine, *Transatlantic Revivalism,* 187, 190. Kent, *Holding the Fort,* 105–6. Wallis, *Happy Warrior,* 65. Booth preached the funeral of John Starkey, a murderer executed in Redcar St., Leicester, ca. 1877, following the hoisting of the black flag. About 2,000 "disreputable, half-drunken persons" came to the service at the Salvation Warehouse.

7. Sandall, *History of the Army,* 1:23 and 1:aPages C.

8. "The Right of Meeting," *The Times* (London), 2 July 1864, 11, reported this July 1 meeting of the committee of metropolitan members and electors appointed to secure the "right of public meeting in parks irrespective of governmental permission." M.P.s Ayrton, Cox, Locke, Whalley, etc., agreed that the police commissioner's orders forbidding park meetings "were totally illegal."

9. Sandall, *History of the Army,* 1:26, 1:29, 1:38–39, 1:74–76, 1:80–85, 1:93–99, 1:104, 1:115, 1:251–52, for the Booths' connection to the Special Services Committee, 1865–70; lists of the Special Services Committee and Evangelisation Society's members indicate interlocking directorates.

10. Ervine, *God's Soldier,* 1:281. For the location of the hall, see George S. Railton, *Twenty-One Years,* 18; and Frederick Coutts, *Bread for My Neighbour,* 34.

11. George S. Railton, *Twenty-One Years,* 18–19.

12. Begbie, *Life of Booth,* 1:341–42. "The East London Christian Mission," *East London Evangelist,* (Oct. 1, 1868), 3–5. George S. Railton, *Twenty-One Years,* 22–23, and *General Booth,* 56. Ervine, *God's Soldier,* 1:283–86. Sandall, *History of the Army,* 1:39–44.

13. Ervine, *God's Soldier,* 1:281–83. *East London Evangelist,* (Oct. 1, 1868), 3. Sandall, *History of the Army,* 1:49–51, 1:39, quotes *Revival,* 13 July 1865. Begbie, *Life of Booth,* 1:335, interviewed an old man who claimed that a

gang of roughs cut the tent cords. Stead, *General Booth,* 67, 72. Booth's rent at 23 New Road, Whitechapel, was £1 per Sunday. George S. Railton, *General Booth,* 63, called the hall an old dancing saloon and low public house.

14. When Samuel Morley died in London in 1886, he left a large fortune made in the textile business founded by his father, who was from Nottingham.

15. Ervine, *God's Soldier,* 1:283, 1:287–88, 1:303–36. Bramwell-Booth, *Bramwell Booth,* 30. Booth-Tucker, *Life of Catherine Booth,* 1:291, 300–332. Bramwell-Booth, *Catherine Booth: The Story,* 321–23. Begbie, *Life of Booth,* 1:317. This extended illness led to nausea and nervous system problems, which caused Catherine to seek a house in the quieter neighborhood of Gore St. A charcoal treatment was her home remedy. P. Whitwell Wilson, *General Evangeline Booth* (New York, 1935), 27. Margaret Troutt, *The General Was a Lady: The Story of Evangeline Booth* (Nashville, Tenn., 1980), 15f.

16. William Booth, *Heathen England,* 29. Sandall, *History of the Army,* 1:52. William Booth, *How to Reach the Masses with the Gospel* (London, 1872), 27–74. "The East London Christian Missions, Past, Present, and Future," *East London Evangelist,* (Dec. 1, 1868), 35. George S. Railton, *General Booth,* 63, 57. George S. Railton, *Twenty-One Years,* 19–20.

17. Sandall, *History of the Army,* 1:57–58, 1:61–64. "The East London Christian Mission," *East London Evangelist,* (Dec. 1, 1868), 35. William Booth, *How to Reach the Masses,* 37–38. George S. Railton, *General Booth,* 63, 57. Begbie, *Life of Booth,* 1:345. George S. Railton, *Twenty-One Years,* 19–20, 27. Ervine, *God's Soldier,* 1:287.

18. Eliza Collingridge began attending mission services at the dancing room in 1865 and continued her work until her death in 1872. Sandall, *History of the Army,* 1:86–88, 1:95, 1:99–104.

19. Booth-Tucker, *Life of Catherine Booth,* 1:330–31. Ervine, *God's Soldier,* 1:296. Sandall, *History of the Army,* 1:111, 1:114; the latter page quotes the *Nonconformist,* 4 Nov. 1868. Gawin Kirkham, in *Revival,* 1868. "The East London Christian Mission," *East London Evangelist,* Dec. 1868, 35.

20. "New Year's Prospects in East London," *East London Evangelist,* (Jan. 1, 1869), 62–63. Sandall, *History of the Army,* 1:124–34. Ervine, *God's Soldier,* 1:306. William Booth, *Heathen England,* 29. A Croydon convert founded the Bromley Station.

21. Ervine, *God's Soldier,* 1:298. Booth-Tucker, *Life of Catherine Booth,* 1:342. Sandall, *History of the Army,* 1:109, 1:124, 1:131.

22. Booth-Tucker, *Life of Catherine Booth,* 1:343–45. Bramwell-Booth,

Catherine Booth: The Story, 239–40. Bramwell-Booth, *Bramwell Booth,* 41–42. Sandall, *History of the Army,* 1:132. Frederick Coutts, *No Discharge in This War* (London, 1974), 25.

23. Sandall, *History of the Army,* 1:46, 1:89, 1:81–82, 1:99–103. Booth-Tucker, *Life of Catherine Booth,* 1:318–19.

24. George S. Railton, *General Booth,* 71. Sandall, *History of the Army,* 1:48, 1:104–11, 1:119–24, 1:131.

25. Bramwell-Booth, *Catherine Booth: The Story,* 234–41. Ervine, *God's Soldier,* 1:288–301, 1:307, 1:389–90. Booth-Tucker, *Life of Catherine Booth,* 1:308–39, 1:346–51, conjectures that Catherine's disorganized notes kept her from publication, but later she published many sermons. Stead, *Mrs. Booth,* 237. Sandall, *History of the Army,* 1:83, 1:96–98. Begbie, *Life of Booth,* 1:324. In 1875, Billups married the Rev. Mr. Irvine and moved to Jersey City Heights, N.J. William Booth, *Heathen England,* 29.

26. Frederick Coutts, *No Discharge,* 22. Sandall, *History of the Army,* 1:75. Ervine, *God's Soldier,* 1:296. Booth-Tucker, *Life of Catherine Booth,* 329–30, 318. Philanthropists included: Samuel Morley, M.P.; Capt. Fishbourne, R.N., C.B.; George Pearse, Stock Exchange; Rev. J. H. Wilson, secretary, Home Missionary Society; Rev. W. Tyler, New Town Chapel; Morgan and Chase; Capt. W. E. Smith, secretary, Evangelisation Society; Gawin Kirkham, secretary, Open Air Mission. Committee members were Nathaniel James Powell, treasurer; Charles Owen, honorable secretary; John Lee Dale; John Alfred Merrington; Edmund Ives; John Eason; C. H. Crispin; George Hamilton; C. S. Mitchell.

27. Sandall, *History of the Army,* 1:74–85, 1:94–108. Booth-Tucker, *Life of Catherine Booth,* 1:318. George S. Railton, *Twenty-One Years,* 21. No sources mention Whittaker's resignation. He does not appear on lists of committee members.

28. C. H. Spurgeon built his tabernacle in 1859, the revival year, and Joseph Parker built his City Temple in 1874, the second year of Dwight Moody's London revival crusade.

29. "Conversion of the People's Market," *East London Evangelist,* Nov. 1868, 17–19. Ervine, *God's Soldier,* 1:304–16. Frederick Coutts, *No Discharge,* 25. Bramwell-Booth, *Catherine Booth: The Story,* 356–57. Henry Reed again offered the Booths his support in 1880, when Catherine told him that his gift had delivered them from dependence on "those who only partially sympathize with our views." When the Booths purchased a Clapton Commons home, she feared that Reed would not like the twenty-five pounds

per year ground rent, but she noted that the neighborhood was improving, so it would be a good investment. When Reed died, the Salvation Army's *War Cry*, "Henry Reed," (Jan. 17, 1881), 13, 20 summarized his theory of charity: get the working classes "thoroughly converted; they will then spend their means more wisely." He had broken with the Wesleyans as "their godly discipline became relaxed" and organized his own mission.

30. David Blackwell, "Tents, Theatres and Other Places," *Officer* 11(July–Aug. 1960): 283–88, says that Booth's early halls held thousands. By 1900, they were partitioned for activities with auditoria of no more than 500 seats. This indicated that by then salvationists were coming to "church" with children and expected something more than massive preaching services. The army no longer expected the masses to attend; by then it had become a sect, not a mission.

31. Sandall, *History of the Army,* 1:72–76, 1:90–92, 1:105–10, 1:124–25, 1:134–35. Bramwell-Booth, *Catherine Booth: The Story,* 237. Booth-Tucker, *Life of Catherine Booth,* 1:329. Begbie, *Life of Booth,* 1:347, wrote that Booth had little interest in social-economic issues at this time. *Saturday Review* is quoted by Frederick Coutts, *Bread for My Neighbour,* 34. Christmas 1867 was a depressing time for Booth, as he compared East End misery to his own family's comforts. In 1868, the Booths distributed 150 Christmas puddings.

32. Sandall, *History of the Army,* 1:104. Ervine, *God's Soldier,* 1:93, 1:99–102, 1:110. Booth-Tucker, *Life of Catherine Booth,* 1:76. Begbie, *Life of Booth,* 1:301, 1:210. No scholar has yet studied the exchange of popular tunes across the Atlantic in this era.

33. Sandall, *History of the Army,* 1:105, quotes the *Morning Advertiser.*

34. "Statement of 'Dedication' and Our Purpose," *East London Evangelist,* Oct. 1868, 1–2.

35. "Conversion of a Penny Gaff," *East London Evangelist,* Oct. 1, 1868, 16. Booth-Tucker, *Life of Catherine Booth,* 1:331. Sandall, *History of the Army,* 1:67. Stead, *General Booth,* 64.

36. Appendix A of this book compares the Methodist New Connexion, Evangelical Alliance, and Christian Mission creeds. See Norman H. Murdoch, "Evangelical Sources of Salvation Army Doctrine," *Evangelical Quarterly* 54 (July 1987): 235–44, for a detailed account.

37. J. Edwin Orr, *The Second Evangelical Awakening* (London, 1955), 126. J. W. Massie, *The Evangelical Alliance* (London, 1847), 160–77.

38. In Christian Mission, 6th Conference, *Minutes,* 1876, this article reads, "We

believe that continuance in a state of salvation depends upon continued obedient faith in Christ." John Coutts, *This We Believe* (London, 1980), 99 in dealing with the mission's rejection of Calvinism, quotes A. M. Nicol, a former Salvation Army officer, who wrote that, even with the change, some salvationists did not take seriously the army's Methodistic articles.

39. John Coutts, *The Salvationists* (London, 1977), 8, argues that, although Catherine Booth condemned "Christian freethinkers," the position on biblical inspiration in the 1870s was loose, permitting liberals and conservatives to coexist in the Christian Mission.

40. John Coutts, *This We Believe,* 122, notes that, in the early Church, wandering prophets gave way to a "fixed system of Church government," with only bishops allowed to ordain men as priests and only priests allowed to celebrate Communion. While Booth avoided ritualism, he instituted rites for swearing in soldiers (lay members) and dedicating babies, that were to be performed only by officers (clergy) whose commissioning the army now refers to as ordination. Ordination itself is performed by a commissioner, the equivalent of a bishop. Hans Kung, in *The Church* (Garden City, N.Y., 1976), 169, 236, 427, 455–65, 488–92, 504–5, 512, 538, 559, writes that by the 3rd century, the church had broken "the people of God" into artificial categories of clergy and laity. John Coutts, *The Salvationists,* 4, observes that swearing soldiers in is a "curiously formal ritual for a Movement which claims earnestly that rituals avail a man nothing at all." See Kessler, *Evangelical Alliance,* 41, 35.

41. "The Legitimate Attraction of Christianity, or, Catching the People's Eye," *Christian Mission Magazine* (Nov. 1873): 164; and "New Ground Occupied, Chatham," *Christian Mission Magazine* (Nov. 1873): 164, 169.

42. Christian Mission, 3rd and 6th Conferences, *Minutes,* 1873 and 1876. English historian John Kent, *Holding the Fort,* 298, 326–29, 339, argues that Salvation Army historians have totally ignored Palmer's influence on its holiness doctrine. William Bramwell, "Flames of Fire," *Christian Mission Magazine* (1 Sept. 1870): 131–35. "In Memoriam: Mrs. Phoebe Palmer," *Christian Mission Magazine* (Jan. 1875): 12–13, said that Phoebe Palmer had done more for "the cause of holiness than any man or woman in this century." James Caughey, "The Striving of the Spirit," *Christian Mission Magazine* (July 1876): 158. James Caughey, "The Standing Doubt," *Christian Mission Magazine* (Apr. 1876): 76–80. Sandall, *History of the Army,* 1:160. Bramwell Booth, *Echoes and Memories,* 42.

43. Catherine Booth to William Booth, 28 Aug. 1860, and Catherine Booth to

her parents, 11 Feb. 1861, see Bramwell-Booth, *Catherine Booth: The Story,* 198–204.

44. Bramwell-Booth, *Bramwell Booth,* 141–42.

45. Bernard Watson, *Soldier Saint: George Scott Railton* (London, 1970), 15–16. George S. Railton again used the phrase "roots of bitterness" in *The Doctrines of the Salvation Army* (London: 1881), and the army included it in its *Handbook of Doctrine* until 1927 (in 1935, in a footnote). In 1959 the army removed it from the *Articles of War* signed by soldiers, and in 1969 struck it from the revised *Handbook of Doctrine.* For the "roots of bitterness" debate, see John Coutts, *The Salvationists,* 7; and Christian Mission, 6th Conference, *Minutes,* 1876.

46. William Booth, "Holiness, An Address at the Conference," *Christian Mission Magazine* (Aug. 1877): 193–203. See also W. Bramwell Booth, "Sanctification," *Christian Mission Magazine* (Feb. 1878): 29–33.

47. Stead, *General Booth,* 64.

4. Failure in East London, 1870–77

1. Ervine, *God's Soldier,* 1:284. George S. Railton, *General Booth,* 66. Begbie, *Life of Booth,* 1:357.

2. Tim Stafford, "Ralph Winter: An Unlikely Revolutionary," *Christianity Today* 28 (7 Sept. 1984): 14–18, finds that Christianity seldom leaps from its own cultural trough to win converts in another.

3. Norman H. Murdoch and Howard F. McMains, "The Salvation Army Disturbances of 1885," *Queen City Heritage: Journal of the Cincinnati Historical Society* 45 (Summer 1987): 31–39. Norman H. Murdoch, "Salvation Army Disturbances in Liverpool, England, 1879–1887," *Journal of Social History* 25 (Mar. 1992): 575–93 and Frank Neal, *Sectarian Violence: The Liverpool Experience, 1819–1914* (Manchester, England, 1988), document Salvation Army and other sectarian violence in this period of Anglo-Irish history.

4. Begbie, *Life of Booth,* 1:98–99. See Paul Thompson, *Socialists, Liberals, and Labour: The Struggle for London, 1865–1914* (London, 1967), 19, for a negative view of London's working-class Nonconformists; see also C. M. Davies, *Unorthodox London* (London, 1873).

5. For Christian Mission history to 1870, see William Booth, *How to Reach the Masses,* 4–6; "East London Christian Mission," *East London Evangelist,* Oct. 1868, 3; Sandall, *History of the Army,* 1:33–34; Frederick Coutts, *Bread for My Neighbour,* 31, 21; and Begbie, *Life of Booth,* 1:341.

6. Frederick Coutts, *Bread for My Neighbour*, 32–34, 19, graphically portrays East London. Benjamin Jowett, *Life and Letters*, 1: 413, qtd. in L. E. Elliott-Burns, *Religion in Victorian England* (London, 1936), 422. William Booth, *How to Reach the Masses*, 4.

7. Sandall, *History of the Army*, 1:28–34. William Booth, *How to Reach the Masses*, 4. Frederick Coutts, *No Discharge*, 19–20, notes that 4,000 deaths in the four districts amounted to 70% of London's total. See E. P. Thompson, *The Making of the English Working Classes* (New York, 1966), 314, on living standards and illnesses of the poor.

8. Thomas Plint, *Crime in England: Its Relation, Character, and Extent* (London, 1851), 26–27, 146, 148–57, describes the criminal class as "a pestiferous canker in the heart of every locality," an "exotic tribe," a "foreign" element that preyed on the "indigenous and really working population," a "moral cesspool into which all the offscourings and dregs of the community settle down and corrupt," and even worse than a "mob." Thomas Carlyle, *English and Other Critical Essays* (London, n.d.), 182–83, qtd. in Gertrude Himmelfarb, *The Idea of Poverty: England and the Early Industrial Age* (New York, 1985), 371, 386–87, scorns the Irish as a major element of a "ragged class" exhibiting "degradation and disorder" worse than those known by the poorest English people. Carlyle's residuum of outcasts, this "curious race" that needed civilizing, is easily equated with Booth's "heathen masses" of the 1860s, 1870s, and 1880s, or with the "submerged tenth" of which Booth wrote in 1890.

9. *East End Evangelist*, 1 Jan. 1869, 62–63.

10. George Scott Railton, "About Culture," *Christian Mission Magazine* (Dec. 1873): 177–79.

11. Sidney Webb and Beatrice Webb, *The History of Trade Unionism* (London, 1950), 45–46. Gareth Steadman Jones, *Outcast London* (Oxford, England, 1971), 337–49. E. P. Thompson, *Making of the English*, 257, 240–41, terms London "the Athens of the Artisan." Henry Pelling, *Social Geography of British Elections, 1885–1910* (London, 1967), 42–59, finds that Limehouse, Mile End, St. George's-in-the-East, and Stepney voted Conservative from 1885 to 1906.

12. G. B. Shaw, *Pall Mall Gazette* (11 Feb. 1886), 4.

13. H. H. Champion, *The Great Dock Strike in London, August 1889* (London, 1890), 11.

14. Lynn Hollen Lees, *Exiles of Erin: Irish Migrants in Victorian London* (Ithaca, N.Y., 1979), 18–19, 56–62. Claude S. Fischer, "Toward a Subcultural

Theory of Urbanism," *American Journal of Sociology* 80 (May 1975): 319–41. Milicent Rose, *The East End of London* (London 1951).

15. Incognito, [pseud.], "Battle of Dorking," *War Cry,* 17 Sept. 1887, 4, claimed that the army's attackers were "an organized system of terrorism." Murdoch, "From Militancy to Social Mission." Victor Bailey, "Salvation Army Riots, the 'Skeleton Army,' and Legal Authority in the Provincial Town," in *Social Control in Nineteenth Century Britain,* ed. A. P. Donajgrodzki (London, 1977): 231–53.

16. Lees, *Exiles of Erin,* 164–69, 190–97, 210–11. Henry Mayhew, *London Labour and the London Poor,* 4 vols., (London, 1861–62), 1:108. Charles Booth, *Life and Labour of the People of London,* (London: 1902–3, Series 3), 3, *Religious Influences,* 7:243–44.

17. Vincent Alan McClelland, *Cardinal Manning, His Public Life and Influence, 1865–1892* (London, 1962), 202–3. J. Derek Holmes, *More Roman than Rome: English Catholicism in the Nineteenth Century* (London, 1978), 122–25, 158–68.

18. Henry Edward Manning, "The Salvation Army," *Contemporary Review* 42 (Oct. 1882), 335–43. "Why Cardinal Manning Thinks the Army Valuable and Hopes for Good from It," *War Cry,* 7 Sept. 1882, 4. Catholic evangelist David Goldstein said in the 1920s, "It would be great if we could organize a sort of Catholic salvation army." Archbishop Ireland in 1889 urged laymen to form "salvation armies to bring God's word to the ear of the most vile." See Debra Campbell, "A Catholic Salvation Army: David Goldstein, Pioneer Lay Evangelist," *Church History* 52 (Sept. 1983): 322–32.

19. Before 1870, members included subscribers to mission funds. By 1870, membership meant actual participation in a station's program, as well as adherence to a strict code of behavior. Therefore the 1870–77 period can be considered a unit for purposes of statistical analysis.

20. Christian Mission, 2nd Conference, *Minutes,* 12–13 June 1871. Donations and book sales supplied income for headquarters. Statistics do not include a mission opened by James Jermy in Aug. 1872 in Cleveland, Ohio. Christian Mission, 3rd Conference, *Minutes,* 30 June–1 July 1873. Christian Mission, 4th Conference, *Minutes,* 22–24 June 1874. "The Reports from the Districts for the Year Ending the 31st March 1874," *Christian Mission Magazine* (Aug. 1874), 226. "The Annual Meeting," *Christian Mission Magazine* (Aug. 1874), 200–205. Christian Mission, 5th Conference, *Minutes,* 14–16 June 1875. "The Annual Meeting," *Christian Mission Magazine* (July 1875), 177. "A Mission to the People," *Christian Mission Magazine* (Mar. 1876),

44–54. Christian Mission, 6th Conference, *Minutes,* 5–7 June 1876. Christian Mission, 7th Conference, *Minutes,* 11–14 June 1877.

21. William Booth, "The State of the Work of God," *Christian Mission Magazine* (Aug. 1877): 212–14.

22. Ibid.

5. Forming a "Salvation Army," 1877–79

1. Christian Mission, 7th Conference, *Minutes,* 11–14 June 1877. "The Conference," *Christian Mission Magazine* (July 1877): 165–66. William Booth, "The Opening Address," *Christian Mission Magazine* (July 1877): 166–81. Catherine Booth, "Letter from Mrs. Booth," *Christian Mission Magazine* (July 1877): 181.

2. William Booth, "Hallelujah Bands," *Christian Mission Magazine* (July 1877): 182–88. Ervine, *God's Soldier,* 1:522.

3. William Booth, "Good Singing," *Christian Mission Magazine* (Aug. 1877): 202–11.

4. George S. Railton, "Torpedoes," *Christian Mission Magazine* (Sept. 1877): 221–24. George S. Railton, "Reinforcements," *Christian Mission Magazine* (Oct. 1877): 249–51. "Christian Mission Work: The Month," *Christian Mission Magazine* (Dec. 1877): 316–19.

5. George S. Railton, "Peace or War?" *Christian Mission Magazine* (Mar. 1878): 57. George S. Railton, "Terms of Peace," *Christian Mission Magazine* (Apr. 1878): 85. George S. Railton, "Rushing to War," *Christian Mission Magazine* (May 1878): 113–16. George S. Railton, "Riots," *Christian Mission Magazine* (June 1878): 141–45.

6. "Gypsy" Smith (1860–1947) left the Salvation Army when Booth asked him to resign for accepting a gold watch, a violation of *Orders and Regulations.*

7. "The Month," *Christian Mission Magazine* (Mar. 1878): 67–69. "The Month," *Christian Mission Magazine* (Apr. 1878): 98–99. "Mr. Booth in the North," *Christian Mission Magazine* (Apr. 1878), 99. "The Month" and "The Christian Mission on the Tyne, Felling," *Christian Mission Magazine* (May 1878): 122–23.

8. "Our War Congress," *Christian Mission Magazine* (Sept. 1878): 227–50. Christian Mission, 8th Conference, *Minutes,* 5–7 Aug. 1878. *The Salvation Army Trust Deeds: The Foundation Deed, 1875; The Annulment Deed, 1878; The Deed of Constitution, 1878; The Supplemental Deed, 1904; The*

Social Trust Deed, 1891 (London, n.d.). Later deeds include the Salvation Army Act, 1968; and the Salvation Army Act, 1980.

9. Arthur W. Watts, *Lion Hearts: Memoirs of the Christian Mission, Afterwards Known as The Salvation Army* (Gillingham, Kent, England, 1929), 10–15, 22–23. In 1875, Booth appointed Watts, "on trial," to Canning Town, then sent him to Stoke Newington and Tottenham in 1876 and back to Stoke in 1877. In 1879, he sent Watts to Salisbury. The *Minutes* and *Magazine* for 1878 and 1880 do not list Watts. John Allen, a senior evangelist, told Watts after the 1878 conference: "I am done, my health is gone, if I had been well, things would have been very different this morning." Watts interpreted the remark to mean that Watts's hand "would not have been the only one raised in protest." Corbridge later told Watts that one of two reasons for his leaving the Salvation Army was "the unnecessary suffering" officers endured, "in fact he mentioned the word starving."

10. William Booth, "Rushing to War," *Christian Mission Magazine* (May 1878): 113–16.

11. Herbert Asquith, *The Volunteer and Other Poems* (London, 1917), 9. John Gowans, "Army," *War Cry*, New York ed., 16 July 1983, 2, gave this contemporary view of Salvation Army origins:

> When we were made
> The sky was full
> Of steeples and of spires,
> With Churches of a thousand kinds
> To suit each man's desires.
> And priests and pastors hurried
> In their thousands to their task,
> Why did you make this 'Army-Church,'
> Am I allowed to ask?
> With bandsmen in the organ loft
> And songsters in the choir,
>
> And brilliant banners blazing
> With the motto 'Blood and Fire'?
> Was it because with incense
> And the chanting of the creed
> You wanted your own shock troops
> Of a very different breed?

And with the more sedate of saints
The rougher sort as well,
Irreverently to shake the living
Daylights out of Hell!!

12. On aggressive Wesleyan Christianity, see Timothy Smith, *Revivalism and Social Reform*, 204, 231–32. On Muscular Christianity, see D. Newsome, *Godliness and Good Learning* (London, 1961), 207–16; and Kauver and Sorensen, eds., *The Victorian Mind*, 91, 176. Walter E. Houghton, *The Victorian Frame of Mind, 1830–1870* (New Haven, Conn., 1957), 214–15, quotes Charles Kingsley, inventor of the term "muscular christianity"— "'If you want to get mankind, if not to heaven, at least out of hell, kick them out.'" W. R. Greg, "Kingsley and Carlyle," *Literary and Social Judgments* (London: Trubner, 1877), 145–46, wrote: "What unspeakable relief and joy for a Christian like Mr. Kingsley, whom God has made boiling over with animal eagerness and fierce aggressive instincts, to feel that he is not called upon to control these instincts, but only to direct them; and that once having, or fancying that he has, in view of a man or an institution that is God's enemy as well as his, he may hate it with a perfect hatred, and go at it *en sabreur!*" Albert Edward Bailey, "The Rev. Sabine Baring-Gould," *The Gospel in Hymns* (New York, 1950), 370–75. Susan S. Tamke, *Make a Joyful Noise Unto the Lord: Hymns as a Reflection of Victorian Social Attitudes* (Athens, Ohio, 1978), 150155. Charles Kingsley, *Hypatia* (London, 1853).

13. Olive Anderson, "The Growth of Christian Militarism in Mid-Victorian Britain," *English Historical Review* 86 (Jan. 1971): 64–72.

14. Maj. Gen. Sir Garnet I. Wolseley, "England as a Military Power in 1854 and in 1878," *Nineteenth Century* 3 (Mar. 1878): 433–56. Brian Bond, "The Late Victorian Army," *History Today* (Sept. 1961): 616–24, quotes Wolseley: "We may not be a military nation, but without doubt, we are the most warlike people on earth." Hugh Cunningham, *The Volunteer Force* (Hamden, Conn., 1975), 28–29, 54, 60, 83–4. *Volunteer Service Gazette* (8 Aug. 1863): 155. *The Times,* (London) 17 June 1878. Rudyard Kipling, *Ballads and Barrack-Room Ballads* (New York, 1892), 46.

15. Gwyn Harries-Jenkins, *The Army in Victorian Society* (London, 1977), 274, quotes Avery's *Report of the Royal Commission on Warlike Stories* (London 1887), with "Evidence of Lord Wolseley."

16. William Harris Rule, *An Account of the Establishment of Wesleyan Methodism in the British Army* (London, 1883), 116–17. H. J. Hanham, "Re-

ligion and Nationality in the Mid-Victorian Army," in *War and Society, 1828–1971,* ed. M. R. D. Foote (London, 1973), 159–81, argues that the Salvation Army adopted military uniform "because it was composed of individualistic eccentrics, who needed to be reminded that they belonged to the same organization," an elitist thesis he got from Olive Anderson.

17. "Our War Congress," *Christian Mission Magazine* (Oct. 1878): 225, 251. "The Month," *Christian Mission Magazine* (Oct. 1878): 253–54. William Booth, "Our New Name," *Salvationist* (1 Jan. 1879): 1–3. The General [William Booth], "The Salvation Army," *Salvationist* (1 Feb. 1879): 29–33.

18. W. J. Pearson, "Come Join Our Army," *Salvationist* (1 Feb. 1879): 33.

19. "The Hallelujah Lasses," *Northern Express,* qtd. in the *Salvationist* (1 May 1879): 115–16. "The Month," *Salvationist* (1 May 1879): 140.

20. "Council of War on the Tyne. Newcastle and Gateshead, May 17th, 18th, 19th," *Salvationist* (1 June 1879): 141–48.

21. "London Council of War, Whit-Monday," *Salvationist* (1 July 1879): 169–73. "Jottings from the Journal of the General," *Salvationist* (1 Aug. 1879): 200–204, and *Salvationist* (Oct. 1879): 252–58. "Field-Day in Whitechapel, from the *Christian,*" *Salvationist* (1 Sept. 1879): 232–33. "Opening of the Millwall Factory," *Salvationist* (1 Dec. 1879): .

22. "Jottings from the Journal of the General," *Salvationist* (1 Sept. 1879): 226–29, and (1 Nov. 1879): 283–87.

23. "Babylonian: The *Secular Review* on The Salvation Army," *Salvationist* (1 Sept. 1879): 229–31. "Netting Sinners in Sheffield Sewers," from the *Sheffield Independent,* 13 Aug. 1879, rptd. in *Salvationist* (1 Sept. 1879): 235–37.

24. "The Nottingham Council of War, November 1st, 2nd, 3rd," *Salvationist* (1 Dec. 1879): 311–14.

25. "Jottings from the General," *Salvationist* (1 Dec. 1879): 314–17.

26. William Booth, "A Good Soldier of Jesus Christ," pt. 1, *Salvationist,* (1 Nov. 1879): 281–83; and pt. 2, *Salvationist* (1 Dec. 1879): 309–11.

27. See Norman H. Murdoch, "The Salvation Army and the Church of England, 1882–1883," *Historical Magazine of the Protestant Episcopal Church* 55 (Mar. 1986): 31–55.

28. Anderson, "Growth of Christian Militarism," 66–69, says that K. S. Inglis, *Churches and the Working Classes in Victorian England* (London, 1963), was wrong when he held that the Salvation Army, Church Army, and Boys' Brigade reflected Britain's paramilitarism in the 1880s. She held that these organizations relied on military devices for "amusement" and "offered in an

acceptable form the means of discipline . . . often needed in such work."
She argues that the army's routines were less a militant expression than a
reflection of a "guerrilla cult" in the late 1850s and in the 1860s which
stressed spontaneous local activity and personal initiative. Booth, she be-
lieves, used military jargon to exploit "popular interest in the Russo-Turkish
war in precisely the way . . . revivalists had been exploiting shipwrecks,
conflagrations and other public sensations for the previous twenty years or
more." But the *Christian Mission Magazine* (June 1877, Oct. 1877, Sept.
1878) did not exploit events in the fear-promoting manner Anderson sug-
gests. Anderson finds the Salvation Army idea in London's Shoeblack Brigades of the early 1860s, who wore red, yellow, blue, or purple Garibaldi
shirts and badges. She rightly notes that parades with banners, music,
sashes, and badges were features of demonstrations long before Booth
adopted them. But in the 1870s, the Volunteers were far more obvious
sources of military inspiration than guerrilla cults of the 1850s and 1860s.

Part III

6. A Christian Imperium's Growth and Stagnation

1. *War Cry* published original songs written by salvationists in the 1880s.
   Tunes were often Anglo-American folk tunes which passed back and forth
   across the Atlantic, and among music halls, pubs, and gospel meetings.
2. A. M. Nicol, *General Booth and the Salvation Army* (London, 1910), xiii,
   points to the Booths' antagonism for Catholicism as the reason for the Salvation Army's failure in France.
3. Sandall, *History of the Army,* 2:216, 2:231–32, 2:5, 2:65.
4. Norman H. Murdoch, "Frank Smith, Salvationist-Socialist, Father of Salvation Army Social Work," paper presented at meeting of the Salvation Army
   Historical Society, New York, 1978. Nicol, *General Booth,* 115–18, discusses
   officer allowances.
5. Nicol, *General Booth,* ch. 10, 212–30.
6. "The London Major Frank Smith's Account of Himself," *War Cry,* 21 Sept.
   1882, 1.
7. Hugh McLeod, *Class and Religion in the Late Victorian City* (Hamden,
   Conn., 1974), 60, 89.
8. Paul Thompson, *Socialists, Liberals and Labour,* 18.

9. *War Cry,* 26 Jan. 1889, 12; and *War Cry,* 13 April 1889, 13.

10. These figures are from *War Cry* accounts, 1887 to 1894; and *Salvation Army Yearbook, 1994* (London, 1994), 41.

11. Lee Krenis, "Authority and Rebellion in Victorian Autobiography," *Journal of British Studies* 18 (Fall 1978): 107–130, shows that multigenerational arrangements were common among Victorians. Nearly all institutions were nepotistic. Bramwell-Booth, *Catherine Booth: The Story,* 297.

12. Arch R. Wiggins, *History of the Salvation Army* (London, 1964), 4:353.

13. Ervine, *God's Soldier,* ii, 342. "Ballington Booth," *National Cyclopaedia of American Biography* (New York, 1917), 14: 54. In 1896, the Ballington Booths refused orders to leave the U.S. After they resigned, they founded a rival organization, the Volunteers of America, led by Gen. Ballington Booth until 1940, by his wife thereafter until 1948, and then by their son Charles. The Volunteers' general was elected, rather than being named by his predecessor, as in the Salvation Army. The Salvation Army adopted this more democratic approach in 1929. Bramwell-Booth, *Catherine Booth: The Story,* 297. Ervine, *God's Soldier,* ii, 666. Wiggins, *History of the Salvation Army,* iv, 82.

14. James Strahan, *The Marechale,* 4th ed. (New York, 1921). Carolyn Scott, *The Heavenly Witch* (London, 1981). Sandall, *History of the Army,* 2:262f. Wiggins, *History of the Salvation Army,* 4:109. When William ordered Ballington and Maud to leave the U.S., he also ordered the Booth-Clibborns to move from France to Holland-Belgium. Some felt that William acted capriciously in these moves. Catherine Booth-Clibborn complained about the lack of influence territorial leaders had in army decisions. Her frustration was shared by other Booth children who resigned and, to some extent, by those who remained in the army. Around 1900, Arthur Booth-Clibborn became a disciple of John Alexander Dowie, founder of Zion City in Chicago, who presented himself as an Elijah announcing Christ's Second Coming. On 10 Jan. 1902, Catherine resigned from her father's army to join her husband at Zion City. She later withdrew from Dowie's sect and began her own evangelistic work. Nicol, *General Booth,* discusses each of the Booth children's resignations. On the Booth-Clibborns, see Nicol, *General Booth,* 255–61.

15. Frederick deL. Booth-Tucker, *The Consul* (New York, 1893), 138. When Emma's health failed in 1891, William Booth appointed the Tuckers as foreign secretaries (1891–96). When he sent them to the U.S. in 1896, Emma took the personal title of consul and had an active public ministry despite

being the mother of a large family. During the Tuckers' American command, the army grew from 2,000 officers and employees in 1896, to 3,284 in 1903; and from 700 corps and institutions to 911. Annual expenditures for poor relief rose from about $20,000 to $800,000 during that time, and the army in the U.S. served 300,000 free Christmas dinners in that 7-year period. In 1927–29, Booth-Tucker joined the rebellion which sought to democratize the army's selection of its general.

16. Ottman, *Herbert Booth*. Bramwell-Booth, *Bramwell Booth*, 186. In 1892–96, Herbert commanded the army in Canada. In 1896, instead of taking Ballington's place in New York as expected, he went to command Australasia, bearing the personal title of commandant. His oratory, musical ability, and gift for fundraising to support ambitious social and evangelical schemes made him, of the sons, most like his father. He resigned on 3 Feb. 1902, despite the fact that William regarded him as his chosen successor, should anything happen to Bramwell. Although Herbert accused his father of undermining his leadership through international headquarters' tyranny, Salvation Army historians treat Herbert well. Wiggins wrote: "His six-year term of command of Australasia was a period of dynamic leadership and all-around progress." *History of the Salvation Army*, 141.

17. Booth-Tucker, *Life of Catherine Booth*, 1:534. Begbie, *Life of Booth*, 1:307.

18. P. W. Wilson, *General Evangeline Booth of the Salvation Army* (New York, 1948). Troutt, *The General Was a Lady*. Sandall, *History of the Army*, 2:98. In 1929, Eva requested that Bramwell not name his successor as the organizational deed required and as William had done in 1912. Bramwell felt compelled to follow his father's will and insisted on naming the next general. As he slipped into his last illness, a council of international commissioners met near London to remove him, arguing that he was physically incompetent to continue as general. Eva had reason to believe that she would succeed her brother, but the high council elected Bramwell's chief-of-staff, Edward Higgins to be the third general. Eva went back to the U.S. to continue her 30-year command, until her 1934 election to succeed Higgins. In 1898, she had taken temporary command in the U.S. after Ballington resigned. See Nicol, *General Booth*, 233–51, on her role in Ballington's resignation. From Canada, Eva went to New York in 1904 to take up Booth-Tucker's work. She became general in 1933, at age 69, and retired to her home in Hartsdale, N.Y., in 1939, where she died on 17 June 1950. She agreed with her disputatious siblings on the need for more federalism in army polity, but, unlike them, she did not resign from the organization.

19. In 1894, Lucy took command of India for a second time, with Booth-Hellberg as her joint commander. In the family shakeup of 1896, the Booth-Hellbergs replaced the Booth-Clibborns in France until 1904. For the next five years, Booth-Hellberg was on sick furlough; he died in 1909. That year Lucy became commander for Denmark, and in 1926 for Norway. She became traveling commissioner in 1928 and resided in Stockholm with her only surviving daughter, Mildred. In 1933, Evangeline sent her to command South America West.

20. *War Cry,* 13 Apr. 1882, 4.

21. "Major Moore," *War Cry,* 18 Dec. 1880, 1.

22. Murdoch, "Frank Smith: Salvationist-Socialist."

23. Suzie F. Swift, sister-in-law of American commissioner Samuel Logan Brengle, left the Salvation Army in 1896 to become a Dominican nun; her papers are at Sinsinawa Dominican Convent, Sinsinawa, Wisconsin.

24. Brindley Boon, "Field Secretary's Notes," *War Cry,* 26 Feb. 1887, 2; 5 Mar. 1887, 8; 26 Mar. 1887, 8.

25. "Minute 44 of October 3" *War Cry,* 13 Oct. 1888, 2; Jan. 1889; and Chief Secretary Boon, "New 'Grade Department,'" *War Cry,* 7 Sept. 1889, 2. William Booth, "The General at the Circus, Bristol," *War Cry,* 12 Mar. 1887, 2. Kent, *Hold the Fort,* notes the army's insensitivity to working-class perspectives.

26. "Our First Examination in the Field Officer's Book," *War Cry,* 19 Mar. 1887, 8; on further development of army rules books see *War Cry,* 2 July 1887, 2; 9 July 1887,10; 23 July 1887, 3; and 3 Nov. 1888, 5.

27. "General Spends a Sunday at Regent Hall," *War Cry,* 4 Feb. 1888, 6.

28. "General's 60th Birthday," *War Cry,* 20 Apr. 1889, 1–4; "May Meeting—Exeter Hall," *War Cry,* 17 May 1890, 1–2.

29. *The Times* (London), 17 Jan. 1889, also asked why Booth had declined overtures from the Archbishop of Canterbury. See Murdoch, "Salvation Army and Church of England," for treatment of the 1882 negotiations.

30. George S. Railton, *Twenty-One Years,* 1886. "Annual Report, 1889," *War Cry,* 4 Jan. 1890, 5.

31. "Our May Meeting," *War Cry,* 14 May 1887, 8; and 8 Oct. 1887, 2; all report that the army had sent out 800 cadets in 12 months. "Training Home Banquet," *War Cry,* 5 Nov. 1887, 5–6; Suzie F. Swift, "The Village War," *War Cry,* 5 Nov. 1887, 1–2.

32. "Field Secretary's Notes," *War Cry,* 11 June 1887, 10. "Junior Soldiers War," *War Cry,* 14 Jan. 1888, 9–10. George S. Railton, "How to Make Junior Soldiers," *War Cry,* 5 May 1888, 2.

33. Nicol, *General Booth,* 309–10.

34. "Justice for Ireland," *War Cry,* 19 May 1890, 5. John Coutts, *The Salvationists,* 97–111. Nicol, *General Booth,* 310–17, on Europe.

35. Nicol, *General Booth,* 317–23. Harry Williams, CBE, FRCS, Edin. (medical certifications), *Booth-Tucker: William Booth's First Gentleman* (London, 1980), 71–99.

36. Harry Williams, *Booth-Tucker,* 121, 80, 56–70, was a Salvation Army medical missionary in India. He quotes from the *1884 Annual Report of the Gujarat Presbyterian Mission, The Times* (London), and *Harvest Field,* 96–97. Ervine, *God's Soldier,* 2, 555–76, 539–44. The author interviewed J. Wascom Pickett in 1965 at Asbury Theological Seminary, Wilmore, Kentucky. Kent, *Hold the Fort,* found that revival sects, at odds with major denominations, pointed out wastefulness and lack of initiative in bringing about conversions. See John Coutts, *The Salvationists,* 140–47. Other biographies of Booth-Tucker include: F. A. MacKenzie, *Booth-Tucker: Sadhu and Saint* (London, 1930); Booth-Tucker, *Muktifauj, or Forty Years with the Salvation Army in India and Ceylon* (London, 1912); Booth-Tucker, *Life Links,* privately published, 1888; and Booth-Tucker, *The Consul.*

37. See Harry Williams, *Booth-Tucker,* 220–46, on Booth-Tucker's dispute with his brother-in-law Bramwell Booth in 1929.

38. "Emigration to Canada," *War Cry,* 14 May and 23 July 1887.

39. My statistics come primarily from *War Cry* (London), and Nicol, *General Booth,* 323–34. The army's failure to develop a membership out of converts began in 1875–77. Statistics show a decline in the U.S. from 1900 to 1910, with periodic resurgence and stagnation since. By 1929, there were 1,052 corps; there were 1,097 in 1990. Thus there was no net growth in half a century. There was an average of 71 soldiers per corps after 50 years in the U.S.; after a hundred years, the U.S. had about the same number of corps as had existed in East London in 1888. Studies show that the army has the same number of members per church as other working-class denominations, around 70, and similar standards for membership. In the level of giving, however, salvationists lag far behind other working-class Wesleyan sects (Nazarenes, Wesleyans, and Free Methodists).

Douglas W. Johnson, Paul R. Picard, Bernard Quinn, *Churches and Church Membership in the United States, 1971* (Washington, D.C., 1974), report that the Salvation Army in the U.S. in 1971 had 74,967 members in 1,043 corps, for an average of 72. The largest holiness denomination, Nazarenes, had 398,714 members in 4,640 churches, averaging 85.93. Free

Methodists had 46,514 members in 1,075 churches, for an average of 43.27. Wesleyans had 76,016 members in 1,792 churches, averaging 42.42. The army's U.S. base was in the western south-central, eastern north-central, and western north-central regions, the fringes of the Bible Belt. Thus the army's original appeal to evangelical Protestants continues. But, unlike other working-class Wesleyan sects, the army's income is from sources outside its membership. For Salvation Army statistics worldwide, see H. Wakelin Coxill, Kenneth Grubb, eds., *World Christian Handbook,* 1968 (Nashville, Tenn., 1967), and later eds.; and *The Salvation Army Year Book, 1994* (London 1994).

40. William Booth, "The General's Letter," #4, *War Cry,* 13 Dec. 1884, 2; and #9, "The One Salvation Army," 24 Jan. 1885, 1.

41. William Booth, "The General's Letter," #23, 2 May 1885; "Neutrality," 12 June 1886, 3; Frank Smith, "With the General," 13 Aug. 1887, 8;

42. "Two Days in Birmingham," *War Cry,* 21 June 1890, 5. "Our May Meeting," *War Cry,* 14 May 1887, 8; The New York *War Cry* also sought out salvationist Jews in late 1887. There was no report of success.

43. "The One Salvation Army," *War Cry,* 31 Jan. 1885, 1; "Yorkshire Division," *War Cry,* 28 Feb. 1885, 1; "The General at Woolwich," *War Cry,* 14 Mar. 1885, 1; and "All Around," *War Cry,* 8 Apr. 1885, 3. "Commissioner Newberry, India," *War Cry* (U.S.), 1 Apr. 1984, observed that India's Salvation Army could not exist without outside funds, most of which were used for the army's social programs.

44. "Great Meeting of Field and Subaltern Officers in London," *War Cry,* 20 Jan. 1886, 2. "The Consecration of the Fifty," *War Cry,* 9 July 1887, 3.

45. "Field Secretary's Notes," *War Cry,* 15 May 1886, 2; "Ex-Colonel Day," *War Cry,* 11 Sept. 1886, 8, 10; "Field Secretary's Notes," *War Cry,* 25 Sept. 1886, 2; and "Field Secretary's Notes," *War Cry,* 9 Oct. 1886, 2. Henry Edmunds, *My Adventures with General Booth,* (London), unpub. ms., British Library, discusses the 1889–91 struggle over administrative democratization. Former ADC Samuel Horatio Hodges also published his quarrel with Booth's autocracy. Several dissidents lost court cases and the Booth autocracy lasted until 1929, when Bramwell lost his case for family control, both in the army's high council and then in court. Parliament passed a new Salvation Army organizational act in 1931.

46. William Booth, "The Future of Missions," *War Cry,* 18 May 1889, 1.

7. Wholesale Salvation: Darkest England's Social Reform

1. Andrew Mearns, *The Bitter Cry of Outcast London* (London, 1883).
2. Warren Sylvester Smith, *The London Heretics, 1870–1914* (London, 1967), 15.
3. See Norman H. Murdoch, "Rose Culture and Social Reform: Edward Bellamy's *Looking Backward* (1888) and William Booth's *Darkest England and the Way Out* (1890)," *Utopian Studies* 3 (1992): 91–101.
4. Frederick Coutts, *Bread for My Neighbour*, 35–38, argues that scholars have ignored and mistreated Booth, whose social concern was continuous throughout his life.
5. Staff Capt. Ewens, "The Salvation Army's Reply to *The Bitter Cry*," *War Cry*, 25 Dec. 1883, 1–2. Catherine Booth, "Brighton," *War Cry*, 2 Feb. 1884, 2. "The General at Winsford," *Winsford and Middlewich Guardian*, qtd. in *War Cry*, 16 Feb. 1884, 1. Booth stated that there is "one remedy," salvation. Eighteen years as a missioner had taught him that salvation will clothe the naked and "change their miserable hearts and make them happy."
6. Frederick Coutts, *Bread for My Neighbour*, 35, 45. Sandall, *History of the Army*, 3:11. E. Drabble, "More Rescue Work," *War Cry*, 17 Mar. 1883, 1. Maj. Henry Edmunds, "Midnight Rescue Work in Glasgow," *War Cry*, 24 Mar. 1885, 1; and 28 Apr. 1883, 1; Capt. Melvena Molland, "Our Midnight Brigade—Why a Home Is Necessary," *War Cry*, 23 May 1883, 2. "Opening of Victoria House Home of Rescue," *War Cry*, 2 June 1883, 1. George S. Railton, *Twenty-One Years*, 208. Bramwell-Booth, *Bramwell Booth*, 178, reported that "Booth at first hesitated" to take on this additional financial burden.
7. Sandall, *History of the Army*, 1:169, 3:3–10. Watson, *Soldier Saint*, 70–79. Bramwell Booth, "Special Efforts Wanted in 1884 for the Salvation of Special Classes," *War Cry*, 25 Dec. 1883, 1. Bramwell Booth listed tradesmen, publicans, and the ill, as well as prisoners. "Our Melbourne Prison-Gate Brigade," *War Cry*, 2 July 1884, 1. Deborah Railton, "Were You Ever in Prison?" *War Cry*, 13 Aug. 1884, 4.
8. B. B. Cox, "In and Out of Seven Dials," *War Cry*, 13 Nov. 1884, 3. "Cellar, Gutter, and Garret," *War Cry*, 25 Dec. 1884, 1; 4 Mar. 1885, 1; 18 Apr. 1885, 1; and 19 Aug. 1885, 1. Cadet Sarah E. Owen, "Cellar, Gutter, and Garret Work in Seven Dials," *War Cry*, 17 Jan. 1885, 4. Frederick Coutts, *Bread for My Neighbour*, 38. Sandall, *History of the Army*, 3:20. Allen F. Davis, *Spearheads for Reform* (New York, 1967), 3–12.

9. "The General's Letter," #31, "Fallen Women," *War Cry,* 11 July 1885, 1, de-
    plored "traffic in the bodies and souls" of 50,000 "young, ignorant, inno-
    cent girls to gratify" the lust of 300,000 "heartless men, many of whom
    boast of superior station and education, and . . . religion," three-fourths of
    them married.

10. The following deal with the Maiden Tribute—Armstrong case. Raymond L.
    Schults, *Crusader in Babylon: W. T. Stead and the Pall Mall Gazette* (Lin-
    coln, Neb., 1972), 133–67. Ann Stafford, *The Age of Consent* (London,
    1964). Madge Unsworth, *Maiden Tribute* (London, 1949). Ervine, *God's
    Soldier,* 2:632–58. Begbie, *Life of Booth,* 2:37–53. Bramwell-Booth,
    Bramwell Booth, 178–84. Bramwell Booth, *Echoes and Memories,* 115–32.
    Frederick Coutts, *Bread for My Neighbour,* 45–62. Rebecca Jarrett, unpub.
    ms., Salvation Army Archives, London, 1926, consists of autobiographical
    fragments written when author was 80 years old. "Babylon: or the *Pall Mall
    Gazette* and The Salvation Army on Corruption, Cruelties, and Crime of
    London," July 1885, unpubished ms., British Library, London.

11. "Protection of Young Girls, Great Mass Meeting of Women in Exeter Hall,"
    War Cry, 29 July 1885, 1. "General's Letter: New National Scheme for the
    Deliverance of Unprotected Girls and the Rescue of Fallen Women," *War
    Cry,* 8 Aug. 1885, 1–2. "Petition and May Day Procession through the City
    to the House of Commons," *War Cry,* 8 Aug. 1885, 1–2. "The General's
    Letter," #34, "The New Act," *War Cry,* 15 Aug. 1885, 1.

12. Catherine Booth, "Letter to Rich Friends," *War Cry,* 11 Sept. 1886, 8. See
    "The Salvation Army in a 'Christian Nation,'" *War Cry,* 7 May 1887, 6; and
    "Slum Work," *War Cry,* 7 Jan. 1888, 9.

13. William Booth, "Socialism," *War Cry,* 27 Feb. 1886, 9. See also Suzie F.
    Swift, "Sociology and Salvation," pt. 1, *All the World* 6 (Jan. 1890): 39–41,
    and pt. 2 *All the World* 6 (Mar. 1890): 110–13. James Vint, "With the Gen-
    eral, Nottingham," *War Cry,* 3 Apr. 1886, 3.

14. "Short Cuts to High Ideals," *Pall Mall Gazette,* 29 May 1886. Francis W. L.
    Adams, *Australian Essays* (Melbourne, 1886).

15. Murdoch, "Frank Smith, Salvationist-Socialist." Jones, *Outcast London,* 337.
    E. I. Champness, *Frank Smith, M.P.: Pioneer and Modern Mystic* (London,
    1942). "Life of Frank Smith, M.P.," *Nuneaton Observer,* 8 Jan. 1943. "Life of
    Frank Smith, Socialist Pioneer," *South London Press,* 17 Jan. 1943. "The
    London Major Frank Smith's Account of Himself," *War Cry,* 21 Sept. 1882.
    "Commissioner Frank Smith, United States," *War Cry,* 29 May 1886, 7; *War
    Cry,* 10 July 1886, 10.

16. Frank Smith, "On the March," *War Cry,* 30 July 1887, 7, 9. On Henry George, see *War Cry,* 6 Aug. 1887, 9. On Glasgow visit, see Frank Smith, "With the General in Scotland," *War Cry,* 24 Sept. 1887, 7.

17. On Smith relapse, see *War Cry,* 22 Oct. 1887, 9. Brindley Boon, *War Cry,* 3 Dec. 1887, 2, continued to oppose social reform as an affirmative to "inner change."

18. M. Gordon Dill, "A Day from the Life of a Slum Officer," *War Cry,* 7 Apr. 1888, 1–2. M. Gordon Dill, "How the Poor Die," 12 May 1888, 1–2. Margaret Allen, "Rescue Facts," *War Cry,* 31 Mar. 1888, 6; Margaret Allen, "Midnight London," *War Cry,* 2 Mar. 1888, 5. Mahlah, "Sharp Practice, *War Cry,* 3 Mar. 1888, 1–2; Mahlah, "Life Sketches," *War Cry* 31 Mar. 1888, 5; Mahlah, "Tanzen: A Gipsy's Story," *War Cry,* 19 May 1888, 1–2. Mahlah, "Horrible London," *War Cry,* 3 Nov. 1888, 1–2. James Cooke, "Slum Warfare," *War Cry,* 12 May 1888, 8; James Cooke, "London Slum Work," *War Cry,* 4 Aug. 1888, 7. For Jack the Ripper's influence on the army's work, see *War Cry,* 13 October 1888, 2; "Another Murder," *War Cry,*17 Nov. 1888, 9; "Latest White Chapel Murder," *War Cry,* 1 Dec. 1888, 1.

19. "Salvation Army Rescue Work," *War Cry,* 23 June 1888, 8. Maj. James Cooke, "To Field Officers and Slum Candidates," *War Cry,* 19 July 1890, 13. Beatrice Webb, *Our Partnership* (New York, 1948), 400.

20. "The Salvation Army and the Sweating System—The Latest Slander," *War Cry,* 12 May 1888, 8; "The Salvation Army and the Sweating System," *War Cry,* 19 May 1888, 8–9, contains Bramwell Booth's response. Norman Longmate, *Milestones in Working Class History* (London, 1975), 70–71. *The Times* (London) 25 Dec. 1888. Ellen Pash, "A Unique Failure," *All the World* 6 (Jan.–May 1890): 5–9, 51–57, 114–19, 184–88, 221–23.

21. "The General and the Home Secretary," *War Cry,* 22 Dec. 1888, 9. See *War Cry,* 5 Jan. 1889, 11, for rejection of the proposal. "Our Food and Shelter Scheme," *War Cry,* 26 Jan. 1889, 3. *The Times* (London) 17 Jan. 1889. "Hanbury St. Shelter for Women," *War Cry,* 25 May 1889, 13. "Fifth Anniversary of Rescue Work," *War Cry,* 1 June 1889, 5–6. *Deliverer,* 22 June 1889, 10. Norman H. Murdoch, *European Idea Sources of William Booth's Darkest England Scheme of 1890* (Lanark, Scotland, 1989), discusses the influence of Meath and others outside the army on Booth.

22. George S. Railton, "My Last Lecture," *War Cry,* 25 May 1889, 10. William Booth, "The Wonderful Salvation Army Machine," *War Cry,* 20 July 1889, 9. *War Cry,* 27 July 1889, 7.

23. On the 1889 Dock Strike, see *War Cry,* 7 Sept. 1889, 2, 9, and 10; 14 Sept.

1889, 7; 21 Sept. 1889, 2, 9, and 10; 28 Sept. 1889, 2, 8, 9, and 13; and 5
Oct. 1889, 8 and 10. On Whitechapel as a food depot, see "Ramblings in
the East End,"*War Cry,* 2 Nov. 1889, 2; and "'272' Becomes Food and Shelter Headquarters," *War Cry,* 9 Nov. 1889, 7. Worldly Wiseman, "The Salvation Army and the Strike," *London Daily News,* qtd. in *War Cry,* 28 Sept.
1889, 2.

24. Suzie F. Swift, "Glimpses of East End Life," *War Cry,* 25 Dec. 1889, 17–18.
Long Fellow, "Our Dockers and Our Army," *War Cry,* 25 Dec. 1889, 22–23.

25. On Barker: *War Cry,* 11, 8; and 18 Jan. 1890, 7. On Boon: "Chief Secretary," *War Cry,* 8 Mar. 1890, 2. On U.S. slum work: *War Cry,* 22 Mar. 1890,
4. On cadets in slum shelters: *War Cry,* 5 Apr. 1890, 8.

26. Smith was at the 24 Feb., 1890 opening of the Westminster Shelter #5. For
Smith's March–June 1890 activities, see *War Cry,* 29 Mar. 1890, 9; 5 Apr.
1890, 8; 12 Apr. 1890, 5; 19 Apr. 1890, 9; 26 Apr. 1890, 4; 10 May 1890, 5
and 8; 7 June 1890, 5, 9; 14 June 1890, 8–9; and 28 June 1890, 5, 16. Smith
could not keep an engagement when he was "wired to Clapton," where
William Booth worked on the social scheme as Catherine Booth lay dying
of cancer. *War Cry,* 24 May 1890, 2.

27. "Booth v. Ferritt," *War Cry,* 17 May 1890, 9.

28. W. T. Stead, *Review of Reviews* (June 1890) quoted in *War Cry,* 14 June
1890, 10. Frank Smith, "All About the 'Wing,'" *War Cry:,*5 July 1890, 6;
Frank Smith, "The Social Reform Wing," 12 July 1890, 4; and Frank Smith,
"Feathers From the Social Reform Wing," 19 July 1890, 6. Frank Smith, "The
Social Reform Wing," *War Cry,* 26 July 1890, 5. Begbie, *Life of Booth,* 2:165.
William Booth, *Darkest England and the Way Out* (Chicago, 1890; rptd.
London, 1970), 107–110, 158–59.

29. *Star,* 2 Jan. 1891, qtd. in Sandall, *History of the Army,* 3:325–26. W. T.
Stead, "The Book of the Month," *Review of Reviews* (Nov. 1890), 492–507,
acknowledged William Booth's reluctance concerning the scheme.
Frederick Whyte, *The Life of W. T. Stead* (London, 1925), 2:13.

30. When Herbert Spencer, in the *Times,* challenged William Booth's control,
Bramwell Booth responded; see his *Echoes and Memories,* 201–8.

31. William Booth, *Darkest England,* 116–17, 306–8. Sandall, *History of the
Army,* 3:101–3.

32. William Booth, *Darkest England,* 118, 182, 158–59. Sandall, *History of the
Army,* 3:136. Walter Besant, "The Farm and the City," *Living Age* 216 (29
Jan. 1898), 306–7. Harold C. Steele, *I Was a Stranger* (New York, 1954),
159, 100.

33. H. Rider Haggard, *Regeneration, Being an Account of the Social Work of The Salvation Army in Great Britain* (London, 1910), 199; on Boxted Colony, see 200–205. H. Rider Haggard, *The Poor and the Land, Being a Report on the Salvation Army Colonies in the United States and at Hadleigh, England with Scheme of National Land Settlement* (London, 1905), xiii, 146.

34. Sandall, *History of the Army*, 3:358. As late as 1907, Bramwell Booth discussed the oversea colony with Winston Churchill. Richard Collier, *The General Next to God* (New York, 1955), 197. Begbie, *Life of Booth*, 2:367, indicates that in 1908, William Booth brought the scheme up in conversation with Lloyd-George. Norman H. Murdoch, "Anglo-American Salvation Army Farm Colonies, 1890–1910," *Communal Societies* 3 (Fall 1983): 111–21.

35. Inglis, *Churches and the Working Classes*, 201–3. Paul Thompson, *Socialists, Liberals and Labour*, 158. Steele, *I Was a Stranger*, 55–56, 128–33. J. Keir Hardie, "Frank Smith, L.C.C.," *Labour Prophet* (Sept. 1894): 113. *In Brightest England (Looking Forward); or, 'General' Booth's Scheme Eclipsed* (London, 1891), 16, 61.

36. *Methodist Times*, 18 Sept. 1890, 956, 958.

37. Murdoch, *European Idea Sources*.

38. T. H. Huxley, *Evolution and Ethics and Other Essays* (New York, 1989). On Charles Loch's Charity Organization Society, see Paul Thompson, *Socialists, Liberals and Labour*, 91–99.

39. Stead, *Mrs. Booth*, 208. Stead nevertheless praised Catherine Booth as "a Socialist of the heart," W. T. Stead, "The Late Mrs. Booth," *Warley*, 11 Oct. 1890, 8.

40. Watson, *Soldier Saint*, 13–15, 121, 128, 144, 179, 238, 181–82.

41. Frank Smith, "Sociology: The Lord's Prayer in Eight Volleys," *War Cry*, 30 Aug. 1890, 4; 4 Oct. 1890, 11; 1 Nov. 1890, 11; 29 Nov. 1890, 6. Hardie, "Frank Smith," 113.

42. "The Salvation Army: A Serious Crisis," *The Times* (London), 26 Dec. 1890, 5. "The Salvation Army: Official Statement on Commissioner Smith's Resignation," *The Times* (London), 30 Dec. 1890, 5. "Frank Smith Resignation," *War Cry*, 3 Jan. 1891. On Smith's 1901 return to the Salvation Army, see: Kenneth D. Morgan, *Keir Hardie: Radical and Socialist* (London, 1975), 111; and "Brigadier Frank Smith," *War Cry*, 30 Nov. 1901. A. M. McBriar, *Fabian Socialism and English Politics, 1832–85* (Cambridge, England, 1966), 198. Morgan, *Keir Hardie*, 45. and Paul Thompson, *Socialists, Liber-*

als and Labour, 158. Frank Smith, *The Betrayal of Bramwell Booth* (London, 1929). Murdoch, "Frank Smith, Salvationist-Socialist."

43. Begbie, *Life of Booth,* 2:183. Peter J. Hoffman, "Social Policy in the Last Quarter of the Twentieth Century," paper delivered at the 1978 Salvation Army Social Conference, London, 2–3.

Bibliographical Essay

Published works on the Salvation Army by professional and amateur historians have depended on access to data held by the army and, on occasion, have been subject to army censorship. Nevertheless, since 1965, serious studies of the army have pierced its secrecy by examining documentary sources. Several books led this trend: Bernard Watson's *Soldier Saint: George Scott Railton* (London: Hodder and Stoughton, 1970) exposed Railton's irate opposition to the army's social emphasis after 1890. R. G. Moyles's *The Blood and Fire in Canada* (Toronto: Peter Martin, 1977) brought a balanced but critical approach to Salvation Army history. Such analyses seek to escape prior Salvation Army censorship by a "literary board." Other works which analyze as well as describe include: Frederick Coutts, *Bread for My Neighbor* (London: Hodder & Stoughton, 1978); John Coutts, *The Salvationists* (London: Mowbrays, 1977); John Coutts, *This We Believe* (London: Challenge Books, 1980); and K. S. Inglis, chapter 5, in *Churches and the Working Classes in Victorian England* (London: Routledge and Kegan Paul, 1963). Other important contemporary historians include Roger Green, George Hazell, Ronald Holz, Glen K. Horridge, E. H. McKinley, Christine Parkyn, David Rightmire, and Harry Williams.

Numerous scholars have written probing essays cited in this book's notes. My attempts at Salvation Army history are several. On Salvationist–Irish Roman Catholic clashes: Norman H. Murdoch, "Salvation Army Disturbances in Liverpool, England, 1879–1887," *Journal of Social History* 25 (Spring 1992): 575–93; "From Militancy to Social Mission: The Salvation Army and Street Disturbances in Liverpool, 1879–1887," in *Popular Politics, Riot and Labour: Essays in Liverpool History, 1790–1940*, edited by John Belchem, 160–72 (Liverpool, England: Liverpool University Press, 1992); and, with Howard F. McMains, "The Salvation Army Disturbances of 1885," *Queen City Heritage: Journal of the Cincinnati Historical Society* 45 (Summer 1987): 31–39. I wrote "Rose Culture and Social Reform: Edward Bellamy's *Looking Backward* (1888) and William Booth's *Darkest England* (1890)," *Utopian Studies* 3 (Fall 1992), 91–101. As managing editor of *Christian History*'s "Booth Edition" (1990), I wrote five articles on the Booths. And I wrote *European Idea Sources of William Booth's Darkest England Scheme of 1890* (Lanark, Scotland: New Lanark Conservation Trust, 1989); "Evangelical Sources of Salvation Army Doctrine," *Evangelical Quarterly* 59 (July 1987): 235–44; "The Salvation Army's U.S.

Arrival," *Organization of American Historians Newsletter* 15 (May 1987): 12–13; "A Protestant Hospital for Covington: Booth Memorial Hospital, 1915–1985," *Journal of Kentucky Studies* 3 (Oct. 1986): 107–49; "The Salvation Army and the Church of England, 1882–1883," *Historical Magazine of the Protestant Episcopal Church* 55 (Mar. 1986): 31–55; *The Salvation Army in Cincinnati, 1885–1985* (Cincinnati, Ohio: Salvation Army, 1985); *The Salvation Army: An Anglo-American Revivalist Social Mission* (Ann Arbor, Mich.: University Microfilms, 1985); "Wesleyan Influences on William and Catherine Booth," *Wesleyan Theological Journal* 20 (Fall 1985): 97–103; "Female Ministry in the Thought and Work of Catherine Booth," *Church History* 53 (Sept. 1984): 363–78; and "Anglo-American Salvation Army Farm Colonies, 1890–1910," *Communal Societies* 3 (Fall 1983): 111–21.

After it observed its centenary in 1965, the Salvation Army began to collect documents at archives in Britain, the U.S., and Canada. Most sources I list here can be found in these archives, where I have done much of my research. Primary sources frequently reveal a movement quite different from the one salvationists and others know. Three years after Booth began his East End mission, he published the *East London Evangelist* (1868–69), a magazine that reported policy statements and statistics, as did its successors: *Christian Mission Magazine* (1870–78), *Salvationist* (1879), and *War Cry*, international and local editions, since 27 Dec. 1879. Particularly useful for the early period are Christian Mission Conference, *Minutes,* 1870–78; and George Scott Railton's *Heathen England* (London: S. W. Partridge, 1877) and *Twenty-One Year's Salvation Army* (London: Salvation Army, 1886).

Salvation Army journals and pamphlets deal with social (*Social Gazette*), rescue (*Deliverer*), and missionary (*All the World*) work; auxiliaries (*Conqueror*); doctrine (*Handbook of Doctrine, The Sacraments, The Salvation Army Directory*); rituals (*Salvation Army Ceremonies*); hymns (*The Song Book of the Salvation Army*); deeds (*Foundation Deed,* 1875; *Annulment Deed,* 1878; *Deed of Constitution,* 1878; *Salvation Army, Certificate of Incorporation and By-Laws,* New York, 1899; *Supplemental Deed,* 1904; *Social Trust Deed,* 1891; *Salvation Army Act,* 1931; *Deed of Variation,* 1965; *Salvation Army Act,* 1968); opinions (*Officer*); *Orders and Regulations* for various ranks and offices; yearbooks (*All About The Salvation Army,* 1882–88; *The Salvation War,* 1882–85; *The Reason Why,* 1887; *The Coming Army,* 1888; and *The Advance of the Salvation Army,* 1893–94, *Year Book* for recent years); and directories (*Disposition of Forces*).

Secondary sources often contain primary sources. Otherwise, because they were written by salvationists who received the army's blessing, they are useful primarily for determining salvationist views at the time of writing. A seven-volume official *History of the Salvation Army,* Sandall, vols. 1, 2, and 3; Wiggins vols. 4, 5; F. Coutts vols. 6–7, (London: Nelson and Hodder and Stoughton, 1947–86) covers the period from 1865 through the 1970s. It is a useful source of facts about the army, but the authors show little curiosity about why the army developed in the way it did. Surprisingly, this official work is the only complete work on the army as an international organization. Other books and articles, some by professional historians, provide army history by city, nation, or program. Biographies fill gaps not treated in general histories, but these works too tend to lack interpretation. Nevertheless, there is hope that recent professional histories will produce a clear picture of why the army has become the kind of organization it is today.

An enormous literature exists by the various Booths and about their roles in the army's history to 1939, when Evangeline retired as general. What remains of the family's papers arrived at the British Library in 1989, but much of the material already was available in published works. Standard biographies of William Booth are Harold Begbie's authorized *Life of General William Booth,* 2 vols. (New York: Macmillan, 1920); and St. John Ervine's more perceptive *God's Soldier: General William Booth,* 2 vols. (New York: Macmillan, 1934). Earlier studies by W. T. Stead, *General Booth* (London: Isbister, 1891); and George Scott Railton, *General Booth* (London: Hodder and Stoughton, 1912), are useful. A more recent uncritical work is Richard Collier, *The General Next to God* (New York: Collins, 1955). William's most important writings are *How to Reach the Masses with the Gospel* (London: Marshall, Morgan, Chase and Scott, 1872), early Christian Mission history; and *In Darkest England and the Way Out* (Chicago, 1890; rptd. London: Charles Knight, 1970), social reform ideas produced by Frank Smith with W. T. Stead. Major journals carried *Darkest England* reviews. Booth's views on the Salvation Army are contained in "What Is the Salvation Army?" *Contemporary Review* 42 (Aug. 1882): 175–82. *Contemporary Review* 42 also published studies of Booth by Randall T. Davidson, Frances Power Cobb, and Cardinal Manning (Aug.–Oct. 1882). Booth also compiled *The Christian Mission Hymn Book* (London, 1876). His ideas on missionary work are in "The Millennium, or, The Ultimate Triumph of Salvation Army Principles," *All the World* 6 (1890): 337–43.

A. M. Nicol, *General Booth and the Salvation Army* (London: Herbert and Daniel, 1910); and Henry Edmunds, "My Adventures with William Booth" (unpub. ms., British Library, London), are critical of Booth. Books criticizing the Darkest England scheme include: Bernard Bosanquet, *"In Darkest England," On the Wrong Track* (London: Swan Sonnenschein, 1898); Helen Bosanquet, *Social Work in London, 1869–1912* (London: John Murray, 1914); Philip Dwyer, *General*

Booth's Submerged Tenth, or the Wrong Way to Do the Right Thing (London: Swan Sonnenschein, 1891); and T. H. Huxley, "Social Diseases and Worse Remedies" (*Times* correspondence, 1891) in *Evolution and Ethics and Other Essays,* (New York: D. Appleton, 1896). Many supported the scheme: H. Rider Haggard, *The Poor and the Land* (London: Longmans, Green, 1905), and *Regeneration, Being an Account of the Social Work of The Salvation Army in Great Britain* (London: Longmans, Green, 1910); Theodore Roosevelt, "Rider Haggard and the Salvation Army," *Outlook* (May–Aug. 1910): 476–77; Arnold White, "The Truth About the Salvation Army," *Fortnightly Review* (July 1892): 111–24; and Arnold White, *The Great Idea* (London: Salvation Army, 1910). A recent analysis of Darkest England is Frederick Coutts, *Bread for My Neighbour* (London: Hodder and Stoughton, 1978).

Catherine's authorized biographer was her verbose son-in-law, Frederick deL. Booth-Tucker, *The Life of Catherine Booth*, 2 vols. (London: Salvationist Pub., 1892; 3rd ed., London, 1924). Granddaughter Catherine Bramwell-Booth wrote *Catherine Booth: The Story of Her Loves* (London: Hodder and Stoughton, 1970). W. T. Stead, *Mrs. Booth of the Salvation Army* (London: Nisbet, 1900); Bramwell Booth, *On the Banks of the River* (London: Salvation Army, 1894); and Mildred Duff, *Catherine Booth* (London: Salvation Army, 1901) are early volumes by admirers. Catherine Booth wrote apologies for her own ideas and for her husband's mission: *Female Ministry: Woman's Right to Preach the Gospel* (1859, now unavailable in its unexpurgated form; abridged ed. (New York: Salvation Army,1975); *Aggressive Christianity* (London: Salvation Army,1880); *Godliness* (London: Salvation Army, 1881); *Life and Death* (London: Salvation Army, 1883); *Popular Christianity* (London: Salvation Army, 1884); *The Salvation Army in Relation to Church and State* (London: Salvation Army: 1883); and pamphlets.

Bramwell Booth's *Echoes and Memories* (London: Hodder and Stoughton, 1925); his *These Fifty Years* (London: Cassell, 1929); and a biography by his daughter, Catherine Bramwell-Booth, *Bramwell Booth* (London: Rich and Cowan, 1933), are less revealing than a debate about his deposition as general: F. A. MacKenzie, *Clash of the Cymbals* (New York: Bertano, 1929); and Frank Smith, *The Betrayal of Bramwell Booth* (London: Jarrold, 1929).

Ballington Booth wrote *From Ocean to Ocean* (New York: Ogilvie, 1891); his wife Maud Booth wrote *Beneath Two Flags* (New York: Funk and Wagnalls, 1889). See "Commander and Mrs. Booth's Statement of Explanation Regarding the Causes which Led to Their Expressing Inability to Take Another Command," unpub. ms., 1896. Susan F. Welty, *Look Up and Hope!* (New York: Nelson, 1961), describes Maud's life.

Catherine Booth-Clibborn recalled *Ten Years' War in the French and Swiss Republics,* (London: Salvation Army, 1891). James Strahan, *The Marechale* (New York: George H. Doran, 1921); and Carolyn Scott, *The Heavenly Witch* (London: Hamish Hamilton, 1981), are her biographies.

Frederick Booth-Tucker penned Emma's life, *The Consul* (New York: Salvation Army, 1893); *Darkest India* (Bombay: Gazette Steam Printing Works, 1891); *The Salvation Army in the United States* (New York: Reliance, 1904); *Muktifauj, or Forty Years with the Salvation Army in India and Ceylon* (London: Marshall, 1912); and articles on farm colonies. Other biographies include: *Life Links,* privately published, at Salvation Army Archives, London; F. A. MacKenzie, *Booth-Tucker: Sadhu and Saint* (London: Hodder and Stoughton, 1930); and Harry Williams, *Booth-Tucker: William Booth's First Gentleman* (London: Hodder and Stoughton, 1980). Ford C. Ottman wrote *Herbert Booth* (New York: Doubleday, Doran, 1928). Eva's biographers are: P. Whitwell Wilson, *General Evangeline Booth* (New York: Revell, 1935); Margaret Troutt, *The General Was a Lady: The Story of Evangeline Booth* (Nashville, Tenn.: Holman, 1980). Lucy and Marian have no biographer, nor do spouses Florence E. Soper Booth, Arthur Sidney Booth-Clibborn, Cornelie Schoch Booth, or Emanuel Booth-Hellberg.

Books by ex-Salvationists that criticize the Booths are: J. J. R. Redstone, *An Ex-Captain's Experiences of the Salvation Army* (London: Christian Commonwealth Pub., 1888); Albert Muspratt, *The Salvation Army: Is It a Benefit to Religion?* (Ripon, England: Harrison, 1884); *The New Papacy: Behind the Scenes in the Salvation Army by an Ex–Staff Officer* (Toronto, Canada: Britmell, 1889); Samuel Horatio Hodges, *General Booth, "the Family," and the Salvation Army* (Manchester, England: n.p. 1890); John Manson, *The Salvation Army and the Public* (London: Routledge, 1906); and Brian Lunn, *Salvation Dynasty* (London: Wm. Hodge, 1936).

On American revivalist influence on Victorian England and the Booths, see Richard Carwardine, *Transatlantic Revivalism: Popular Evangelicalism in Britain and America, 1790–1865* (London: Greenwood, 1978); and John Kent, *Holding the Fort: Studies in Victorian Revivalism* (London: Epworth, 1978). Others hint at transatlantic influences, but Carwardine and Kent include the Booths as prominent among those who fell under the American spell. In the 1880s, Frank Smith transmitted to William reform ideas Smith had encountered in England, America, and on a European tour, proposing them as the answer to the army's failure to save the wretches of the urban slums, as it had claimed to do. Urban workshops, back-to-the-land programs, and emigration all are proposed in the 1880s utopian literature. Smith's interest in social reform was sparked by his reading of Henry George's *Progress and Poverty* (1879; reprint, New York: Robert Schalkenbach Foundation, 1981) and by personal meetings with George ("Henry George on the Salvation Army," *War Cry,* New York, 26 Dec. 1890). Smith also was inspired by Edward Bellamy's *Looking Backward* (1888; reprint New York: Penguin, 1985).

Smith has not received credit for ideas he contributed to the Salvation Army's social program. E. I. Champness, *Frank Smith, M.P.: Pioneer and Modern Mystic* (London: Whitefriars, 1942), focuses on Smith's spiritualism, which he shared with Keir Hardie and, by Champness's account, with the Booths. J. Keir Hardie, Smith's political mentor, wrote "Frank Smith, L.C.C.," *Labour Prophet* (Sept. 1894), 113–14. Smith's second-fiddle position, in both the Salvation Army and the Independent Labour Party (where he was second to Hardie and to George Lansbury), has made it difficult to identify his contributions.

Tension between the army's early revivalism and late social reform impulses is implicit and explicit in its literature. A recent "Memorandum on the Indivisibility of the Socio-Religious Structure of The Salvation Army for the Confidential Guidance of Salvation Army Officers," Salvation Army Archives, Alexandria, Virginia, points to the constant need to explain the dual mission. This document holds that "religion makes the difference" and reigns as the army's primary purpose: "Take away our budgets and leave us our religion and The Salvation Army will continue to flourish and to serve wherever there is a need." But the memorandum, like the army's official history, ignores the fact that Booth found that revivalist religion could not penetrate urban slums. The army's love for revivalism lingers, but social services remain the answer to its difficulty surviving in cities.

Index

Aberdare, 96, 109

abolitionism, 11, 15, 16, 22, 45, 63, 185

abstinence. *See* temperance

Adams, Francis W. L., 152, 210

adherents, 121

advertise, handbills, showbills, 9, 14, 29, 37

Africa, x, 103, 111, 136

Agar, Louise, 108

Agar, Rachel, 106, 108

aggressive Christianity, x, 3, 6, 8, 21, 26, 28, 29, 34, 37, 64, 71, 76, 79, 80, 82, 85, 87, 89, 94, 113, 122, 200. *See* revivalism

Aitken, Robert, 10, 15

alcohol, 22, 55, 63, 75; William Booth on benefits of, 188; brandy, wine, cider, perry, gin, 30, 74–75. *See* drunkards

All the World, 129, 216

Allen, John, 99

America, x, xi, 34, 45, 64, 96, 111, 118–20, 124–31, 136, 139–40, 143, 145, 163, 169, 204–5; civil war, 16, 74; English prejudice against, 68; influence on social reform, 146–67; a "Mighty England," 129; political bosses, 77; Salvation Army roots in American revivalism, 1–4, 5–20, 21–39, 45, 64, 68, 80, 182. *See* revivalism

anarchy, 72, 76, 151

Anderson, Olive, 101, 201–3

Angel Alley, 154

Anglo-American, x, xi, 4, 21, 42, 45–46, 65, 67, 75, 79, 81, 84, 100, 112, 129, 141, 164–65, 203, 216

Anglo-Wesleyan culture, 19, 84

animals, cruelty to, 77

Apollo Music Hall, 55, 63

archives, 216

Argentina, 137

Armenians, 71

Armstrong, Eliza ("Lily"), 150–51

Armstrong, Mrs., 150–51

Armstrong Case, 149–51, 210

Arnold, 110

Arnold, Matthew, 32; "Hebraist," *Culture and Anarchy* (1869) ideas disputed by G. S. Railton, 76

Arthur, William, English revivalist, *The Conversion of All England; May We hope for a Great Revival,* 19

artisans, 77–78

Ashbourne, Derbyshire, 22

Asia, 103, 136

Asquith, Herbert, 101

atheist, 82, 106, 158, 187

Atherton, Staff Captain, 121

Australia, 118, 119, 123, 140, 143, 145, 150, 152, 155, 157, 164

Australasia (includes New Zealand, Tasmania), x, 136, 140, 205

autocracy, authoritarianism, despotism, xi, 3, 6, 26–27, 35, 93, 105, 115, 117, 120, 122, 129–31, 133–34, 136, 141, 143–44, 146, 161, 164, 166, 170, 208; military system of 1877, 3, 88–112
auxiliary leagues, 125
Avery, L. S., 103

"Babylon," 150
back streets, alleys, "Irish islands," 79, 80
back to the land movement, 146, 162–63, 219
backslider, 127, 134. *See* sinner
ballroom, 82
Band of Hope, 65
baptism, 11, 21–22, 38, 66, 138. *See* sacraments
Baptists, 13, 15, 19, 74, 89, 120, 131
Baring-Gould, Sabine, 101, 201
Barker, James, 157
Barnsley, 120
Barrow, 120
Basford, 110
Batley, 38
bazaars, 90
Begbie, Harold, 21, 25, 32, 34, 160, 217
begging, 139; "letters," 57; Tucker's begging bowl, 143
Belgium, 136
Belgravia, 73, 77
Bellamy, Edward, *Looking Backward* (1888), 146, 220
Berlin, 73
Bermondsey, South London, 39
Bernardo, Thomas, 56
Besant, Annie, 158
Besant, Walter, 162
Bethnal Green, 45, 50, 55, 73, 74, 120
Bible, 2, 19, 22, 25, 31, 52–53, 55, 57, 62, 64–66, 91, 145; biblical inspiration, 195. *See* Eliza Collingridge
bigotry, 19

Billups, Mrs., 49, 55, 57; J. E., 98; Mary Coutts, 55, 193
Birmingham, 8, 10, 14, 17, 35, 142
"Black Country," 15, 37, 190
Blackfriars, 126
Blandy, Tom, 98
Blind Beggar Pub, Bethnal Green, 47
Blue Ribbon Army, 104
Bolton, 96, 132
Bombay, 139
Boon, Brindley, 131–32, 136, 153, 157, 158, 211
Booth, Ballington, 106, 118, 124–26, 130; baptized, 11; schism, 127; Volunteers of America, 204, 218
Booth, Bramwell, 13, 33–34, 37, 54, 67, 69, 71, 93–94, 98–99, 123, 125–26, 143–44, 154–55, 158, 160; deposed, 122; "Maiden Tribute," 150–51; sanctification, 69; Frank Smith defends, 166, 170; works, 218
Booth, Catherine (Mrs. Booth-Clibborn)*(Marechale)*, 88, 98, 118, 124–25, 204, 219
Booth, Catherine Mumford, ix, 1, 2, 6, 11, 37–38, 99, 123; apologist, 32, 108, 110; charcoal treatment, 192; conversion, 22–23, 31, 185; died of cancer (1890), 154; education, 31; family's financial support, 32, 37–38, 48, 98; *Female Ministry* (1859), 188; first sermon, 33; meets William, 27–28; opposed ambition, emotionalism, 29–30; role in New Connexion resignation, 34; sanctification, 68–69; social reform, 27, 148, 154, 165–66, 213; tabernacle, 184; temperance, 30; West End-resort preaching, 48, 56–57; works, 218
Booth, Charles, *Life and Labour of the People of London* (1889), 17 volumes, 73, 80

Booth, Charles Brandon, the Booths'
first grandson, 124
Booth, Cornelie Schoch (Mrs.
Herbert), 125
Booth, Emma Moss (Raheeman), 118,
125, 139
Booth, Eveline Cory (Eva,
Evangeline), 49, 119, 125, 205,
217, 219
Booth, Florence Soper (Mrs. Bramwell
Booth), 148, 152
Booth, Herbert Howard, 34, 119, 125,
205, 219
Booth, Lucy Milward (Mrs. Booth-
Hellberg), 126, 205
Booth, Marian Billups, 123, 125
Booth, Mary Moss, 21, 22
Booth, Maud Charlesworth, 124, 204,
218
Booth, Samuel, 21, 22, 186
Booth, William, ix, 1, 5–6, 37, 187;
anti-illectual, 32; autocrat, 38–39,
51, 59, 61, 144; call to preach and
East London, 24–25, 36, 38–39,
47–48, 71–73, 182, 187; Caughey
influence, conversion to
revivalism's American methods,
7–12, 21–39; conversion, 22–23,
31, 183, 185; crises, 186; critics,
Henry Edmunds, Samuel Horatio
Hodges, Brian Lunn, John
Manson, Albert Muspratt, A. M.
Nicol, J. J. R. Redstone, 217, 219;
education, 31; expelled by
Wesleyan Conference, 26; failure
in London, 72–87, 97, 169; *How
to Reach the Masses with the Gospel* (1870), 72; *In Darkest England and the Way Out* (1890),
76, 160; met Catherine Mumford,
27–28; ordained, 36; pawnbroker,
22, 25, 72; poverty, 21, 32; resignation from Methodist sects, 26,
34–36, 39, 46, 190; resolutions,

25; restitution, 23; Salvation
Army, 88, 112; Frank Smith influences conversion to social reform, 146–67, 212; wilderness
years, 37–39, 72
Booth-Clibborn, Arthur Sydney, 125,
204
Booth-Hellberg, Emanuel Daniel, 126,
205
Booth-Tucker, Frederick St. George
de Latour (Fakir Singh), 34, 58,
125–27, 138–39, 204–5, 207;
works, 219
Booth family: correspondence, 187–
90, 217; discipline, 31, 90, 98,
123, 189, 215; education, 31, 123;
finances 22, 27, 32, 37–38, 41,
48–50, 89, 189; health, 24, 30, 49–
51, 56–57, 59–51, 188; imperial
dynasty, xii, 111, 117, 123, 126,
130, 136, 143, 144, 170; Jenner's
vaccination, 57; move to London,
39, 43; nepotism, 126, 204; novels, 31; theater, 31
Booth v. Ferritt, 1890, 159. *See* court
cases
Boston, Lincolnshire, 8, 22
Bow, 155
Bow Common, 53, 79
Boy Scouts (1908), Boys' Brigade
(1883), Boys' Life Brigade (1899),
and Church Lads' Brigade (1890),
104
Bradford, 35, 95, 108, 110; Pullan's
Hall, 95
Bradford, Mr., 18
Bradlaugh, Charles, 106
Bramwell, William, 8, 10, 29, 68, 184
Bramwell-Booth, Catherine, biogra-
phies, 218
Brengle, Samuel Logan, 206
Brighouse Chapel (New Connexion),
33, 35
Bright, John, 125

Brighton, 52, 57, 68; Grand Concert Hall, Dome, 57

Bristol, 11, 35, 120, 132

Britain, xi, 8, 15, 33, 73, 125, 129, 140, 154, 156, 160; army, 89, 91, 97, 101–4; colonies, 116; evangelicals, 6, 12, 18; imperium, a model for Salvation Army, xi, 88; "pieces of" overseas, 163; royalty, Queen Victoria, aristocracy, 126, 134, 145, 152–53

British Weekly, survey, 120, 121, 133, 151

British Workman, 62

Brixton, 38, 72

Bromley, 74, 192

Brooklyn, New York, 127

buildings, property, 41, 48, 50, 51, 52, 55, 58, 90, 99, 108, 109, 120, 127, 131–32, 141, 154–55, 194; unconsecrated, 13

Bullard, Henry, 139

Bullwell, 110

Bunting, Jabez ("High Church" Wesleyan), 10, 26

bureaucratic, 6, 18, 34, 35, 47, 115. *See* denominational, sectarian

"Burned Over District," New York state, 6, 7, 11. *See* England's Midlands and North

Burns, John, 79, 157

Burrell, Mrs., 98

Burslem, 35

Bury, 37, 38

Butler, Josephine, 112, 149

"cab horse charter," 161

Cadman, Elijah, 1, 4, 93, 96, 98, 106, 166

Calcutta, 139

Calvinism. *See* theology

Camborne, Cornwall, 37

Cambridge Music Hall, 55, 62

camp meetings, 6, 9, 16, 53, 63

Campbell, John, 14, 27, 59; Moorfield Tabernacle, 14, 184

Canada, 119, 125, 127, 140, 143, 163, 164, 205

Canning Town, 50, 53, 85

capitalists, 161

Cardiff, Wales, 37, 109

Carey, Brother, 22

Carey, William, 143

Carlyle, Thomas, 32, 73, 161

Carter, William, 18

Carvosso, William, 68

Carwardine, Richard, Anglo-American revivalism, 182, 184–85, 219

casuals, 77–79, 84, 87; casual wards, 63

Catholic Salvation Army, 198

Caughey, James, 1, 3, 5–12, 16, 18–20, 23, 25–26, 29, 33, 35–36, 39, 42, 48, 68, 73, 113, 115, 117, 126, 131, 145, 182–84; banished from Nottingham, 187; income, 10; independence, 10–11; methods, 9–10; Salvation Army connection, 184; social reform, 9

Cavendish-Bentinck, George, M.P., 151

Chadwick, Edwin, 75

Champion, H. H., 79

Champness, E. I., *Frank Smith, M.P.* (1942), 220

charismatic, 41, 42, 92, 117, 123, 128

charity, Salvation Army as, 140, 160. *See* social reform

Charity Organisation Society, 62, 78, 149, 165, 169

chartism, 9, 10, 15, 78, 151

Chase, Samuel, 43, 45, 46

Chatham, 67

Chester, 35, 46

Chesterfield, 8

Chicago Tribune, 131

children, 10, 75, 81, 136, 137; abduction, 151; homes, 81, 171

China Inland Mission, 143

"Chinaman," 106

cholera, London epidemic of 1866, 50, 62, 74, 139

Christian Community (Huguenot), 45, 47

Christian Mission, 1, 20, 41–42, 52, 55, 93, 113, 117–18, 166, 169; becomes Salvation Army, 87, 113; *Christian Mission Magazine* (1870), 52, 64–68, 84–86, 99, 216, becomes *Salvationist* in 1879, 104; Conference *Minutes,* 216; districts, city and country (provincial), 85; doctrines, Appendix A and B, 174, 176–77; failure in London, 71–87, 121; organization, 41–42

Christian primitivism, 3, 24, 28, 64, 70, 110, 116

Christian Revival Association (1865), 39, 41, 48, 50–51

Christian Times, 44

Christian World (1857), 44, 63

Christian Yearbook (1868), 44, 52

Christmas dinners. *See* social reform

Christmas meeting (1876), 88, 90

Christ's second coming, 142

Church of England, anglican, anglo-catholic, 8, 63, 67, 121, 123, 134–35, 164; bishops' committee 1882 negotiation with William Booth, Church Army (1882), 111, 206, 216; high church ritual, 66; low church evangelicals are pro-Booth, 15

Churchill, Winston, 213

Cincinnati, Ohio, 18, 215–16

circuit, 187; rider, 8

city colony, 159, 161–62, 165; food and shelter depots, household salvage brigades, rescue homes, creches, 159. *See* social reform

City of London Theatre, 55

City Temple, 154

Clapton Congress Hall, 120–21

Clare, Job, 98

clergy, clericalism, xi, 1–3, 13, 17, 24–25, 28, 36–37, 57, 66, 73, 81, 132, 136; ordained "regular" minister or preacher "on the plan," 24, 71; "Reverend," 115, 166

Cleveland, Ohio (1872), xi, 20, 45, 118, 191, 198

clothes, dress, fashion, feathers and flowers, 31, 91, 97–98

Cobb, Frances Power, Salvation Army article, 217

Collier, Richard, *The General Next to God* (1955), 217

Collingridge, Eliza, Biblewoman, 52–53, 55, 62, 192

Colombo, 139

colonialism, colonies, colonists, xi, 129, 146, 159, 161, 163

committees, 41, 46, 48, 51, 58–61, 70, 143

concert, concert hall, 73, 82, 90

conference, debates, representative principle, 17, 84 88–89, 90, 91, 97, 99–100, 105, 143; stationing committee appoints evangelists to stations, 90–91. *See* Christian Mission

Congregationalists (1831), independents, 15, 19, 27–28, 32, 37, 74, 120, 131

Conqueror, 216

Conservative Party (Tory), 77, 79, 150, 163, 197

conversion, converts, salvation, 1, 2, 5–13, 15, 22–24, 31, 36, 47–48, 57–58, 62–63, 65, 67, 69, 71, 74, 80, 84, 86, 96, 104–5, 111, 116–17, 134–35, 138–41, 145–46, 149, 152, 161, 169, 171, 209; nurturing, 120, 132. *See* proselytizing

Cooke, James, 154, 211

Cooke, William, 28, 34, 72, 187–88

Coombs, Commissioner, 140
copyrights and patents, 127
Corbridge, William, 92, 99, 144
Cork, 8
Corn Act, 75
Cornwall, 14, 15, 36, 37, 93
corps, 104, 115, 131, 135, 140
Cory, John and Richard, 49
"corybantic Christianity," 126, 164
cottage meeting, 24, 62
Cottrill, Mrs., 148
Council of Gentlemen, 51, 58–61
councils. *See* war congress
court cases, 144, 208; Old Bailey, 151.
    See Booth v. Ferritt, 1890
court marshal, 126
Coutts, Frederick, disputes American
    influence on the Booths in theol-
    ogy and social reform, 185, 197,
    209, 215, 218
Coutts, John, Salvation Army doctrine
    and ritualism, 195, 215
Coventry, xi, 118
Covington, Kentucky, 216
creches, 165
Craig, E. T., 164
Crimean War, 100
Criminal Law Amendment Bill, 149
Criminal Tribes Settlements in India,
    139. *See* farm colonies
Crispen, C. H., 193
critics, Booth's, 38, 63–64; Anglican
    clergy as, 151, 155, 164
Croydon, 52, 57, 84, 97, 191
Crystal Palace, 81
cult, 142
culture, 76–84; influence on conver-
    sion, 196. *See* Irish Catholics
Cunningham, Hugh, 102, 201

Daily Chronicle, 159
Daily News, 157
Daily Telegraph, 159

Dale, John Lee, 193
dance, 82, 104
dancing hall, 48–50, 81, 192
Darkest England Social Scheme
    (1890), 76, 146–67, 169, 170, 215–
    16; critics, Bernard Bosanquet,
    Helen Bosanquet, Philip Dwyer,
    T. H. Huxley, 217–18; supporters,
    H. Rider Haggard, Theodore
    Roosevelt, Arnold White, 218. *See
    In Darkest England and the Way
    Out*
Darwin, Charles, evolution, 31–32,
    145
Davidson, Randall T., Salvation Army
    article, 217
Davies, Llewellan, 134
Davis, Annie, 52
Day, W. F., 144, 208
decline of movements, 110–11, 169
deeds, 199–200, 208, 216; 1873 and
    1878, 98, 199–200
Deliverer, 216
democracy. *See* freedom
Denmark, 136, 205
denominationalism. *See* sectarianism
deposit bank, 165
depression, economic (1884–86), 144
Deptford, 39
Derby, 46, 47
deserter, defector, traitor, resignations,
    39, 51, 90, 95, 97, 99, 111, 133,
    143–44, 166
Dewsbury, 35
Dimberline, Brother, 97
discipline, Methodist, x, 3, 6, 10, 24,
    26, 31, 34, 36, 39, 51, 78, 89, 92–
    93, 103, 105–6, 111–12, 115–17,
    133, 163, 202–3
Disposition of Forces, 216
Disraeli, Benjamin, *Sybil* (1847), 73, 75
doctrine. *See* theology
dole. *See* handout

Dorchester, 8
Dorking, Battle of, 198
dossers, 159, 166
Dow, Lorenzo, 5–6, 10, 36
Dowdle, James, 53, 95, 98
Dowie, Alexander, of Zion City, 125, 204
drunkards, 58, 92, 96, 106, 113, 134, 147, 149, 163, 165, 169
Dublin, 8
Dunn, Samuel, 24, 26, 186–87

Eagle Tavern and Grecian Theatre, 120
Eames, Francis, 24, 186
Eason, John, 45
East End Dock Strike (1889), 78, 146, 156–57, 169 197, 211–12
East London, x, 36, 41–43, 51–52, 116–17, 138, 149, 157, 169; Booth's failure in, 71–87, 91, 95, 97, 103, 108, 113, 120–22
East London Christian Mission (1867), 2, 51–52, 147
East London Evangelist (1868), 52, 64–65, 75, 216
East London Observer, 55, 60
East London Revival Association (1865–67), 18, 41
East London Special Services Committee, 36, 39, 43, 45–47, 191
East London Theatre, 53
Eastern Alhambra (penny gaff) Limehouse, 55
Eastern Star, 55
Easton Hall, 58
Ebbw Vale, Wales, 109
ecumenism, xi, 45, 66, 67
Edinburgh, Scotland, 52, 54
Edmonton, 121
Edmunds, Henry, 144, 208
education, schools, 10, 13, 21–22, 27–88, 31–34, 36, 54, 65, 73–74, 76–77, 81, 145, 147; compulsory edu-cation and literacy, 129; ministe-rial, 2; reform, 188; science, 32; "unintelligent bluster," 14
efficiency, 3, 29, 92, 100, 119, 131, 133, 145, 162
Effingham Theatre, later New East London Theatre, 55, 59–60, 62–63
emigration, Emigration Society, 81, 130, 160, 163–64, 219
emotionalism, sensationalism, 9, 15, 29, 36, 188
employment bureau, 81
engagement, 144
England, 1, 18, 57, 68, 69, 73–77, 79–80, 87, 121, 127, 129, 130, 134, 142–43, 150, 157, 161, 163; "can-ker in the rose," blight in Chris-tian England, 75; "English" Salva-tion Army, 5; evangelists, 8, 15; Methodism, 6–7, 19, 21; Midlands and North, growth of Booth's mission, 11, 14–16, 34–35, 37, 64, 71–87, 95, 103; Protestant, 82, 84; revivals, 11, 34; spiritual decline, 81, 133
Engles, Friederich, 78
enquirers, anxious, 10, 13, 19, 53, 86. *See* penitents
entertainment, amusements, philistinism, sports, 32, 90
enthusiasm (espirit d'corps), 119, 123, 138
Erikson, Erik H., 24
Ervine, St. John, 21, 37, 58, 64, 93, 98, 124, 126, 138, 217
Europe, x, 8, 16, 79, 111, 119, 136, 140, 161
evangelical, nonconformist. *See* prot-estant
Evangelical Alliance, 45–46, 52, 65–66, 191
Evangelisation Society (1864), 45–46, 51, 55–59, 61, 72, 191

evangelism, x, 13, 19, 28

evangelist, itinerant, Christian Mission
    preacher, ix, 2, 7, 11, 18, 23, 29,
    35–36, 39, 41, 48, 63, 84, 88–89,
    97–98, 113–16, 147–48, 152, 155,
    166, 169, 171; "field officer," 104;
    salary, 98; wife, 91. *See* revival-
    ism, laypersons

Evening News and Post, 159

exam system for officers and soldiers,
    133

excursions, 53, 81

Exeter, 12

Exeter Hall, London, 15, 133, 145

experience meetings, public, 49, 63, 86

extradenominationalism, 45, 56, 51,
    115, 191

Eyre Arms Assembly Rooms, St. John's
    Wood, 56

failure, Booth in East London, x, xi,
    71–87, 89, 91, 95, 120, 122, 128,
    133–34, 142, 144, 147, 151, 169;
    overall decline, 135–36; "settling
    down," 131–32; "unique failure,"
    155, 211

fallen men, 150; fallen women, 43, 49,
    147, 152, 169, 210; Midnight
    Movement for, 43, 45; unwed
    mothers, 170

farm colony, India and America, 139–
    40, 159, 160, 162–63, 165, 216

Fawcett, Captain, 106, 110

federal system (interdependent
    whole) v. centralized govern-
    ment, xi–xii, 26, 28, 129, 130,
    141–44, 162, 170

Felling-upon-Tyne, 95, 96

female ministry, x, 1, 3–4, 7, 14, 16–
    17, 27, 28, 32–33, 39, 52, 56, 91,
    95, 98–99, 106, 108, 117–18, 152;
    Catherine Booth's *Female Minis-
    try* (1859), 33, 216; social ser-
    vices, 113, 146, 148–49, 169; "sur-

plus womanhood," 149; "women
    of gentility," 124; women writers,
    136. *See* Booth, Catherine,
    Palmer, Phoebe

Fenton, 35

finance, 41, 45–46, 50, 52–53, 54–61,
    67, 74–75, 91, 113, 116–19, 121–
    22, 138, 140–41, 143–44, 148, 162,
    166, 170–71, 209; Christmas ap-
    peal, 62; debt, 98; fund raising,
    70; members, subscribers, maga-
    zine sales, 51–52, 77, 85–86, 89,
    94–95; sale of books, etc., 10;
    social programs income, 220. *See*
    self-support

Finney, Charles G., 1, 3, 5–6, 16, 18–
    20, 22, 25, 27–29, 33, 35, 39, 42,
    48, 54, 57, 113, 115, 117, 126,
    145, 184; works, 3, 12–14

Fishbourne, Capt., R. N., C.B., 193

fishing, 183

flag, banner, 80, 95, 106, 110–11, 115,
    203; symbolism of, 108

Fletcher of Madeley, 22

folk beliefs, superstition, 80, 82

food and shelter depot, 154–57, 159,
    161–62, 165–66, 212. *See* city colony

"Food for the Millions" shops, 19

foreign secretary, Salvation Army, 136,
    139, 204

Forlong, Gordon, 18

France, 68, 111, 124, 125, 136, 137,
    150, 166

"free and easy" in pubs, 63. *See* music,
    singing

Free Church, Mile End Newtown, 55

Free Methodist, 17, 39

free thinking, 2, 82, 195

freedom, revivalist-lay independence,
    x, xi, 3, 6, 8, 10–11, 14, 18, 24,
    27–28, 34–35, 38–39, 45, 47–48,
    51–52, 67, 96, 99–100, 117–18,
    129, 131, 141, 150, 208; v. settled
    ministry, 41, 113

gambling, 19, 87
Garrick Theatre, 36
Gateshead, 8, 33, 35, 37, 106;
    Catherine Booth's first sermon, 33
general, 5, 26, 39, 88, 94, 105, 118,
    127, 130, 136, 142, 166, 170
general superintendent, 41, 88, 99
George, Henry, 112, 160–61, 164–65,
    211; works, 220
George's Yard, 154
Germany, 106, 136
Gilton, P. T., 28
Gladstone, William, 150
Gladwin, Captain, 138
Glasgow, Scotland, 111
Goddard, Sister, 95, 96
"godly parents," 87
government, British, 94, 151; aid to
    Salvation Army, 150, 155, 157,
    163, 164, 170; Bramwell Booth
    opposes "legislative remedies,"
    155; House of Commons, 46, 149,
    150, 151; House of Lords, 145;
    Parliament, 151, 155, 166. See
    "Maiden Tribute"
Grahamism, 188
Grant, Hay McDowell, 18
Green, Roger, 215
growth (success) and decline, x, xi,
    50–53, 70, 71–87, 113, 115, 116–
    18, 126, 134, 140–42, 163, 166.
    See failure
Guiness, Harry Grattan, 18
Gujerati, India, 138, 139

Habershon and Pite, architects, 60
Hackney, 49, 121
Hadleigh, Essex, colony, 162–63
Haggard, H. Rider, 112, 152, 163, 164–
    65; works, 213, 218
Haggerstown, 121
half-heartedness, 143–44
Halifax, 35, 37
Hallelujah Band sensationalism, 1, 37,

63, 92–93, 115, 190
Hallelujah Lasses, 96, 106, 118
Hameline, Bishop, 16
Hamilton, George, 193
Hammersmith, 38, 49, 97, 108
Hanbury, Truman, and Brixton (brew-
    ers), 55
handout charity, dole, indiscriminate
    charity, Poor Law, 62, 65, 74, 147,
    149, 160, 165, 159. See social reform
Hanley, 11, 35
Hanson, Samuel, 46
Hardie, Keir, 164, 166; "Frank Smith,
    L.C.C.," (1894), 220
harlotry. See prostitution
Harries-Jenkins, Gwyn, 103, 200
Harrison, Brian, 30
Harrison, Frederick, 152
Harvest Field, 138
Hastings, 52, 84, 97
Havelock, Gen. Henry, 103
Hayden, W. Jones, 47
Hayle, Cornwall, 36
Hazell, George, 215
headquarters, London's International
    staff, tyranny, xi, 1, 55, 119, 120,
    129, 132–33, 142, 144, 205; oppo-
    sition to Frank Smith, 153; social
    headquarters, Upper Thames
    Street, 159
health. See Booths
"heathen masses," x, 34, 36, 39, 41–
    43, 45–48, 51–52, 55, 65–67, 91,
    101, 103, 108, 110, 113, 117, 121,
    134, 147, 155, 169, 171; failure to
    convert, 71–87; pagan, 145. See
    poor, masses
"heathenism," 45, 80, 138; defined, 76
heaven. See theology
"Hebraist," 32
hell. See theology
heretics, 81
high council, 122, 170, 208
higher criticism (German), 14, 31

Hindu, 138
history, myth, and hagiography of
    Salvation Army, ix, xii, 34, 64–65,
    72, 97, 110, 163, 195, 181
Hobsbaum, Eric J., 79
Hodges, Samuel Horatio, 144, 208
holiness doctrine, entire sanctification,
    perfectionism, perfect love, con-
    secration, full salvation, Holy
    Ghost baptism, 2, 6, 8, 10–11, 14,
    16, 19, 25, 28–29, 31, 39, 43, 45,
    64, 66–70, 90, 105, 108, 127, 165,
    171, 183, 188; holiness meeting,
    69, 89; influence on Booths, 31,
    195; instantaneous, 68; "roots of
    bitterness," controversy, 69, 196
Holland, 136
Holloway jail, 157
"Holy Monday," 30
Holz, Ronald, 215
home rule, 144
homeless, hotel, lodging house, 159,
    166
homeopathic medicine, 188
homosexual, 151
Horbury, Yorkshire, 101
Horns Assembly Room, Kensington, 49
Horridge, Glenn K., 215
hospitals, 170
Hottentot, 76
Houses of Commons and Lords. See
    government
Houses of Enquiry, 150
Houses of Refuge, overseas, 150. See
    rescue homes
Houghton, 14
Huddersfield, 8, 10
Hughes, Hugh Price, 164
Hull, 8, 10, 11, 35, 120
humanitarian, 32, 145, 165
humor, 63
Hunslet, 35
Huntington, Frederic Dan, 16

Huxley, Thomas H., 126, 145, 152,
    164, 218
Hyde, 37, 38
Hyde Park, dockers' rally in (1889), 158
hydropathy (cold water baths), 30–31,
    37

Ignatius, Father, 57
imperium, Christian, xii, 45, 71, 88,
    98–100, 103, 106, 110–13, 115,
    126, 129, 131, 133, 136, 141–46,
    169, 170; imperialism, xi, 111–12,
    161–62, 164; influence of W. T.
    Stead and Cecil Rhodes, 163
In Darkest England and the Way Out
    (1890), 114, 145; authorship, 114.
    See Darkest England Social
    Scheme
incorporation, Salvation Army in U. S.
    (1899), 127, 216
independence. See freedom of revival-
    ists and lay preachers
Independent Labour Party, 164, 220
Independents. See Congregationalists
India, x, 111, 118, 125, 126, 137–40,
    143, 145, 205, 207; Booth-Tucker,
    Darkest India (1890), 219; civil
    service, 139; mutiny, 100, 103,
    145; Presbyterians in, 138; settle-
    ments, 140; Tamil, 138
indigenous leadership, 143
indoor poor relief, 149. See social re-
    form
Inebriates Home, 159, 165. See drunk-
    ards
infidels, 7, 10, 15, 45, 66, 73, 76, 96,
    98, 105, 108–10, 141, 151; "error
    and superstition," 64;
    "nothingarianism," 105; "unbe-
    lievers and doubters," 145
Inglis, K. S., 163, 203, 215
insurance company, 165–66
interdenominational cooperation, 15,

18, 19, 37, 43; union prayer meet-
ings and revivals, 18. *See* Evan-
gelical Alliance, YMCA, YWCA
international, ix, xi, 15, 113, 118, 126,
128, 130, 136, 141, 143, 170. *See*
missions, Anglo-American, trans-
atlantic
Ireland, 7, 111, 161; Irish-American, 9
Irish in England, 15, 50, 71, 74, 82, 87;
"Hottentots," "heathen," "devil-
ish," 76, 79–81; "papists," Catho-
lics, 82, 87; *War Cry* articles by
Mrs. Commissioner Carlton:
"Brigit," "Mad Julia," 82
"Irregular Agencies," 44, 191
Israel. *See* Jews
Italy, 106, 136, 137
Ives, Edmund, 193

Jack the Ripper, 121–22, 154
Jackson, Lizzie, 106, 108
jail, 120
James, John Angell, 191
Janes, Bishop, 16
Jarrett, Rebecca, 150–51
Jarrow, synagogue, 106
Jennings, Sister, 139
Jermy, James, 45, 198
Jersey, 35
Jerusalem, 142
Jesus, 110, 133; as Salvation Army,
142
Jews, 32, 69, 79, 142, 145, 208; Salva-
tion Army as "Hallelujah Jews,"
133
jingoism, 94
Jones, Gareth Steadman, 78
Jones, Sam, 131
Jowett, Benjamin, 73

Kensington Assembly Rooms, 45
Kent, John, 68, 182, 185, 219. *See*
Frederick Coutts

Kern, Peter, 109–10
King's Cross, 121
Kingsley, Charles, *Hypatia* (1853),
101, 201
Kipling, Rudyard, 102, 201
Kirkham, Gawin, secretary, Open Air
Mission, 53, 192
Knight, Mr., 56
knee drill, 183

Labour Bureau, 158–59, 164
Lahore, India, 139
Lampard, Colonel, 126
Lamplough, Jeremiah, 108
Lancashire Mill Riots, 94
land, laws, 153; colony, 161
Lansbury, George, 220
laypersons, laity, x, xi, 2, 3, 9, 11, 14,
15, 16, 22, 24–27, 46, 51, 53, 66,
86, 92, 115, 116, 118, 132, 140,
141, 148, 169, 185; governance
participation, 91; "irregular ministers," evangelists, 11, 16, 19; lay
delegates, 88, 95; lay speakers,
86; local preachers, 3, 22, 24–26,
39, 46, 65, 89; non-officers, 144;
probationary preacher, 7. *See* soldiers
League of the Cross, 81
Leeds, 8, 35, 37, 38, 43
Lees, Lynn Hollen, 80
Leicester, 110, 191
Liberal Party, 77; Liberal government,
163–64. *See* government
Limehouse, 50, 53, 55, 59, 74, 84–85,
97, 106, 121, 154
Limerick, Ireland, 8
Lincoln, 8
"Lion of Judah," 93
literature "trashy," 91; novels, 31; ob-
scene materials, 151
Liverpool, 8, 46, 130, 139, 152, 215
Lloyd-George, David, 213

Loch, Charles, 149. *See* Charity
    Organisation Society
lodging houses, 79, 159. *See* homeless
London, 12, 14–15, 25, 38–39, 43, 106,
    118, 122, 125, 127, 130, 132, 135–
    36, 147; County Council, 166;
    Fields, 53; Grecian Corps, 143;
    Orphan Asylum, 120; Trades
    Council, 164
London, Jack, *People of the Abyss*
    (1903), 73
Longton, 35
Lord's Prayer, 166
Louth, Lincolnshire, 11, 38
Love Feasts, 9, 66, 89, 95, 104, 110
Luther, Martin, 105

Macclesfield, 8, 35
machine, 98, 103, 115, 156–57, 163;
    Booth's mission as a machine
    that manufactures converts/sol-
    diers, 152
Madras, 139
Maesteg, Wales, 109
"Maiden Tribute," 150–52. *See* W. T.
    Stead
management, efficient, 92, 100
Manchester, 8, 11, 35, 124
Mangus (Chiricahua Indian chief),
    130–31
manifest destiny, 45
Mann, Tom, 79
Manning, Henry Cardinal, 81
Mansion House Committee, 150
Marathi, 139
marches, parades, processions, 24, 37,
    47, 49, 53, 80–81, 96, 103, 109–
    10, 120, 157
Margate (Royal Assembly Rooms), 56
marriage, 27, 29, 37–38, 56
Marsden, Isaac, 23
Mary Magdalene, 152
Marylebone, 125, 134; Police Court, 150
mass, 82

the masses v. the classes, 10, 12, 14,
    18, 36, 42–43, 47, 52, 65–66, 71,
    153
Masterman, C. F. G., *From the Abyss*
    (1902), 73
matchbox factory (Bryant and May's
    Strike, 1888), 74, 155
maternal society, 62, 65
Matlock, Smedley's Spa, 37
May meeting, 133
Mayhew, Henry, 78, 80
McAll, John, 60
Mearns, Andrew, *The Bitter Cry of
    Outcast London* (1883), 73, 114,
    121, 146–47, 161, 169
Meath, the Earl of (imperial migra-
    tion), 155–56, 164
Melbourne, Australia, 150
Melrose, John, 54
membership, xi, 8, 10, 15, 19, 41, 51–
    53, 77–78, 84–85, 118, 120–22,
    127, 132, 140–41. *See* statistics
Merthyr, Wales, 96, 109
Methodist (Wesleyan), 5–10, 1315, 19,
    21, 35, 41–42, 80, 84, 86–87, 92–
    93, 97, 111, 116, 121, 131, 135,
    141, 147
Methodist New Connexion, x, 3, 16,
    18, 19, 28, 29, 34–36, 39, 50, 64,
    65, 72, 173–74
Methodist Sunday School Association,
    7
Methodist Times, 28, 164
middle-class, 14, 17; "decorum," 21,
    33, 41, 72, 152, 159
Midlands and North of England, 10–
    11, 14–16, 34–35, 37, 64, 71–87;
    growth of mission in, 95, 103
migration, 76, 140
Milbourn, James Codd, 18
military, xi, 1, 3, 42, 81, 88–112; a
    "salvation army" formed, 100,
    104–6, 108, 111–13, 115–16, 146
Mill, Herbert, 164

Mill, John Stuart, 19
millennialism, 7, 19, 45, 64, 111, 141–42
Millerites, 7
Missing Persons Inquiry Bureau, 165
missions (foreign), 4, 42, 45, 104, 136, 138, 139, 142, 145
mobs. *See* "roughs"
model dwellings, 147
Monica, 152
Monod, Theodore, 68
Morning Advertiser, 64
Moody, Dwight L., 14, 68, 117, 131, 139. *See* Ira Sankey
Moore, Thomas E., Moore schism (1884), 127, 129–30, 142, 152
Morgan, Richard Cope, 43, 45
Morley, Samuel, 49, 60, 152
Morrison, Dr. John Reid, 88
Mossley, 35
mothers' meetings, 55, 65, 81
"Mothers of the Nation Petition," 150
Mousehole, Cornwall, 36
Mow Cop Camp Meeting, 1807, 6
Mumford, John (brother of Catherine Booth), 22
Mumford, John (father of Catherine Booth), 22, 29–30, 58
Mumford, Sarah (mother of Catherine Booth), 22, 57–58
Murphy, Howard R., ix–x
"muscular Christianity," 101
music, 42, 56, 63–64; brass bands not used till 1880, 96, 102, 104, 109, 110, 111, 115, 132–33, 157; use of popular tunes, 81, 93
music hall, penny gaff, 18, 55–56, 58–60, 62–64, 67, 74, 90, 92, 98, 109
Muslim, 138
Myddleton Hall and Priory, Islington, 45

"narrow escapes," 24, 87
native cultures, 141
"negroes," "coloured," 5, 106, 128

New Brunswick, New Jersey, 12, 127
New York City, 5, 16, 106, 118, 126, 131
New York Herald, 5
New York State (Salvation Army incorporation in), 19, 127
New York World, 157
New Zealand. *See* Australasia
Newburgh, New York, 7, 127
Newcastle-under-Lyme, 35
Newcastle-upon-Tyne, 35–36, 106, 108
Nicol, A. M., 120, 136–38, 140, 157
Nightingale, Florence, 75
Nonconformist, 44, 53, 75
non-officers, 144
nonsectarian, nondenominational, 15, 28, 37 44–45, 48, 59, 65, 151, 170
Norman, Arthur, 139
North, Brownlow, 18
North Ormsby, 97
Northampton, 93
Northern Express, 106
Norway, 136
Nottingham, Meadow Platts, Sneinton Market, 3, 8, 10, 21–22, 24, 35, 37, 39, 49, 110, 147
novels, 31
Nuneaton, 166

obscene materials, 151
obstruction of streets, 120
O'Connor, Fergus, 151
Old Bailey, 151
Old Ford, 53
Oldham, 35
"Onward Christian Soldiers," 101
Open Air Mission (1853), 45
open-air preaching, street services, 10, 24, 37, 45, 47–48, 50, 56, 62, 64–65, 86, 96, 108–9, 120, 127, 132, 139, 147, 171
"opiate of the people," 75
opposition, 46, 55, 79–82, 96–99, 108, 120, 122, 155, 166. *See* mobs
ordination, 2, 66

Oriental Music Hall, Poplar, 56, 58–59
Orr, J. Edwin, 66
outsiders, 146, 160
overseas colony, 160, 163–65
overseas expansion, 123, 126, 133–40
Owenite, 164
Oxford University, 2

Packington Street Chapel, Britannia
    Fields, Islington, 29
palace, 152
Pall Mall Gazette, 114, 149–50, 152, 161
Palmer, Phoebe, 1, 3–6, 16–20, 27,
    33–37, 39, 67–69, 113, 115, 117,
    126, 131, 145
Palmer, Walter, 16–17, 131
Parker, Joseph, 59
Parliament. *See* government
Parsi, 138
Paton, J. B., 37; Nottingham Theologi-
    cal Institute, 34
Paton, Robert, 88
patriotism, 102–3
Pavilion Theatre, 59
Pearse, George, 18, 36, 46
Pearson, W. J., "The Salvation Army is
    Marching Along," 105
penitent form, mourners' bench, com-
    munion rail, 2, 9–10, 19, 65, 120,
    132
Pennefather, William, 18
Pennsylvania, 68
penny banks, 65
"pentecost" prayer sessions, 96, 108
Penzance, Cornwall, 37, 82
Peoples' Hall, 57, 59–61, 90
perfectionism. *See* holiness
Philadelphia (founding of Salvation
    Army in the U.S.), xi, 20, 68
philanthropy, 58, 61, 65, 163–64. *See*
    charity, social reform
phossy jaw, 74
Pickett, J. Wascom, 138
Plymouth Brethren, 43, 56

police, 1, 46, 96, 106; police courts, 81
political parties, politics, 62, 100, 106,
    151; Salvation Army involvement
    in, 166; *see* Conservative Party,
    Independent Labour Party, Lib-
    eral Party
polytechnic, 45
Poole, Joshua, 18
Poole, Richard, 15, 28
Poona, 139
the poor, 15, 21, 24, 35, 37, 41, 42–43,
    46–47, 62–63, 71–75, 78, 79, 149,
    150, 151, 163, 171
Poor Law Committees, 62
Porth, 109
Portsmouth, 120
poverty, 22, 32, 34, 73, 75, 114, 117,
    147, 152–53, 155, 166, 169
Powell, Nathaniel J., Esq., 88
prayer, 5, 8, 9, 12–13, 15, 18–19, 23,
    25, 52, 68–69, 80, 104, 110, 149
preachers' plan, "on the plan," "on
    trial," 24, 91
predestined, 166
Presbyterians, 3, 13, 19
press, religious and secular, 18, 52,
    144–45, 159
Primitive Methodist (1811), 6, 17, 89–
    90, 96; women, 33, 189
Printing House Square, 134
prison, 91, 134, 149, 153, 158, 165,
    169; Prisoners' Brigades, 113,
    147–48; Prisoners' Homes, 157
prize fighters, 92
prodigal son, 147
property, barracks, hall. *See* buildings
proselytizing, church members lured
    by Salvation Army, 81, 87, 96,
    134, 138
prostitutes, harlots, 14, 19, 79, 92, 104,
    134, 147, 149–51, 163
Protestant, x, 5, 8, 10, 12, 15–16, 19,
    45, 68, 71, 73–74, 77, 81–82, 84,
    87, 103–4, 116, 126, 133–35, 137

protracted meetings, 7

provincial towns, "country" stations, 85–86, 94, 97, 99, 103, 108, 113, 117, 120–21, 134–35

public house, pub, tavern, 63, 71, 73, 79, 102, 108–9, 133, 140, 143; allurements of, 190; disturbances by publicans, 1, 96; gin palaces, 73, 81. *See* opposition

Pudsey, 38

puritanism, 10, 32

Pye, Brother, 50

Quakers, Society of Friends, 19, 45, 62, 66, 145; Open Air Mission (1853), 45, 53; Whitechapel Burial Ground, 45–46, 50

Queen's Hall, London, 166

Rabbits, Edward, 26, 49, 187

Radcliffe, Reginald, 18, 46

Rader, Paul A., 170

radicalism, 79; revolution and riots, 78

Railton, George Scott, 13, 76, 84, 94, 99, 123, 129, 130, 134, 142, 156–57, 165–66; in America, 5, 118, 126, 127, 129; anger at social reform, 215; sanctification, 69; *General Booth* (1912), *Heathen England* (1877), *Twenty-One Year's Salvation Army* (1886), 216–17

Railton, Marianne Parkyn (Mrs. G. S., "Deborah"), 148, 209

Ralahine, Ireland, Owenite communal farm experiment, 164

Ramsgate, 56

Redruth, Cornwall, 37

Reed, Henry, 49–50, 53, 60–61, 193–94

Rees, Arthur Augustus, 17, 33

Rees's *From Poverty to Plenty*, 164

Reform Methodism, 3, 11, 26–27, 28, 39, 45, 115

Regent Hall Corps, 120, 133

rehabilitation centers, 171

relief agencies, 81

religious-people, 22, 75, 153; census, 15. *See* "respectable"

Renan, Joseph Ernest, 31

Renan, M., 152

repent, 5, 81

Rescue Homes for Fallen Women, 113, 146, 148, 149, 152, 154–57, 161, 165; refuge for "friendless, penniless girls," 55

resignations, of officers, 144, 204; of Frank Smith, 163–64. *See* William Booth's resignations, deserters

resorts, seaside, Catherine Booth preaching at, 56

"respectable" christians, 9, 14, 19, 29, 37, 49, 103, 108, 110, 148; "better sort," 74; educated classes, 73; ladies and gentlemen, 5, 51, 53–54, 56, 70, 77; wealthy, 45, 51, 54; well-dressed, 5

Revival, 43, 45, 47, 52–53, 59; *The Christian* after 1870, 44, 127

revivalism, American methods, scientific "new methods," influence on the Booths, x, 1–3, 5–20, 24, 28, 33, 36, 42, 52, 62, 65, 80, 92, 115–17, 126, 131–32, 143, 145–47, 151, 155, 157, 165–66, 169, 171, 184, 188, 219; the Booths as Wesleyan revivalists, 17–39; British prejudice against, 68; *See* bible, Caughey, James, emotionalism, female ministry, Finney, Charles G., freedom, social reform, theology doctrine, tracts, visitation

Rhodes, Cecil John, 112, 161, 163

Rhondda Valley, Wales, 120

the rich, 26, 57, 78, 150, 151; "uncaring," "dangerous classes," 152; "hard-hearted," 153. *See* "respectable"

right of public meeting in parks, 191

Rightmire, David, 215

Ripon, Yorkshire, 38
ritual, 66, 80, 171, 195; Salvation
    Army, 216
Roach (Cardiff suburb), 109
Roberts, Robert, R., 8
Robinson, J. W., 106
Roman Catholic, popery, papists,
    priests, catholic, 7–8, 10, 15, 19,
    45, 50, 66, 71, 76, 79–82, 87, 96,
    98, 108, 116, 136, 157, 203
Rome, Italy, 137
Roosevelt, Theodore, 112
rosary, 81
Rotherham, 98, 108
Rotherhithe, South London, 38
roughs, 41, 102, 120, 157, 192
Rugby, 142
rules. *See* orders and regulations, dis-
    cipline
Rumford, Count, 164
Russia, 94, 142

sabbatarianism, 16, 24, 31, 45, 73, 87
sacraments, 49, 57, 66, 95, 105, 165,
    216. *See* baptism, female minis-
    try, ordination, rituals
St. Georges, 74
St. Giles, London, 79, 80
St. Hilda's Hall, 1
St. Ives, Cornwall, 36
St. Just, Cornwall, 36
St. Patrick's, Soho, 81
St. Paul, 43, 146
salaries, officers', 144. *See* finances
salvage, 161, 165; "sell goods sent for
    the benefit of the mission" at
    "used retail shops," 65
salvation, conversion, "being saved."
    See conversion
Salvation Army, 1, 3, 18–21, 24, 31,
    34–35, 38–39, 41–42, 57, 59, 66,
    68, 81, 84–85; bureaucratic, 18;
    chapters, 5, 6, 7; "English," 5; for-

mation of, 88–113; health rem-
    edies, 30–31; name, 1, 41–42,
    104, 118, 145; official history, 34;
    salvationists, names, 109; as so-
    cial agency, 140–41, 151–52, 159,
    161, 166, 169. *See* failure, growth
    and decline, orders and regula-
    tions, temperance Salvation Army
    of America
Salvation Army Yearbook, 122
Salvation Life Guards, 150
salvation "wholesale," 158
Salvationist, 105, 109, 216
salvationists, as social wing agents,
    159
Samurai, social officers as, 154
Sandall, Robert, 63, 163
Sankey, Ira, 93, 110. *See* Moody and
    Sankey
Sansom, Will, 24, 186
satan, devil, 7, 63, 111, 131
Saturday Review, 62, 194
Scandinavia, 126, 137
Scarborough, 8, 120
scientific "new methods" of revival-
    ism. *See* revivalism
schism, 16, 28, 43, 52, 53, 70, 108–9,
    111, 118, 127; (1884 and 1896),
    128–30, 141, 143
schools. *See* education, training homes
Scowby, Thomas, 34
Seaman's Grove, 74
sectarianism, sect, denominationalism,
    opposite of revivalism and free-
    dom, spawns violence, x–xi, 15,
    18–19, 35, 39, 45–46, 48, 66–67,
    81–82, 115–17, 132, 134, 141, 151,
    196. *See* freedom, revivalism
secular, xi, 74, 80, 170, 171
Secular Review, 109
self denial, 25, 119, 144
self-support, self-help, self-sufficient,
    self-sustaining, 46, 51, 70, 82, 85;

(defined), 102, 104, 136–38, 140, 143, 161, 162, 208; self-rule, 129–30, 143; self-preservation, 151
seminaries, 2, 13, 34, 39, 68
settled ministers, 8, 11, 29, 34–36, 38, 39, 41. *See* clergy
settlement house. *See* Toynbee House
Seven Dials, 149
Shaftesbury, Earl of, 91
Shaw, George Bernard, *Major Barbara* (1905), 78
Sheffield, 8, 9, 11, 30, 35, 37–38, 95–96; Hall of Science ("infidels"), 95; *Sheffield Independent,* 110; Temperance Hall, 95
shelter. *See* food and shelter depots
Shepherd, Kate, 109
Shirley family, 118
Shoreditch, 46, 50, 55, 84, 85, 121
Sims, G. R., *How the Poor Live* (1889), 73
singing, *Song Book of the Salvation Army,* 216. *See* music
sinners, penitents, drunkards, blasphemers, thieves, gamblers, infidels, harlots, pleasure seekers, slum-dwellers, backsliders, money-getters, "vilest and roughest people," 1, 5, 23, 47, 69, 72, 104–5, 110–11, 134, 145, 147–48, 169, 171
slavery, 11
slums, Booth's failure to evangelize, x–xi, 1, 24, 37, 72, 74, 80, 82, 101, 103, 108, 116–17, 125, 128, 131, 133–35, 147, 149, 152, 155, 157, 169, 220; slum corps, 152, 157; slum posts, 152, 154, 161, 165; slum sisters, 113, 148, 154
smallpox, 74
Smith, Frank, 114, 118, 120, 124, 128, 130, 145–46, 152–54, 158–60, 165–66, 169–70, 203, 208, 210–11, 217; *The Betrayal of Bramwell Booth* (1929), 218; *Darkest England* authorship, 160, 163–64, 219–20; led Salvation Army social program, 158; "Red Major," 152; resigned 163–64, 166, 213–14; Trafalgar Square & Hyde Park docker rallies, 158
Smith, Hannah, 67–68; *The Christians' Secret of a Happy Life,* 68
Smith, Robert Pearsall, 67
Smith, Rodney "Gypsy," 95, 199
Smith, Timothy, Wesleyans and reform in America, 189
Smith, Capt. W. E., secretary, Evangelisation Society, 193
Smith, W. H., 150
Smith, William Alexander, 104
Smithies, T. B., 62
Soap and Water Brigades, 149
Social Gazette, 216
social reform, social christianity, social salvation, social service, x, 6–7, 9, 16, 19, 21, 27, 43, 45, 51, 59, 72, 75–76, 103, 113–14, 116–17, 122–23, 134, 136–37, 141, 145, 161; evangelicals attack prostitution, wife-beating, theatre-going, gambling, 19; legislation, 75; mission "outdoor" relief, "breakfast and coal christians," "soupers," handouts, meat and bread tickets, teas, Christmas dinners, maternal societies, 61–62, 64–65, 74, 81; Salvation Army split into social and spiritual wings, social v. evangelical, Booth-Smith dispute, xi; 153–57, 159, 165, 170–71, 209, 220; scientific social work, 62, 152, 165, 169; social reform organization, 146–67. *See* Darkest England Scheme, Smith, Frank, Stead, W. T., Swift, Susie F.

socialist(s), 10, 15, 72, 76, 78–79, 146,
    150; Catherine Booth as, 213;
    William Booth on "Socialism of
    Infidelity" v. "Salvation Social-
    ism," 151–52, 210; "paradise mon-
    gers," 145; Frank Smith, 161; So-
    cial Democratic Federation, 77–78
society: aristocracy, artisans, casual
    poor, shopkeepers, 77
Society of Friends. *See* Quakers
sociology, 166
soldiers (laypersons), xi, 81, 111, 130–
    36, 140, 142–45, 155; junior sol-
    diers, 136, 206; sergeants, 121–22.
    See membership, statistics
solicitor, 99, 100
soul-winners, 116. *See* evangelists
soup kitchen, 60–62, 65, 116–17, 147,
    154; soup and soap v. salvation,
    165–66
South Africa, 76, 145, 164
South America, 206
South Wales Daily News, 109
Southwark, London, 39, 79, 81
Spalding, Lincolnshire, 28
Spencer, Herbert, 32, 212
spiritualism, 220
Spitalfields, 45, 74, 96
Spurgeon, Charles H., 15, 59, 184–85;
    Metropolitan Tabernacle, 193
Stabb, John, 36, 45, 46, 47
Stafford, 35
stagnation, x, 8, 84–85, 87, 103, 115,
    117, 126, 132, 145, 147. *See* fail-
    ure, growth and decline
Stalybridge, 37
Stanley, H. M., *In Darkest Africa*
    (1890), 76
Star, 159, 161
"Starvation Army," 157; the starving,
    75, 78
stations, Christian Mission, 41, 48, 50–
    51, 53, 56, 69, 75, 84–55, 89, 91;

become corps, 104; station super-
    intendent, 91
statistics, "Methodist Bookkeeping," 8,
    10–12, 14, 16, 19, 38, 47, 51–53,
    58, 84, 86, 91, 104, 108, 110, 118,
    120–22, 126–28, 130–36, 138–40,
    198, 204, 207–8; social, 152, 156–
    57; Statistical Department, 132
Stead, W. T., xi, 62, 70, 112, 114, 145–
    46, 149, 159, 160–61, 165, 210;
    General Booth (1891), 217; influ-
    ence on William Booth, 163, 212;
    "Maiden Tribute" and Armstrong
    Trial, 146, 149–51, 169; *Mrs.
    Booth of the Salvation Army*
    (1900), 218; *Pall Mall Gazette*
    editor, 152
Steele, Harold C., 163
Stepney, 50, 74; Alfred Street Chapel,
    55
stock exchange, 145
Stockholm, 206
Stockton, 86
Stockwell New Chapel Congregational
    Church, 27, 29
Stoke-Newington, 35
stores, 162
Stowe, Harriet Beecher, 31
Stratford, 53
stratification. *See* laypersons, officers,
    ranks
"Street Arabs." *See* poor
Stroud, Wales, 109
Strout, Cushing, ix
submerged masses. *See* poor
suburbs, 52
suffrage, women and workers, 16,
    100, 129
summer camps, 171
Sunday school, 15, 33, 45, 91, 109,
    113, 134
Sunday School Times, 136
Sunderland, 4, 8

superstition. *See* folk beliefs
"surplus womanhood," 149. *See* female ministry
Surrey Gardens Music Hall, London, 15
Swansea, 96
Sweden, 106, 124, 136
Swift, Suzie Forest, 129, 157; became Dominican nun, 206
Switzerland, 124, 136

tabernacles, 14, 15, 27, 56, 59–60, 110, 184
Taylor, James Hudson, 143
temperance, teetotal, abstinence, the pledge, 9, 11, 16, 19, 21–22, 27–28, 30, 39, 42, 45, 65, 81, 87, 91, 96, 98, 142, 188
Temperance Permanent Land and Building Society, 60
tent meetings, 47–48
territorial command system, 103, 115, 136, 141, 170. *See* federalism
testimony, testify, witnessing, 5, 13, 63, 92, 109, 110, 132
Thackeray, William Mackpeace, 110
theater, 9, 15, 59, 67, 73, 82, 90; theater-going, 19, 31
theology, doctrine, 27, 42, 52, 57, 64–69; antinomian, 110; William Booth, 2, 18, 22, 28–29; Calvinist, 2, 13, 27–28, 43, 54, 56, 66–67, 187, 195; depravity, fall, 32, 165; free thought, transcendental, trinitarianism, 2; heaven, 5, 19, 73, 82, 110, 145–46; hell, 9, 19, 29, 80, 105, 110; sources of Christian Mission-Salvation Army creed, 65–66, 215; speculative, 9, 31, 33, 64–65; Wesleyan Arminian, 2, 6, 19, 65, 67, 89. *See* conversion, holiness, revivalism
thieves, 74, 158, 163

Thomas, David, 27, 29, 32
Thomas Passage Hall, London, 55
Thompson, E. P., 9
Thompson, Henry, 46
Thompson, Mary, 139
Tillett, Ben, 78, 157
The Times (London), 46, 102, 134, 138, 155, 163–64, 166
tobacco, 31, 97, 98
Toynbee House, 149
tracts, distribution of, 18–19, 42, 45–46, 52, 62, 64, 84, 142
trade unions, 62, 100, 129, 133, 155, 157; labor unrest, 163, 177; Trade Union Council, 78
Trafalgar Riots (1886), 151
training, for lay speakers, teachers, visitors, 65
training homes, officer cadets (1880), 2, 102, 118, 124–25, 135 (new program), 139, 169, 171; "manufacture" a civilian army, 102
traitor. S*ee* deserter
transatlantic, x, 10, 15, 182, 203. *See* Anglo-American
transcendentalism, 2. *See* theology
Tredegar, 96; Temperance Hall, 109
trinitarianism, 2. *See* theology
Troutt, Margaret, 219
"turning point," 69–70
Tunbridge Wells, 49
Tyler, Rev. W., New Town Chapel, 193

underground, 74
unemployment, 62, 74–78, 81, 97, 117, 146, 153–54, 158–59, 161–62, 165
uniform, includes badges, sashes, 1, 98, 102–3, 111, 133, 202–3
Unitarians, 19, 22, 24, 60, 105
United Kingdom, 116, 118. *See* Britain, England, Scotland

United Methodist Free Church (1850), 11, 15, 16, 26
Universalism, 105, 187
University of Humanity, 2
Upham, Thomas C., 16
Upper Norwood, Gypsy Hill Colony, 52–54
urban home mission, 7, 15–16, 29, 36, 41, 51, 61–62, 65, 72, 116; See Christian Mission, Christian Revival Association, East London Christian Mission, East London Revival Association, Salvation Army

Vassar College, 157
Vaughan, Cardinal, 81
vegetarianism, 31, 188
vice, crime, criminals, 75, 78, 153
Victoria, Queen, 27, 106, 150
"vilest offender," 152
villages, 132, 135
Vint, James, 137
visitation, door to door, 1, 12–13, 24, 29, 42, 52, 62, 65, 81, 147
voluntary agencies, 16, 45–46, 51, 65, 165, 191
Volunteer Army (British), "Volunteers," 100–101, 103, 104
Volunteer Service Gazette, 102
Volunteers of America, 124, 130, 204
voting, in Salvation Army, 143

waifs and strays, 102
wake, 81
Wakefield, 8
Wales, 17, 19, 37, 96
Walsall "Black Country," 17, 37, 47, 92, 190
Walworth, 25, 26
Wandsworth Jail, 148
Wapping, 72
war council, congress, 88, 90, 94, 104, 108, 110, 115, 143
War Cry (1879), 81–82, 115, 118, 121, 130, 137, 139, 152–54, 166; sales and circulation, 121–22, 127, 133, 140, 143
"war memories," 96
Ward, Sgt. and Mrs., 148–49
waste labor and waste lands, 146
Watson, Bernard, 69, 165, 215
Watts, Arthur, 99–100, 118, 200
Watts, Kate, 96
Waugh, Thomas, 8
Weaver, Richard, 18, 28
Webb, Sidney and Beatrice, 27, 78, 112, 152, 154–55
Welty, Susan F., biography of Maud Charlesworth Booth, 218
Wesley, John, 12, 22, 25, 54, 63, 68, 89, 99, 105, 117, 132; creed, 165; secular tunes, 189. See Methodist
Wesley Chapel, City Road, 45; Bethnal Green, 53; Merthyr, Wales, 96; Spitalfields, 96
Wesleyan, 1, 169, 171; American Methodism, 6, 11, 15, 19, 68; British Methodism, 2, 6; influences on the Booths, 216; "Shopkeeper Wesleyanism," 10. See Methodist, discipline, theology
Wesleyan (British) Methodist Conference, 3, 8–11, 15–16, 36, 39, 43, 45, 97; excommunicated William Booth, 26
Wesleyan Times (Free Methodist), 44, 48
Westminster, 81
Whig Morning Chronicle, 10
Whitby, 1, 93
White, Arnold, 112, 152, 164
White Slave Trade, 150
Whitechapel "mother corps," 1, 36, 48, 50, 74, 79, 84–86, 94–97, 108–9, 120–21, 148, 154, 156; becomes food depot (1889), 157, 212; Friends Burial Ground tent, 46–47. See Quakers

Whitefield, George, 12, 25, 63, 105; secular tunes, 189
Whitehaven, 108
Whittaker, Frederick, mission secretary, 58; resignation, 193
"wholesale" salvation. *See* social reform
wife-beating, 19
Wiggins, Arch R., 123
Willard, Frances, 112, 125
Williams, Harry, 138, 215; *Booth-Tucker* (1980), 219
Wilson, Rev. J. H., secretary, Home Missionary Society, 193
Wilson, P. Whitehall, *General Evangeline Booth* (1935), 219
Winthrop, John, 100
Wolesley, Maj. Gen. Garnet, 101–2, 201
Wolverhampton, 17
Women's Christian Temperance Union, 104
women's equal status and pay in Salvation Army, 165
Woodhouse Carr, 38
Woolwich, 79
Worcester, Worcestershire, 14, 127

Workers' Agricultural University, 163
workhouse, 159
working class, xi, 7–10, 14–16, 18–19, 21, 34, 42, 53, 59, 64, 70, 74, 77–78, 85, 100, 102–3, 110, 117, 121, 129, 131–32, 134, 140, 143, 146–47, 152, 155, 163, 206; laundry workers, 155; unrest, 163. *See* East End Dock Strike, trade unions
workshops, as part of city colony, 146, 158, 161, 165; "Hallelujah" workshops' products, 159
worldliness, 28, 57, 90, 133, 166. *See* sinners

Xavier, Francis, 138

Yarmouth, 35
yearbook, Salvation Army, 216
YMCA, YWCA, 15, 45
York, 8, 35
Young Soldier, 136
Ystrad, Wales, 109

Zulus, 150